Manga Studio For Dummies®

Cheat Sheet

Tools Palette

Tool	Shortcut Key	Tool	Shortcut Key
Hand	H	Zoom	/
Rotate Page	R		
Rectangle/Elliptical Marquee	M	Lasso/Polyline Marquee	L
Magic Wand	W	Move Layer	K
Object Selector	O	Layer Selection	D
Line/Curve/Polyline	U	Rectangle/Ellipse/Polygon	U
Pen	P	Pencil	P
Magic Marker	P	Eraser	E
Fill	G	Airbrush	B
Gradation (EX)	G	Pattern Brush	B
Panel Maker	F	Panel Ruler Cutter	F
Text	T	Join Line	J
Eyedropper (EX)	I		
Smooth (EX)	;	Dust Cleaner (EX)	;
Width Correction	@	Line Lever	@
Line Smoother	:		
Black Color	4	White Color	5
Transparent Color	6	Tone (EX)	7

Page Shortcuts

Command	Shortcut Keys (Windows)	Shortcut Keys (Mac)
Move Page	spacebar	spacebar
Rotate Page	Shift+spacebar	Shift+spacebar
Page Zoom Out	Ctrl+- (number pad)	⌘+- (number pad)
Page Zoom In	Ctrl++ (number pad)	⌘++ (number pad)
Actual Size	Ctrl+Alt+0 (zero)	⌘+Option+0 (zero)
Fit Page to Window	Ctrl+0	⌘+0
Print Size	Ctrl+Shift+0 (zero)	⌘+Shift+0 (zero)
New Layer	Ctrl+Shift+N	⌘+Shift+N
Change Layer Type	Ctrl+Alt+E	⌘+Option+E
Show/Hide Rulers	Ctrl+R	⌘+R
Show/Hide Transparency	Ctrl+4	

For Dummies: Bestselling Book Series for Beginners

**BESTSELLING
BOOK SERIES**

Manga Studio For Dummies®

Cheat Sheet

Tool Shortcuts

Tool Action	Shortcut Keys (Windows)	Shortcut Keys (Mac)
Undo Action	Ctrl+Z	⌘+Z
Redo Action	Ctrl+Y	⌘+Y
Increase Brush/Line Size	]	]
Decrease Brush/Line Size	[	[
Draw Straight Line/Maintain Shape Tool's Aspect Ratio	Shift+drag	Shift+drag
Switch to Black Color	4	4
Switch to White Color	5	5
Switch to Transparent Color	6	6
Switch to Tone	7	7

Selection Shortcuts

Command	Shortcut Keys (Windows)	Shortcut Keys (Mac)
Select All	Ctrl+A	⌘+A
Deselect All	Ctrl+D	⌘+D
Invert Selection	Ctrl+Shift+I	⌘+Shift+I
Convert Selection to Layer	Ctrl+Shift+D	⌘+Shift+D
Convert Selection Layer to Selection	Ctrl+F	⌘+F
Quick Mask (EX)	Ctrl+M	⌘+M
Quick Select (EX)	Ctrl+Shift+M	⌘+Shift+M

Show/Hide Palettes

Palette	Shortcut Key	Palette	Shortcut Key
Tools	F2	Tool Options	F3
Layers	F4	Navigator	F5
Tones	F6	Properties	F7
History	F8	Gray (EX)	F9
Materials (EX)	F10	Custom Tools (EX)	F11
Actions (EX)	F12	Show/Hide Active Palettes	Tab

For Dummies: Bestselling Book Series for Beginners

by Doug Hills and Michael Rhodes

Wiley Publishing, Inc.

Manga Studio® For Dummies®

Published by
Wiley Publishing, Inc.
111 River Street
Hoboken, NJ 07030-5774

www.wiley.com

Copyright © 2008 by Wiley Publishing, Inc., Indianapolis, Indiana

Published by Wiley Publishing, Inc., Indianapolis, Indiana

Published simultaneously in Canada

For general information on our other products and services, please contact our Customer Care Department within the U.S. at 800-762-2974, outside the U.S. at 317-572-3993, or fax 317-572-4002.

For technical support, please visit www.wiley.com/techsupport.

Wiley also publishes its books in a variety of electronic formats. Some content that appears in print may not be available in electronic books.

Library of Congress Control Number: 2007926397

ISBN: 978-0-470-12986-9

Manufactured in the United States of America

10 9 8 7 6 5 4 3 2 1

WILEY

About the Author

Doug Hills has been drawing ever since high school. Originally influenced by the superhero comics of the early- to mid-1990s, his style has adapted towards his other favorite genre: manga. Learning and studying techniques from both the East and West, he's constantly striving to create a style that can truly be called his own.

In recent years, he has taken that love and desire for comics onto the Internet with two webcomics: *Place Name Here* and *Chibi Cheerleaders From Outer Space,* which he works on with his wife, Stacey. His webcomic work led him to Ten Ton Studios, where he worked on a story for their book, *Anthologica*, and eventually became a member of the group.

Originally from Chatham, NY, Doug now lives in Logan, UT, with his wife of seven years and their three-year-old daughter, Brady. All told, Doug's a pretty happy and lucky guy.

Dedication

To Ben Tassinari, who taught me what it means to live for today and enjoy life to its fullest.

Author's Acknowledgments

Jeez, where to start.

Special thanks go out to my wife, Stacey, and my daughter, Brady, for their never-ending support and patience. To Mom, Dad, and my entire family for their support and always pushing me to do my best. To the guys at Ten Ton Studios — if it weren't for you guys and your support (and pushing me in front of the right people), I wouldn't have had this opportunity. To Fahim Niaz and the folks at e frontier for offering this project. To Jean Rogers and Steve Hayes at Wiley Publishing for their infinite patience during this whole project.

Special thanks go out to Jason Masters, Joe Brudlos, Lincy Chan, and Teyon Alexander for providing additional artwork for this book. I wanted to show how Manga Studio works for all different artistic styles, and these guys stepped up to the plate. Thanks so much!

Publisher's Acknowledgments

We're proud of this book; please send us your comments through our online registration form located at www.dummies.com/register/.

Some of the people who helped bring this book to market include the following:

Acquisitions, Editorial, and Media Development

Project Editor: Jean Rogers

Senior Acquisitions Editors: Melody Layne, Steve Hayes

Copy Editor: Heidi Unger

Technical Editor: Sarah Vaughn

Editorial Manager: Kevin Kirschner

Media Development Project Manager: Laura Atkinson

Media Development Assistant Producer: Josh Frank

Editorial Assistant: Amanda Foxworth

Sr. Editorial Assistant: Cherie Case

Cartoons: Rich Tennant (www.the5thwave.com)

Composition Services

Project Coordinator: Lynsey Osborn

Layout and Graphics: Stacie Brooks, Reuben W. Davis, Melissa K. Jester, Barbara Moore, Christine Williams

Proofreader: Evelyn W. Still

Indexer: Sharon Shock

Anniversary Logo Design: Richard Pacifico

Publishing and Editorial for Technology Dummies

Richard Swadley, Vice President and Executive Group Publisher

Andy Cummings, Vice President and Publisher

Mary Bednarek, Executive Acquisitions Director

Mary C. Corder, Editorial Director

Publishing for Consumer Dummies

Diane Graves Steele, Vice President and Publisher

Joyce Pepple, Acquisitions Director

Composition Services

Gerry Fahey, Vice President of Production Services

Debbie Stailey, Director of Composition Services

Contents at a Glance

Table of Contents

Introduction

*I*t's amazing to think about how much the industry of creating manga and other forms of comics has changed in such a short period of time. It wasn't all that long ago that the sole purpose of computers in the process was to add colors and word balloons to the page. Things like penciling and inking were left to traditional tools because the technology wasn't quite there yet to accurately reproduce the subtle pen and pencil strokes artists use when creating their work. Or if it *was* there, it was pretty darn expensive.

With the advent of the consumer-priced drawing tablet in the late 1990s and the popularity of programs such as Photoshop and Painter, the revolutionary idea of producing art without the need of a traditional pencil, pen, and paper was possible. I certainly thought that it was revolutionary when I decided to go all-digital with my work back in 2003.

Unfortunately, the available art programs still had (what I found to be) frustrating limitations in refining the work. Sure, many of these programs had tools to help draw straight lines or simulate French curves, but they lacked a certain organic feeling in the drawing process. Small things like the ability to rotate the page while drawing (something Photoshop lacks) or being able to lay down a ruler or curve and use that instead of the line and curve tools had a tendency to take me out of the experience. Needless to say, I found myself trying program after program that would have one aspect or another right, but would miss a great deal more.

Then came Manga Studio. Originally a program created and used in Japan for several years, it was translated and brought over to the United States in early 2006. When I finally got my hands on the program, I couldn't believe what I had missed out on. Manga Studio had everything I needed to work on my comics from beginning to end — and then some! I could now treat the canvas like I would a regular piece of paper. I could add all kinds of rulers and guides and use them like their analog counterparts. The pencils felt like pencils, and the pens felt like pens. Manga Studio was *exactly* what I'd been hunting for these past few years.

Manga Studio comes in two flavors: Debut and EX. Manga Studio EX is the full-featured, full-price version. Manga Studio Debut has all the basic tools, commands, and functions that the EX version does, but it lacks a few of the higher-end tools that EX provides. Because of that, Debut is less expensive than EX. This book will work just fine for you, regardless of which version of Manga Studio you're using.

About This Book

To say that Manga Studio is feature rich is a bit of an understatement. If you've used Photoshop before, much of how Manga Studio works will seem somewhat familiar, if not exactly the same. But if the realm of digital art is a brand-new concept to you, you might become overwhelmed at first. Rightly so — Manga Studio is a very dense and robust program. Heck, while going over the program for the purposes of this book, I discovered that I had previously used only about 30 to 40 percent of its full potential.

I think that's actually a great feature of the program; you can use as much or as little as you'd like and still produce the same quality pages. It just depends on what you're looking to do with the program. Still, if you're new to this process, you might not know where to begin so that you *can* create those quality pages.

I had a few goals in mind while writing this book:

- ✔ To help you create your first page in Manga Studio, from beginning to end.
- ✔ To show how you can work either 100 percent digital or use a combination of digital and traditional tools.
- ✔ To explain how the various features in the program work and how they can help save you some time and energy.
- ✔ To explain the differences between Manga Studio Debut and Manga Studio EX and help figure out which version is for you. (If you haven't already bought it, of course.)
- ✔ To go over both the basic and advanced methods that Manga Studio provides.

Above all, I want to show that while Manga Studio is a lot to take in when you first fire it up, after you get used to how the system works and what tools work best for you, it becomes as intuitive as working with traditional tools. Plus you get to save a few trees. And that's not a bad thing, now is it?

Foolish Assumptions

I don't really know who you are or what your goals are. Hopefully *you* know who you are. (If not, might I suggest *Freud For Dummies?*)

So I can only assume that if you've picked up this book, you:

- ✔ Like manga and/or comics.
- ✔ *Really* like manga and/or comics.

✔ Like to draw. Or ink. Or work with screen tones.

✔ Regularly draw using your computer — or have at least dabbled with it.

✔ Have purchased or otherwise legally obtained a copy of either Manga Studio Debut or Manga Studio EX. If you haven't bought the program yet, you can install a 30-day demo of the program right from the CD that comes with this book.

✔ Have installed said program on your computer. (This book is intended for Macintosh and PC versions — that goes for you Linux users running the program under Wine, as well.)

✔ Aren't sure where to start or are looking to see if there's something you missed after looking through the user manual.

✔ Aren't sure yet if you want to purchase the program and hope this book will answer any lingering questions you have.

If one or more of the above assumptions fits you, then this book is just the right thing for you. By the way, if you haven't tried drawing or inking digitally, and you're looking to try that out, I highly recommend purchasing a drawing tablet. It's a lot easier to draw with one of those than with a mouse (unless you *really* like a challenge).

Conventions Used in This Book

Throughout the book, I present instructions in a consistent, easy-to-follow format to help you navigate through the program. For example, when I explain how to navigate through the main menu, you'll see an ⇨ icon. I use this arrow to define a transition as you go from one menu to another. So when you see something like File⇨New⇨Page, it means when you use your mouse or drawing tablet stylus, you click File, click New, and then click Page as each respective menu pops up.

Also, because I cover both the PC and Mac versions of the program, I give you keystroke commands for both as I go along, with the Mac commands in parentheses or separated by a slash. For example:

Press Ctrl+C (⌘+C on the Mac).

Press Enter/Return when done.

Oh, and keep in mind that I'm a PC user. (Sorry, just can't make the switch!) I primarily use Windows terminology (for example, I call it a *drop-down list* instead of a *pop-up window),* both for the sake of simplicity and because I just don't know all the proper Mac terms — and I'd hate to screw them up and anger you Mac fans out there.

How This Book Is Organized

The book is written in such a way that you can read it however you want or need to. Each chapter (and section within each chapter) is set up to be independent of the others. So while I may reference other sections of the book that you should check out (and I do that a lot), you can read each section and chapter just as easily as if you read it from cover to cover.

I broke the book down into six parts, each one covering an essential aspect of knowing and understanding Manga Studio.

Part I: Welcome to Manga Studio!

Seems like a pretty good place to start, right? Like I mention earlier, using a program like this for the first time can be pretty intimidating. So this part of the book goes over the basics of the program and the essential and helpful tools you need to know how to use to get your first page started.

Part II: Roughing It

Now, we're getting somewhere! This part of the book is devoted to getting your idea down onto (virtual) paper and chipping away at it until it's exactly how you want it. The chapters in this part take you from starting a new blank page, through the first rough pencil sketches, to creating and working with layers, panels, and rulers, and selecting and transforming objects.

Part III: Refining and Exporting Your Work

When you have your drawing or page exactly how you want it, it's time to polish it up and make it all pretty for everyone to see. The chapters in this part show you how to ink your work, add tones for "color" and dimension, create word bubbles and add text, and export and print your finished pages.

Part IV: Advanced Tips and Tricks

After you know the basics of drawing and refining your page, that's all fine and good, but that can't be all that Manga Studio can do, can it? Nope! You've only scratched the surface of what this program can do to help you streamline your work and potentially speed things along in the process. The chapters in this part of the book cover tips and tricks for making your work easier and quicker, and using Manga Studio EX-only tools.

Part V: The Part of Tens

All For Dummies books include top ten lists. My goal in this part is to include items, ideas, and tips that assist you not only with using Manga Studio, but also to help you as an artist and creator. The part of tens chapters provide you with ten (plus some) great books and online resources, and they discuss ten tips and tricks to make working in Manga Studio quicker, easier, and more fun.

After the Part of Tens chapters is the Appendix, which covers the CD-ROM included with this book. Turn to the Appendix for the lowdown on what's included on the CD-ROM and instructions on how to use it.

 The CD also includes three bonus chapters. Bonus Chapters 1 and 2 cover the advanced topics of using vectors and importing 2D and 3D objects. Bonus Chapter 3 gives you background information on manga that may help you if you intend on publishing the comics you create in Manga Studio.

Icons Used in This Book

Every now and then, I have a few "oh yeah, check this out!" moments. It can be something really important to watch out for, or some cute little trick you may not have thought of trying. To help point these out, I give you a few road signs.

 This is where I stop you and say, "Hey, you know what? Try this out." You know that the paragraph next to this icon gives you information that can save you time, improve your work, or make your hair shinier.

 Here's where I point out something very important that you should keep in the back of your mind while working with the program. Read any warnings carefully — they'll help you avoid losing time and work.

 I may be an artist, but I'm also a techie geek. Here's where I go all out with some technical jargon that's only going to matter to you if you're also a techie geek.

 I use the Remember icon to point out information you'll want to keep in mind as you're using Manga Studio.

 In addition to the book you have in your hands, I provide some sample artwork and photos on the enclosed CD-ROM. The CD also includes a free, 30-day demo version of Manga Studio EX, brought to you courtesy of e frontier. So keep an eye out for this icon — it means more goodies for you!

Where to Go from Here

If you're raring to go create your first comic, jump ahead to Chapter 3 for a quick run-through of creating a page from start to finish. If you've got stacks of drawings on paper and you want to scan them into Manga Studio, turn to Chapter 5. If you're looking for inspiration or further resources on drawing, flip to Chapter 16.

If you'd like to drop me an e-mail, you can head over to my Web site at www. pnhcomics.com and click the Contact Us! link. While you're there, you can check out some of my artwork, as well as two webcomics that I've worked on for a few years.

Part I
Welcome to Manga Studio!

The 5th Wave   By Rich Tennant

DENISE AND JERRY LEVIN — AUTHORS OF "LOST IN THE MALL PARKING LOT," "THE MISPLACED GALLERY INVITATION," AND, "THE BAD HAIRCUT—WHY ME?"

Truthfully? If it weren't for Manga Studio, many of these stories would have remained untold.

In this part . . .

So, you either bought a copy of Manga Studio and picked this book up because you aren't exactly sure where to go from here, or maybe you saw this on the bookshelf and would like to know exactly what Manga Studio is. This first part of the book gives you some understanding as to what this program is and what it can do to help you create comics on your computer.

Chapter 1 goes over the basics of Manga Studio, including what you can (and can't) do in the program, as well as a breakdown of the new workspace you'll create your art in. Chapter 2 offers a bit of help to the beginning artist, with some suggestions on what you should buy to make your experience with the program a pleasurable one. I also discuss several comic terms that you'll run into as you continue down this potential career path, as well as offer a few suggestions when you start to feel a bit frustrated at the whole "creating comics" thing. (It'll happen; trust me.)

Finally, for those that are just chomping at the bit and raring to get right to work in the program, Chapter 3 is your quick-start guide. This chapter takes you from concept to completion, covering all the basic tools you need to create art and prepare it for mass consumption, either in print or on the Internet.

Chapter 1

Getting to Know Manga Studio

*W*hen you buy a new program, do you actually read the instruction manual? It's okay. You can be honest — I won't tell anyone. The problem with skipping the instructions is that sometimes you miss out on many interesting tidbits you didn't know you could do with the program.

Well, you can think of this chapter as your Manga Studio cheat sheet — so you don't *have* to go read the instructions. This chapter is your general overview of the program. I discuss how it differs from other drawing programs, and I do a run-through of the Manga Studio workspace, along with all the cool toys that you can use when producing your manga or comic.

And if you haven't yet decided which version of Manga Studio to purchase, I discuss how the Debut and EX versions differ and which may be the one that best suits your drawing needs.

How Manga Studio Differs from Other Drawing Programs

In many ways, Manga Studio is similar to other drawing programs available, such as Adobe Photoshop or Corel Painter. Each of these programs is good in its own right, but because Manga Studio is first and foremost a comic creation program, it has a few functions that set it apart from other drawing programs — and that help make your life as a digital artist easier.

Don't let the name fool you!

The one critique I have about the program is that its name was changed from the original Japanese name of Comic Studio to Manga Studio here in America. I'm not really sure why the name was changed, aside from catching the eye of manga fans and artists. The problem with this name change is that when I talk to my Western-based comic book artist buddies, they think that the program is for the production of manga only. Far from it.

So let me reassure you — you can use Manga Studio to draw manga, superhero comics, or any other style or genre of sequential art. In the following figure, you can see three different styles of comics, all done in Manga Studio. The thing to keep in mind when using this program is that it's a tool to create art. It's no different than using traditional pens and pencils.

Artwork courtesy of Michael Rhodes, Teyon Alexander (characters © Merge Comics), and Jason Masters (God Complex © Brandon Thomas and Jason Masters).

Finding out what Manga Studio can do for you

Over the years of producing art digitally, I've tried out a *lot* of different programs. Each program would get the job done for me in one way or another, but many times I would find myself feeling very frustrated while working with them. Don't get me wrong, I think there are some flat-out awesome art programs on the market. The problem that I was having was while they're good *art* programs, I didn't find them to be very good *comic drawing* programs. As I experimented with these programs I could never find a good comfort level to create my work digitally from start to end. More often than not, I found myself working with multiple programs just to get a page done.

What I found when working in Manga Studio is that comfort level. It was the first program that I felt let me take advantage of the digital medium, while also having the "real world" feeling I normally had when working with real pencils and inks.

So, I thought I'd list a few features of Manga Studio that I found to be the most helpful to my work, and possibly will help you out as well.

Adding a personal touch to line work with custom rulers and guides

When using a program such as Photoshop or Painter, your ability to draw straight lines or custom curves can be a bit limited. You can always use the Line, Curve, or Pen tools, but because the lines all end up uniform, there's definitely a loss of personality. What you need are *virtual rulers* that can guide you in creating and adjusting straight edges, curves, and polygons of any size and shape. Then all you need to do is draw on them, much like their real-world counterparts, adding your own personal touches to the line work as you go along.

Manga Studio provides such a feature with its Ruler Layers feature, which lets you create as many rulers as you need for your page. Straight or curved, rectangular or polygonal, you can make any kind of ruler you need. In addition, you can scale and rotate the rulers. Do you find that your curved ruler isn't quite how you want it? Grab an endpoint and adjust it. It's just that simple.

To me, the best part is that when the ruler is set, you can vary your line weight as you draw along the ruler. It probably doesn't sound like much, but it's a great thing if you want to be able to add a bit of a personal flair to your technical line work. (See Chapter 8 for the details on using the Rule Layers feature.)

Eliminating shakiness in line work

If you've ever tried drawing or inking in Photoshop at anything less than 200% zoom, I'm sure you've noticed you need unnatural steadiness to draw anything resembling a straight line. Even at your steadiest, you notice some wobble to your line work. The only way to remedy that is to zoom in close to the page, but you risk losing sight of the picture as a whole as you work.

Manga Studio provides the ability to set a *variable correcting* to the line work. What this means is that as you work, the line adjusts itself to reduce or eliminate shakiness. The setting is variable, so you can make the correction as strong or as light as you like.

If you like to work while zoomed out but have been unhappy with how your line work has been coming out, this function may be just the remedy you need. (I tell you how to use this feature in Bonus Chapter 1 on the CD.)

Having thousands of screentones at your disposal

Manga Studio comes preinstalled with thousands of *screentones* (patterns of dots or other shapes that are used in black and white artwork to represent shades of gray) that you can't get with other drawing programs. In addition, these tones are *vector based,* which means that you can adjust the size of your finished page to any size you want, and the quality of the tones remains the same. This is something that even the Computones package for Photoshop can't do. (Incidentally, EX users can use Computones in addition to the program's main tones, so there's another advantage.)

Chapter 11 covers all you need to know about adding screentones to your work.

Working with multiple-page story files

What if you could contain all of the pages in your story or chapter in one place, which you could then easily preview as you go along? Manga Studio provides that with its story files. Here, you can create as many pages as you'd like, and they're organized in one location. You can then rearrange the pages, add new ones, or remove excess ones. And because all the page files are collected within one story file, all you need to do to view your story is just open one file, instead of several. Chapter 4 discusses how to work with these files.

Manga Studio EX users also can combine two consecutive pages into a spread — for those large action pieces you want to draw. (Conversely, you can split a spread into two separate pages.)

Knowing your page dimensions with print guides (preinstalled and custom)

Manga Studio includes page templates of various shapes and sizes that are useful if you're planning on printing your comic. In addition, for several of those templates, a set of print guides is included.

The print guide helps you keep track of what areas of the page are safe and what areas are cut off by the printer when preparing it for the final book. It's a very useful way to make sure any important artwork or dialogue isn't accidentally cut because you didn't keep track of where the cut-off points were. I go over the basics of the print guide in Chapter 4.

Creating custom word balloons (EX only)

Many programs offer the ability to add text to a page, but Manga Studio EX provides you the option of adding word balloons as well. These vector-based balloons can be squashed, stretched, and fitted to whatever dialogue you want to add. EX comes with a wide variety of balloon shapes to choose from, but if you don't see what you're looking for, you can always create your own! Check out Chapter 12 for more information on how the word balloon function works.

Knowing what Manga Studio can't do (easily)

The one thing Manga Studio can't do, at least as easily as other drawing programs can, is color work. That's not to say it's *impossible* to do, it just isn't really as intuitive as your traditional digital coloring programs. The reason for this is simple — at its heart, Manga Studio was designed for black-and-white use. While it can convert a layer from black and white to custom colors, the intention is more to adjust your draft work color to differentiate it from your finished work.

You can do simple cell-shaded-style color work, as well as some airbrushing, to add highlights and shadows to a drawing. However, you can't alter a layer's settings like you can in Photoshop. This means you can adjust only the layer's opacity; functions like multiply or overlay don't exist in Manga Studio. The other thing to keep in mind is that each color has to be on its own separate layer. This can certainly bloat the size of your page file if you're planning on doing detailed color work.

In Chapter 14, I go over how you can do some simple color work in Manga Studio. It's a fun little trick that you can experiment with. However, if you're looking to do some serious color work for your comic, this is the one area that Manga Studio lacks, compared to other programs.

Debut versus EX: Which Is Right for You?

Manga Studio comes in two flavors: Debut and EX. Choosing the right version for you comes down to what features you're looking for in a drawing program, what ones you can do without, and (most importantly) how much money you're willing to spend:

- ✔ **Manga Studio Debut** is the introductory-level version of the program. There are no bells and whistles to this version of the program; it contains all the basic tools you need to create your manga from start to finish. Debut works as a fairly accurate simulation of all the traditional tools you would use for producing a comic, all in one convenient package.

  If you're looking for a straight-forward drawing and screentoning art program, you may want to consider this version instead of EX. At a lower price point than the EX version, Debut is easy on your wallet.

- ✔ **Manga Studio EX** helps you take advantage of the fact that you *are* working on a computer. This version provides shortcuts and functions that you simply can't do with traditional tools or even Manga Studio Debut. The EX version also allows you to work with *vectors,* which let you expand or shrink your artwork to whatever size you need, without any loss of quality. (The Debut version, by comparison, is *raster-based only*. This means that you will lose line quality if you try to enlarge the image.)

If you have the money to spend and would like a few shortcuts to help speed up and streamline your creative process, this may be the version for you.

If you haven't purchased either version yet, be sure to pop the CD-ROM that accompanies this book into your computer. e frontier, the company that brings you Manga Studio, has generously included a 30-day demo version of Manga Studio EX. (You can also download the demo version from www. e-frontier.com/go/mangastudio.) It's a good way to test-drive the program if you're still on the fence regarding which version to purchase.

Getting to Know Your New Workspace

Provided you've installed your program (and if you haven't yet, you probably should), you're now staring at your brand new workspace (shown in Figure 1-1), with no idea where to start.

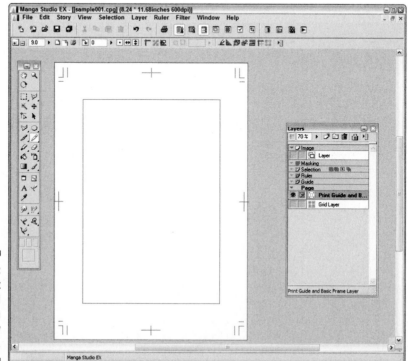

Figure 1-1:
Time to get acquainted with your new workspace.

This is as good a time as any to familiarize yourself with the basic tools, functions, and palettes that you'll be using in Manga Studio. You're going to be using them a lot, so it's best to get to know them.

This section is intended to be a general overview; I explore the functions in much more detail in later chapters. Remember, this is your cheat sheet; I can't give you all the information right off the bat!

Recognizing the Main toolbar

Much like many other programs (both drawing and nondrawing) you may have used, the Main toolbar (shown in Figure 1-2) contains your basic file and clipboard buttons. You can save, print, cut, paste, undo, and redo pretty easily from here. As you can guess, this toolbar is pretty straightforward.

Figure 1-2:
The Main
toolbar.

The Main toolbar also has buttons you can use to hide and show the various palettes available. Because things can get pretty cluttered on your workspace when you have too many palettes open at once, having the ability to quickly turn them on and off is handy.

Table 1-1 lists all the functions on the Main toolbar.

Table 1-1		The Main Toolbar Buttons
Icon	*Name*	*Description*
	New Page	Creates a new page file.
	New Story	Creates a new story file.
	Open	Opens an existing Manga Studio file.
	Save File	Saves your page or story file.

(continued)

Table 1-1 *(continued)*

Icon	Name	Description
	Save All	Saves all of your open Manga Studio files.
	Cut	Cuts a selection from the page to the computer's clipboard.
	Copy	Copies a selection from the page to the computer's clipboard.
	Paste	Pastes a selection from the computer's clipboard to the page.
	Clear	Deletes a selection from the page.
	Undo	Reverses the preceding action.
	Redo	Replaces an Undo action.
	Print	Sends the page to your printer.
	Tools palette	Opens/hides the Tools palette.
	Tool Options palette	Opens/hides the Tool Options palette.
	Layers palette	Opens/hides the Layers palette.
	Navigator palette	Opens/hides the Navigator palette.
	Tones palette	Opens/hides the Tones palette.
	Properties palette	Opens/hides the Properties palette.
	History palette	Opens/hides the History palette.

Icon	Name	Description
	Gray palette *	Opens/hides the Gray palette.
	Materials palette *	Opens/hides the Materials palette.
	Custom Tools palette *	Opens/hides the Custom Tools palette.
	Actions palette *	Opens/hides the Actions palette.

* Available in Manga Studio EX only.

Adjusting your view with the Page toolbar

The Page toolbar, shown in Figure 1-3, contains general page-viewing and manipulation tools. These allow you to adjust on-the-fly without the need to constantly switch to different tools or palettes to do the same thing. Table 1-2 breaks the functions down for you.

Figure 1-3: The Page toolbar.

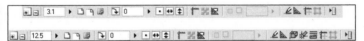

Table 1-2		The Page Toolbar
Icon	Name	Description
	Zoom In	Increases the size of the page's viewing area.
	Zoom Out	Decreases the size of the viewing area.

(continued)

Table 1-2 *(continued)*

Icon	Name	Description
12.5 ▶	Custom Zoom	Allows you to manually enter the size of the viewing area by percentage.
	Fit to Window	Resizes the viewing area to fit within the page window.
	Actual Pixels	Resizes the viewing area to its actual size in pixels.
	Print Size	Resizes the viewing area to fit within the user-defined print size.
	Rotate	Rotates the viewing area 90 degrees clockwise.
0 ▶	Angle	Allows you to enter a manual viewing angle for the page.
	Normal View	Adjusts the viewing area to its default setting.
	Flip Image Horizontally	Horizontally inverts the viewing area.
	Flip Image Vertically	Vertically inverts the viewing area.
	Show/Hide Page Rulers	Sets the visibility of any rulers on the page.
	Show/Hide Transparent Area	Allows you to see the transparent (non-inked) areas of the page.
	Show/Hide Ruler Manipulator	Used to adjust any rulers on the page.
	Snap Mode On/Off	Sets ability for a drawing tool to automatically snap to any ruler or guide.
	Snap to Rulers	Snaps drawing tool to any rulers on the page.
	Snap to Perspective Rulers *	Snaps drawing tool to any perspective rulers on the page.

Icon	Name	Description
 	Snap to Focus Line Rulers *	Snaps drawing tool to any focus line rulers on the page.
	Snap to Parallel Lines *	Snaps drawing tool to any parallel line rulers on the page.
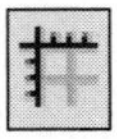	Snap to Guides	Snaps drawing tool to any guides on the page.
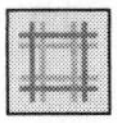	Snap to Grid	Snaps drawing tool to any grids on the page.

* Available in Manga Studio EX only.

Accessing your core set of tools

Out of all the various functions, actions, and palettes that come with Manga Studio, there is one that I'm sure you'll use more than any other — the Tools palette, which you can see in Figure 1-4.

This is your toolbox. Or more specifically, this is your art box. This palette contains all the drawing tools you need to rough out your page, cut out unnecessary sections, ink it up, and erase any mistakes you made along the way. In Table 1-3, I compile a list of the tools in the palette, along with short descriptions of what they do. I discuss most of these tools in later chapters.

Figure 1-4:
The Tools
palette.

You can access any of the tools from your keyboard by pressing the shortcut key noted in Table 1-3. As you go through the table, you'll notice that some tools share the same shortcut. That allows you to cycle quickly through these similar tools by pressing the shortcut key multiple times. For example, you would press the P to select the Pen tool, press P again to select the Pencil tool, and P once more to select the Marker tool. To go back to the Pen tool simply press P again.

Table 1-3		The Tools Palette	
Icon	**Name**	**Shortcut**	**Description**
	Hand	H	Moves the page around the workspace.
	Zoom	/	Enlarges or reduces the page viewing area.
	Rotate	R	Rotates the page in the workspace.
	Rectangle/ Ellipse Marquee	M	Creates a rectangular or circular selection.
	Lasso/Polygonal Lasso	L	Creates a custom selection.
	Wand	W	Creates a selection within an enclosed area of a drawing.
	Move Layer	K	Moves the highlighted layer around the page.
	Object Selector	O	Selects and moves an endpoint of a ruler.
	Layer Selection	D	Highlights the layer of the line work, screentone, or any other object on the page you selected.
	Line/Curve/Polyline	U	Creates a straight line, curved line, or custom shape.
	Rectangle/Ellipse/ Polygon	U	Creates a rectangular, elliptical, or polygonal shape.
	Pen	P	Used for inking/finishing a drawing.
	Pencil	P	Used for roughing out a drawing.

Icon	Name	Shortcut	Description
	Marker	P	Used for inking a drawing.
	Eraser	E	Used to erase a drawing.
	Fill	G	Fills an enclosed area of a drawing with foreground or background color.
	Airbrush	B	Used to add spattering/noise to a drawing.
	Gradation *	G	Adds a color gradient to the page.
	Pattern Brush	B	Paints a design pattern onto the page.
	Panel Maker	F	Creates a new panel layer on the page.
	Panel Ruler Cutter	F	Divides a panel into two (used on a Panel Ruler only).
	Text	T	Adds text to a page.
	Join Line	J	Joins two lines.
	Eyedropper *	I	Samples a screentone for use elsewhere.
	Smooth *	;	Smooths/blurs an image.
	Dust Cleaner *	;	Removes excess particles from a scanned image.
	Width Correction *	@	Adjusts the width of a vector line.
	Line Lever *	@	Adjusts the position of a vector line.
	Line Smoother *	:	Smoothes out a shaky vector line.

* Available in Manga Studio EX only.

Exploring various palettes

While the Tools palette is probably the one you'll use the most in Manga Studio, it isn't the only one available. When you opened the program for the first time, you were bombarded with palettes and windows, as shown in Figure 1-5. It's a lot to weed through at first, but as you get to understand each of the palettes in the program, you may find them as indispensable as the Tools palette.

If at any time you'd like to remove some of the clutter from too many palettes open at once, press the Tab key on your keyboard to hide them all at once. Press the Tab key again to make them all visible again.

Tool Options

Each tool in Manga Studio is customizable in one way or another. The Tool Options palette shows you all the options available with the currently selected tool. This allows you to tweak the tools to your heart's content, until they're set in such a way that they feel as comfortable to use as their real-world counterparts.

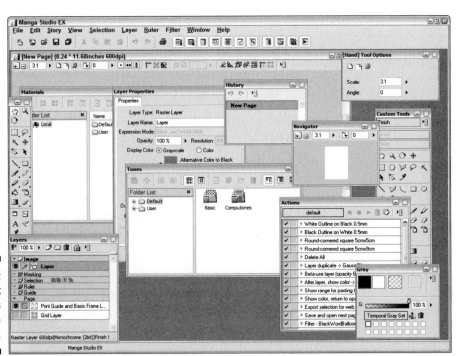

Figure 1-5:
That's a lot of palettes on the screen.

Layers

Looking at the Layers palette, you can see a whole slew of layer types that you can (and probably will) use as you create your pages. The Layers palette helps to keep all the various layer types organized. This way, you not only know what layer you're currently working on, but also keep track of the other layers and layer types you create. I go over layers in much more detail in Chapter 6.

Navigator

The Navigator palette works much like the functions available on the Page toolbar; you can zoom in and out, as well as rotate the page (or enter manual values for each).

You'll also notice a miniature representation of your page, as well as a red rectangle. This allows you to move around the page, much like using the Grab tool from the Tools palette. All you need to do is click within the rectangle with your mouse or stylus and drag it around the preview pane. As you can see, manipulating the preview pane also moves the main page as well. This is a good way to maneuver around the page without having to switch to the Grab tool every time you need to adjust its placement.

Tones

The Tones palette is your repository for all the tones that come installed with your program, as well as any customized tones you create. Each type of tone available is filed into its own folder. All you need to do is dig into those folders and find the tone you need! For more information on using tones on your page, be sure to check out Chapter 11.

Layer Properties

Each layer type in Manga Studio has its own set of properties to go along with it. The Layer Properties palette shows you all the options available for that particular type. (Options you can't adjust are grayed out.) Adjusting the properties can range from simply renaming the layer, to setting the layer-specific ruler properties. Chapter 6 covers the various layer properties available to you, depending on the layer type.

History

The Undo function in Manga Studio is a great way to quickly erase a mistake you may have just made. But what happens if you need to go back several steps? You could always undo a few extra times — or if you happen to own Manga Studio EX, you can take advantage of the History palette.

The History palette keeps track of a set number of previous actions (which you can set in the System Preferences of the program) in a list. You just look through the list to the action you'd like to go back to and click it with your mouse or stylus. Instantly, you travel back in time to the point you want to start over from. And you don't even need a DeLorean to do it!

(Just a quick note to you Manga Studio Debut users out there — the rest of the palettes are exclusive to the EX version of the program.)

Gray (EX only)

The Gray palette gives you a bit more fine-tuning for the color of your ink as you're working on a layer. Much like the opacity setting determines how opaque or transparent a layer can be, the Gray palette adjusts how dark or light a shade of gray you'd like to work in.

This is useful for those who like to work loosely and lightly with their pencils and then go back and refine the work with a darker pencil. If you don't want to create a brand-new layer for the tight pencils, you can just adjust the grays as you go along. You can try setting the gray color to a lighter shade for your loose roughs. Then, when you're ready to tighten the pencils up, darken the grays and start refining! It's a great alternative to those who feel some "life" from their work is lost when traced on a separate layer.

Materials (EX only)

The Materials palette is your repository for all the various tools and samples that you can use in your drawing. These include:

- Two-dimensional images that you can use with the 2DLT importing function (which I explain in Bonus Chapter 2 on the CD).
- Three-dimensional objects that you can use with the 3DLT importing function (which I explain in Bonus Chapter 2 on the CD).
- Custom Ruler shapes, such as French Curves, Elliptical and Circular rulers, and others.
- Preset Layer Types, such as a Black Only Raster pen layer.
- Word balloons.

You can place each of these materials on the page by clicking and dragging it using your mouse or stylus. In addition, you can save your own custom images, rulers, and layer types in the User folder. I discuss the Materials palette in a bit more detail in Chapter 15.

Custom Tools (EX only)

While the Tools palette provides all your important drawing tools, EX users can take that idea a bit further. The Custom Tools palette allows you to customize exactly which tools you want to have at the ready. Don't want to have to hold down the Pencil tool in order to switch them? Add all the pencils you want right onto the palette. Want to quickly access functions without having to go through a series of nested menus? You can add those as well. There's no limit to what you can add!

To help you organize things a bit further, you can switch between custom sets. If you'd like to have a custom palette of rough work tools and one with nothing but vector tools, it's easy to set up and switch. This palette is yet one more way you can streamline the way you work digitally by quickly accessing to the tools and functions you use most frequently.

Actions (EX only)

Have you ever run into instances where you find yourself repeating the same series of functions over and over? It can prove to be quite tedious and boring if you have to export a series of pages one at a time, for example. If you're an EX user, you may find the Actions palette can help relieve you of these doldrums.

Actions (or *macros,* as they're often called in other programs) are a series of recorded commands and functions. What's special about these actions is that instead of repeatedly going through a series of steps manually, you can use actions to quickly perform those steps automatically.

The preinstalled actions can range from automatically setting up the properties of an imported image to adding an outline to exporting your page for the Internet. What's more, you can always record your own actions to use at a later time. When using the preinstalled actions — or creating your own — you may find these to be another way to shave a few seconds or minutes off of your production — time you can then use to focus on more creative things.

Chapter 2

Help for the Beginning (Manga Studio) Artist

his chapter is aimed squarely at the new wave of digital artists out there who pick up this book. Maybe you're the person who always dreamed about drawing comics but didn't know where to begin. Or you could be the person who received this book and a copy of Manga Studio as a gift (if that's the case, Happy birthday/Christmas/Kwanzaa/Chanukah/Festivus/or whatever) and aren't sure where to go from here.

The chapter's broken down into, I'd say, one-third useful computer hardware information to help you use Manga Studio and two-thirds (hopefully) useful suggestions on comics and manga creation and storytelling in general.

Acquiring Useful Tools

I'll take the leap of faith and assume that you already have a computer running some flavor of Windows or Mac OS X (sorry, Linux users! You can always see if the program will run though Wine), or else you probably wouldn't be reading this book.

However, there are a few pieces of hardware, both internal to your computer as well as external, that you may find useful to have. What's more, you don't need to go on a massive spending spree to get them.

You can never have too much RAM!

Appendix A to this book contains the absolute minimum requirements you need to run Manga Studio on your PC or Mac. It may run a bit *sluggishly*, but it'll run. So here's what I suggest you do to make your Manga Studio experience that much better:

- ✔ **Buy a new computer!** (Just kidding.) The truth is, you don't need the latest and greatest machine on the market in order to use Manga Studio.

- ✔ **Buy more RAM.** This is the one piece of equipment that I consider to be the most vital upgrade for your machine. You can have the fastest processor possible in your machine, but it doesn't mean much if you don't have enough RAM. And because you're working primarily in two dimensions (unless you have Manga Studio EX and are planning on using the 3DLT import function — see Bonus Chapter 2 on the CD), you really don't need an expensive graphics card.

The system requirements suggest a minimum of 256 to 512MB of RAM in your machine. Some users also suggest that you have at least 1GB. Considering how relatively inexpensive RAM is nowadays, I suggest maxing your machine out with as much RAM as it can use. At the *very* least, I suggest boosting your memory up to about 2GB of RAM (if your computer can handle that much RAM).

You can purchase relatively inexpensive RAM at several Web sites. I happen to like Newegg (www.newegg.com) for my computer purchases, but you can also purchase from RAM manufacturers such as Crucial (www.crucial.com).

Time to create some art — But with what?

The most important tool to have when working with Manga Studio is your computer. The *second* most important tool is what you use to create the artwork in the program. If you're thinking of drawing with the computer itself, you're going to need something other than your mouse (unless you're really *really* good). If you're thinking of finishing up the work you started on paper, you're going to need something to get the drawing to the computer, and then when you're done, back out of it.

A drawing tablet, scanner, and printer are three tools that I think are just as important to your Manga Studio experience as the program itself. The following sections explain why.

A drawing tablet

Drawing with a tablet is much easier than drawing with a mouse. However, whether you need a drawing tablet depends on what you plan on doing with Manga Studio. If you're going to scan your pencil or ink work into the computer and you're using the program solely to add screentones and do some touch-up work, you can get by with just your mouse. But unless you're adept at drawing with a brick, I wouldn't suggest trying to use a mouse for *drawing* anything. You'll find it much easier and you'll get better results if you draw with a tablet.

If you've never used (or even heard of) one before, a *drawing tablet* is a means of reproducing natural drawing on the computer. It actually works like a mouse, except that you use a special pen on a drawing surface that's connected to your computer. Unlike a mouse, the pen has *pressure sensitivity*. (That is, the line size and/or opacity of the line you're drawing increase and decrease, depending on how lightly or heavily you press the pen tip on the tablet.) So when you draw with a tablet in Manga Studio, the pen and pencil lines should look like what you'd draw with a normal pencil and paper.

A scanner

If you aren't planning on doing any digital drawing (or are planning on scanning in one stage of the process and finishing the rest with a drawing tablet), a scanner is *the* piece of equipment (outside of the computer itself) that you need to own. It's the only way you're going to get your pencil or pen work into Manga Studio.

A printer

I think that if you're looking to create a physical comic book for your family and friends to read, the easiest and simplest method is to print it, fold it in half, and staple it together. In one of the more obvious statements you'll read in this book, in order to do that, you're going to need a decent printer.

Odds are that you probably already have a printer. If you don't, you can get a relatively inexpensive one from your local office supply or electronics supply stores. Because Manga Studio produces black-and-white art, you don't necessarily need to worry about the most photorealistic color printer on the market. But you should look into a printer that prints at a *high resolution*. (That is, the more dots that can fit in an inch, the sharper the line art looks.) You can purchase good quality laser or inkjet printers without putting a large dent in your wallet at your local office supply store.

You also need to look into paper that doesn't cause the ink to bleed together, resulting in a messy looking page. Fortunately, most regular typing paper should work just fine.

Understanding the Essentials of Comic Creation

While the following subsections can apply to Manga Studio, they cover the art of manga and comic creation in a more general (and abbreviated) sense. I guess you could call this section Sequential Art 101.

Basic terminology

Over the course of the book, I throw around a lot of comic terminology. Some terms you may be familiar with, others may be new. I even try to throw in a few terms that I think you should be familiar with in general, as you're going to encounter them as you go along on your artistic career. (And you'll definitely encounter them as you work in Manga Studio.)

- ✔ **Panel:** Where the magic takes place. These tiny (and not so tiny) boxes of various shapes and sizes contain all the action and dialogue of a scene. (See Figure 2-1.)

- ✔ **Gutter:** The white (or black) space between panels, columns, and the inner margins between two facing pages. (See Figure 2-1.)

- ✔ **Bleed:** A panel that extends all the way to the edge of a page. (See Figure 2-2.) When the pages are cut after being printed on, any art extending into the bleed is cut off. This makes the panel extend to the edges of the finished pages.

Panels

Figure 2-1:
Manga and comic pages are comprised of panels and gutters.

Gutters

✔ **Trim:** When you work on pages that will be printed by a professional printer, consider a small area around each page disposable. The *trim* is the area that is cut after the pages are printed — anything past the trim is lost.

✔ **Safe area:** The area of the page that's in no danger of getting trimmed by the printer. It's suggested that you keep all of the dialogue and most important artwork inside this area.

✔ **Spreads:** Art that spans over two pages in a book. (See Figure 2-3.)

✔ **Layout:** Usually a very rudimentary sketch placing what you want on the page, including the number of panels and the basic action you want to show in each. (See Figure 2-4.)

Figure 2-2: A bleed panel extends all the way to the edge of a page.

Bleed panel

Figure 2-3: You can really get your reader's attention with a two-page spread.

✔ **Roughs:** A term for the unrefined pencil or pen sketches that you use to get a "rough" idea of how you want the page to look. Roughs tend to be more detailed than layouts but can still be pretty messy, compared to the final work. (See Figure 2-5.)

✔ **Loose pencils:** Very rough pencil sketches. You aren't worried about the sketch being clean — you're more focused on getting the general "feel" of what you want to draw on the page. (See the leftmost image in Figure 2-6.)

✔ **Tightened pencils:** Cleaner, more refined pencil work. These tend to look more refined than loose pencil work. (See the middle image in Figure 2-6.)

✔ **Screentones:** Tiny dots that are used in black-and-white artwork to depict shades of gray. (See Figure 2-7.) Screentones are featured quite heavily in manga and some independent comics.

✔ **Breaking the border:** This refers to panels where a figure or object "breaks" beyond its borders. This causes the illusion that the figure is "popping" out of the confines of the page. (See Figure 2-8.)

Figure 2-4:
You use layouts to get a basic idea of the page down on paper. And I mean *basic.*

Figure 2-5:
Roughs add some detail to the layouts but can still be pretty messy.

Figure 2-6:
The difference between loose pencils (left), tight pencils (middle), and line work (right).

✔ **Establishing shot:** A panel that depicts where the scene you're drawing is taking place. It gives the reader an anchor of sorts. This can be a city skyline, a country meadow, or the exterior of a futuristic spaceship flying through space. (See Figure 2-9.)

Figure 2-7:
Screentones
are heavily
featured in
manga.

Figure 2-8:
A character
popping out
of a panel is
"breaking
the border."

*Artwork courtesy Jason Masters (character
©Brandon Thomas and Jason Masters)*

Figure 2-9:
An establishing shot can help set up the scene on a page.

Storytelling basics: It's harder than it looks

Drawing comics can be hard. Telling a story can also be hard. Telling a story in comic book form is extremely difficult. You might be thinking, "What's he talking about? I draw panels of people fighting or talking and I'm good to go!" Actually (while I do love a good fight scene) there's a bit more to storytelling than just a series of boxes on a page.

I'm certainly not going to pretend I'm an expert in the field of storytelling. (In Chapter 16, I mention a few books that you can check out that offer a *much* better and thorough explanation on the subject.) But, I thought I'd mention a couple of tips that I've picked up over the years that you may find useful as you start working on your first pages.

- **Panels aren't just images in boxes.** When I draw (what passes for) comics or manga, I tend to not think that I'm drawing comics. Instead, it's more like I'm storyboarding the scene of a movie. So, as I lay a page out, I try to think about how the camera would capture what's going on in the page.

  When working on my own comic, I've found that this helps me visualize how the page should be laid out. (Actually, this helps when I'm working from someone else's script as well — just in a more structured "this is how many panels you're to draw" way.) By thinking this way, I get a better feel for how I want to pace the story, where the characters should be in the scene, how the scene should be lit, and so on. I also know not to confuse the reader by suddenly switching character positions or drawing from crazy angles just because I think it looks cool. If it wouldn't work in a movie, it probably wouldn't work in a comic.

As you start laying out your first pages, try to think about *why* you want the page to look a certain way as much as *how* you plan on drawing it. That way, if it makes sense to you, it will make sense to the reader.

✔ **You're going to have to draw backgrounds to help the reader understand the scene.** Backgrounds aren't the easiest things in the world to draw. They can be downright maddening to work on, especially if you're working on something that's incredibly detailed. It's much more fun to draw figures — after all, that's what the readers will be focusing on, right?

To a degree, yes — the characters you draw on the page are what entice the readers to read the comic. But if you don't give the readers a basis for where the characters *are*, they aren't going to know the context of what the characters are doing.

In *Making Comics: Storytelling Secrets of Comics, Manga and Graphic Novels* (published by Harper Paperbacks), Scott McCloud suggests that you shouldn't look at backgrounds as backdrops to a scene. Rather they're environments that you're creating for your characters to live within. So try not be afraid to draw them, as difficult as they may be. You don't want your characters to exist in limbo, do you?

✔ **Take as many pages as you need to tell your story.** If you plan on being the artist for someone else's book, odds are you'll get a pretty tight script telling you exactly how many pages will be in the book and how many panels per page. If you work on your *own* book or webcomic, you get a bit more freedom.

One of the ways that I feel manga differs from the DC or Marvel comics of the world is the impression that there is more freedom in the way the artist tells the story. What an American creator may tell in one or two pages, a manga artist may tell in ten or twelve. I always felt when reading certain manga that there was more of a "cinematic" pacing, almost like I was reading a movie (if that makes any sense).

If you're planning on creating your own book or webcomic, try not to feel as though you *have* to tell your story within a set number of pages. It's your story to tell — tell it however you'd like, with as many (or few) pages as you want to.

If you decide to become an independent creator, keep in mind that you have the freedom to use as many panels and pages you want as you work on your story and eventual layouts. It goes back to the first suggestion I make in this section: Try treating the comic as though it's a movie and you're the director. You get the chance to tell your story exactly as you want it to be told.

A few other odds and ends you might find useful

These suggestions don't really have anything to do with Manga Studio. You don't need a computer program, or even a *computer,* for these tips. For the beginning artists out there reading this, I can only guess how excited you must be about hunkering down and getting to work drawing everything that you have going on in your imagination. As you go along though, you may find times where this isn't quite as fun as you thought it would be. I hate to say it, but it may even feel like *work.* You may get frustrated that things aren't coming out quite as you want them to. You may, after a while, just decide to throw your hands up in the air and walk away.

It's natural. Every artist goes through that at one point or another. I know *I* do on a regular basis. But I try to keep at it, even when I feel like I don't want to anymore, and I'm sure you can do the same thing, too. So, in the following subsections, I compiled a few suggestions and tips you may find useful if you start to feel frustrated or stressed that things aren't going quite as well as you hoped.

Practice!

I used to hate that word, if only because I really hated to actually *do* it. I found it extremely mundane and boring, going over something again and again and again. I just figured that if I drew a figure once, that's all I needed to do. As I grew older, I finally started to realize why practice can be a good thing.

The only way to get better is through repetition and practice. Whether it's drawing hands, eyes, heads, or buildings, as you repeat the process again and again, it becomes second nature. Eventually you may get to the point where you can draw a cityscape or large group of characters without breaking a sweat.

But you aren't going to get there unless you keep working away at improving those skills, and the only way to do it is to go over the process again and again and again and again and again.

Find your voice

Take a look through some various comics and manga. What's the one thing you notice? I'll bet the major observation is the difference between how artists draw and/or pace their work. If you look at Ken Akamatsu's style (*Love Hina*), his work looks nothing at all like Yasuhiro Nightow's (*Trigun*), who's work in turn is completely different from Jim Lee's (*All-Star Batman and Robin*), who's art doesn't look at all like John Romita Jr.'s (*World War Hulk*), who's style looks absolutely nothing like Joe Madureira's (*Battle Chasers*).

That's because each of those artists has found what I call his "voice." This is the artistic style that each artist has developed and nurtured over the years. They took what they learned or admired and built upon it, creating something uniquely their own, this fueling the next generation of artists to do the same thing.

There's nothing wrong with emulating the style of your favorite artist at first. (Heck, I started out as a Jim Lee clone when I first started drawing comics in high school.) But if you want to really stand out from the hundreds and thousands of other artists out there (and not be constantly called a "so-and-so clone"), you'll eventually need to find the style of drawing manga and comics that you can truly call your own.

Above all else, as you find your voice, don't be afraid to take chances. If you really want to create a unique style, you may have to push your artistic boundaries in ways you never thought of doing before. Who knows? Maybe as you grow and mature as an artist, you too will influence someone else to get into the business. And how cool would it be to say someone is a "clone" of you?

Look for inspiration

For those times when you feel artistically drained or you feel like you're out of ideas, try flipping through some comics, art magazines, or even the Internet. See what others are doing. You may feel yourself getting jazzed up just by looking at new and different kinds of comic or non-comic-related art styles and techniques.

Getting a fresh perspective on how others do their work may help you to look at your own work in a new light, allowing you to tackle things in a way you never thought of before. Besides, you may even find you can do a *better* job than what they've done, and a little artistic competition is never a bad thing.

Don't be afraid to use references

When you get stuck on how to draw a particular figure, background, or object correctly, use a reference image! It could be a photo of your friends acting out the scene or an image you've taken off of the Internet of a cityscape, tank, or airline jet. Whatever the case may be, using some kind of reference material as you draw gives your art that much more realism and believability, which may help your readers become more engrossed in the world you've created.

Accept and learn from criticism

I believe the old saying goes, there are no wrong answers. Well, *that's* wrong.

Of *course* there are wrong answers! It's the yang to the yin: You aren't going to know or understand what the right answer is if you don't stumble upon the wrong answer. It's probably odd to suggest that there is a wrong way to draw a manga or comic, when it's such a subjective genre in and of itself. But as you go along your artistic journey, you're going to encounter times when you work on a piece of art, take a step back, and you (or someone else will) say, "Well, *that* didn't work at all!"

It happens. Not everything you create can be a touchdown. There will always be instances when you throw an incomplete pass or worse yet, fumble the ball. (You can probably tell that football season started at the time of this writing.) I think, more than anything else in this book, that ground rule needs to be established because (hopefully) that will help you as you try to push your artistic boundaries.

Criticism is one of the things that you face when you create art for public view. For every one person that likes what you make, there's someone that hates it and dissects every little nuance that's "wrong" with what you've done. It comes with the territory. Some are going to be harsher than others, and it can be very easy to get discouraged when you get a scathing e-mail or message board post stating that you "stink."

When that happens, you just pick yourself up, dust yourself off, and decide if there are any nuggets of information within the criticism that you can use to learn and improve from. Of course, I could be completely wrong about this.

It's a marathon, not a sprint

The longer you work on a comic, the more you may become bored and tired of it. That's understandable; it's a grueling and daunting task to crank out page after page after page. I think that's why many independent comics out there don't seem to go past three or four issues — eventually the creator just gets bored and decides to stop.

My only suggestion when you feel like you don't want to do this anymore is to try to focus on one page or issue at a time. It's a long, arduous process, to be sure. But if you can mentally prepare yourself for what could be a very long road ahead, you may find yourself at the end looking back at all you've accomplished before you know it.

Always remember why you're doing this

I'd say that if you purchased this book and the Manga Studio program (at the very least if you purchased the program) that you want to be a comic/manga artist. You want that chance to live out your dream — and hopefully at some point, you'll get to do that. Always remember that feeling because there will be times when you wonder why you're doing this to yourself.

Being a comic artist is, I believe, one of the luckiest jobs in the world, even if you don't get paid for it. (Although, making some money is nice.) You get to create brand-new worlds and characters. If you're fortunate, people will get to read and enjoy what you've put your heart and soul into. If you get the chance to create something that will make people laugh and/or cry, I feel that's what makes all the sleepless nights and marathon drawing sessions worth it. Never forget that.

Chapter 3

Creating Your First Manga Page: A Quick-Start Guide

*W*hile the rest of this book is devoted to a detailed look at the ins and outs of Manga Studio, sometimes a person just wants to know the absolute basic things needed to create a comic from start to finish.

Ask and ye shall receive — this chapter is just for you. This chapter is all about starting down your path to manga creation quickly and easily. I go through only the vital information you need to know about Manga Studio, as well as the basic tools you need to get the job done. If you need more detailed information . . . well, that's what the rest of the book is for!

As I go through the basic steps to create a page, I make sure to point out which chapters in the book you can turn to in order to get a closer look at how certain tools and functions work within Manga Studio.

For the purpose of this quick-start guide, I'm using Manga Studio Debut. This is for simplicity's sake, as the goal here is to show a means of creating a page that both versions of the program (Manga Studio EX and Manga Studio Debut) can do easily.

Opening a New Page

After you install the program and enter your serial number, you should see Manga Studio's workspace. The next order of business is to create a new page to start drawing on by following these steps:

1. **From the main menu, choose File⇨New⇨Page.**

   A New Page dialog box appears, as shown in Figure 3-1. You're presented with a lot of choices for page types, as well as an option to create your own page. I go over pages and page templates in Chapter 4, but for now, you can just pick a basic page template to work from.

2. **If it isn't already selected, click the Page Templates tab located at the top of the dialog box.**

   Off the bat, you see various types of page templates, separated into folders. You also see two standalone pages above the folders, one of which you use for this exercise.

3. **Select the Size A4 Paper Finish B5 5mm template and click the OK button.**

   Now you have a page to start drawing on, as shown in Figure 3-2. The blue lines you see on the page are the print guide. These help you know what area of the page is safe to draw on and what art will be cut off by the printer. I break down the print guide in further detail in Chapter 4.

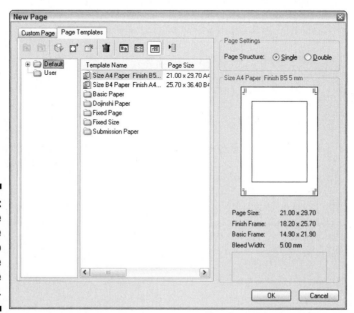

Figure 3-1:
Select the template you want to use from the New Page dialog box.

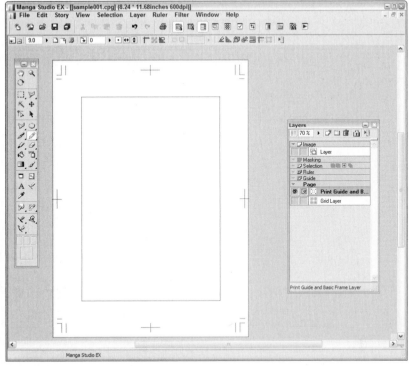

Figure 3-2:
Your new
page, all
ready for
you to
unleash
your
creativity.

Roughing the Page Out

After you have a new page created, the next order of business is to draw! The rest of the figures you see in this chapter demonstrate the type of work you can do in Manga Studio, but this is as good an opportunity as any for you to have fun and let your imagination go crazy.

Before you start laying out your page, you should set up the image layer you'll be drawing on as your Roughs layer. This is a good practice to get into with not only this roughs layer, but later on as you add new layers for inks and other effects.

1. **Using your mouse or stylus, make sure that the image layer is high-lighted. (It's marked Layer on the palette.)**

    If the Layers palette isn't visible, press F4 on your keyboard.

2. **Double-click the image layer on the Layers palette.**

    When you do that, the Layer Properties palette opens, if it isn't already visible.

What you want to do now is set the layer up so that you will know later that this is your roughs layer. Changing its name and drawing color will help you when you start inking.

3. **When the Layer Properties palette opens, click on the Advanced View button to bring up the additional layer options.**

4. **Type** Roughs **in the Layer Name text box.**

5. **To change the drawing color, select Color from the Display Color radio buttons.**

    Now when you start drawing on this layer, all the work is the default color. You can always change the color later by clicking the Alternative Color to Black color box and selecting your preferred color.

6. **Select Sketch from the Output Attribute radio buttons.**

    Changing the Output Attribute is useful when you're going to print or export your work. Besides, it's a good habit to get into when it comes to setting up which layers you want to use for sketching and which layers you'll use for your finish work.

    The properties should now look like the settings in Figure 3-3. At this stage, you don't need the Layer Properties palette anymore, so feel free to close it, if you'd like the extra screen space.

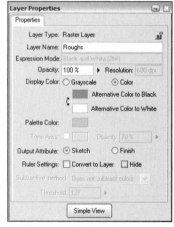

Figure 3-3: The properties for your rough sketch layer should look something like this.

7. **On the Tools palette, select the Pencil tool.**

    For the purpose of roughing your page out, the default pencil should suffice. If you'd like to change it, however, just hold down the Pencil tool button for a couple of seconds and a selection of pencils pops up, as shown in Figure 3-4. Select the pencil you'd like to use from that drop-down list.

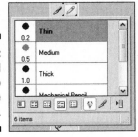

Figure 3-4:
Additional
pencils to
choose
from.

8. Start drawing!

I'm sure I don't need to go into too much detail in this step. All you need to do is use your drawing tablet or mouse to start roughing out your layout. Figure 3-5 shows what I came up with.

Figure 3-5:
Time to start
roughing out
the page.

Adding a New Layer

Using additional layers on a page in Manga Studio is much like putting tracing paper on top of a regular sheet of paper; it allows you to work on top of your roughs, while leaving the original art untouched. Refining your work on a new layer not only keeps your various art stages separate, it makes it so that you don't need to go through and erase all the rough pencil work from the finished line art. That saves you some extra time.

Follow these steps to add a new layer to your page:

1. **From the main menu, choose Layer⇨New Layer.**

   A New Layer dialog box appears, as shown in Figure 3-6. The default settings for the layer suffice for this exercise, so you don't need to change anything here.

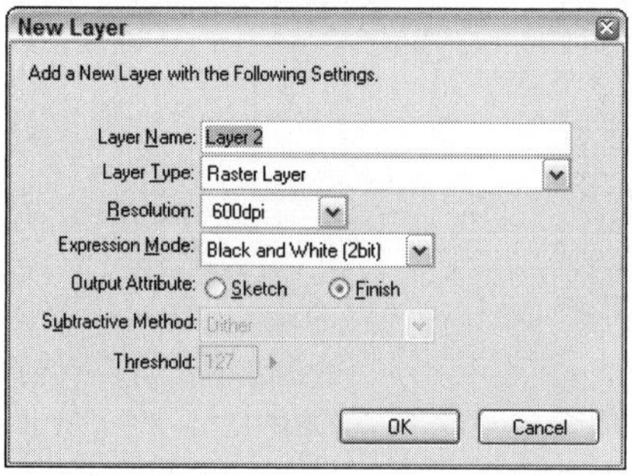

Figure 3-6:
The New
Layer dialog
box.

New Layer
Add a New Layer with the Following Settings.
Layer Name: Layer 2
Layer Type: Raster Layer
Resolution: 600dpi
Expression Mode: Black and White (2bit)
Output Attribute: ○ Sketch ⊙ Finish
Subtractive Method: Dither
Threshold: 127
OK   Cancel

2. **Click OK.**

Your new layer is all set for you to refine your roughs.

Try not to go to crazy with layers, as it will increase the size of your file and may have an adverse effect in your computer's performance.

Inking Your Work

When done right, inking can bring out things on a page that the penciler never even thought of doing. Done poorly, inking can instantly ruin even the best pencil work. Fortunately, you can practice your inking as much as you want in Manga Studio, and you don't have to touch the roughs! That's because the inks are placed on a different layer than the roughs. (See the preceding section for the steps to create new layers.)

To use the pen, just click the Pen tool button on the Tools palette with your mouse or stylus. When you first start using this program, the pen defaults to its G Pen setting. This is a good all-around pen to start inking with, but it isn't the only one available to you. If you hold down on the Pen tool icon for a few seconds, a drop-down list appears with all of the other pen types available to use, as shown in Figure 3-7. Just scroll through the list and select the pen you'd like to use.

Figure 3-7:
Inking with
the Pen tool
is a breeze!

 If you're the type that prefers to work with markers or Rapidograph-style pens, Manga Studio has that covered as well. If you click the Marker tool button on the Tools palette, you can use its set of markers to ink with. Once again, if you would like to see the selection of markers available to you, hold down on the Marker tool button for a couple of seconds. A drop-down list appears with the list of all the markers at your disposal, as shown in Figure 3-8. Select the marker you want to use and ink away!

Figure 3-8:
If working
with
markers is
more your
style, use
the Marker
tool.

In addition to the pens and markers that are set in the program, you can create your own pens to use. (Check out Chapter 14, where I discuss how to customize and create your own drawing tools.)

Erasing Your Mistakes

It happens to the best of us. As you're working with your inks, a mistake is bound to happen. If this happens while penciling, you grab an eraser and remove the mistake. When inking, however, you have to grab your bottle of correction fluid, cover the mistake, and hope you won't have to fix that mistake again. (Multiple layers of correction fluid can become a problem to ink on after a while.) Being able to use an eraser would be a nice thing when inking, I'm sure.

This is where working digitally has its advantages. You can use the Eraser tool — that you normally use when penciling your work — on inks and practically every other drawing tool you use in Manga Studio.

To use the eraser, click the Eraser tool button located on the Tools palette. As shown in Figure 3-9, you can use your mouse or stylus and erase away your mistakes just like you're using the pencil or pen tools.

Figure 3-9: It's very easy to erase inks in Manga Studio.

If you're using a drawing tablet and you happen to have a stylus with an eraser tip, you can use that as well. Keep in mind that the eraser tip is the same size as your current drawing tool. It's good to use when you want to do some precision erasing of an area.

If you want to make a quick removal of an errant line you've just drawn, just undo it! Press Ctrl+Z (⌘+Z on the Mac), and the program removes your last step. If you want to go back several steps, you can continue to press Ctrl+Z. Keep in mind that you will only have a set number of Undos available, which you can set in the System Properties (explained in Chapter 14).

The Eraser tool is especially useful when you're working with screentones. It's perfect for removing excess tones, as well as adding highlights to a character or scene.

Readying Your Panels

Here's the reason I suggest adding panels to your roughs earlier in the chapter: You can use a panel layer to not only create the borders for you, but also clean up any excess art that may have bled past the boundaries of your panels.

What's great about this tool is that you can create practically any kind of panels you'd like. Whether you like to work with purely square or rectangular panels, or like to skew things up, you can make them on the Panel Ruler layer with no problems.

To create your panel borders:

1. **From the main menu, choose Layer⇨New Layer.**

2. **Select Panel Ruler Layer from the Layer Type drop-down list and click OK.**

   A thick blue rectangle appears around the inner rectangle of your print guide. That's your Panel Ruler Layer. That's what you use to shape and ultimately draw your panel borders.

3. **On the Tools palette, select the Panel Ruler Cutter tool.**

4. **Using your panels as a guide, drag the tool along the panel ruler, bisecting each area into two panels, as shown in Figure 3-10.**

5. **On the Tools palette, select the Object Selector tool.**

   Depending on how you drew the panels, the Panel Rulers you created may still be the wrong size. The Object Selector helps you shape the Panel Rulers further so that everything matches up.

Figure 3-10:
The Panel
Ruler Cutter
does exactly
what it says.

6. **Click one of the Panel Ruler edges (it turns red), and drag it until it meets your border, as shown in Figure 3-11.**

Repeat as necessary.

Figure 3-11:
The Object
Selector
tool helps
you stretch
the panel
rulers to
match your
panels.

Now that the Panel Rulers match what you roughed out, it's time to turn them into finished borders.

 7. **From the main menu, choose Ruler⇨Panel Ruler⇨Rasterize.**

    A Rasterize Panel Ruler dialog box pops up, as shown in Figure 3-12.

    In this exercise, I want you to keep things simple, so I have you create a simple raster layer. If you're interested in more complicated techniques, such as creating individual panel layers to work on, be sure to check out Chapter 7.

 8. **Select the Convert Panel Image to Raster Pen Layer check box.**

 9. **Type Borders in the Layer Name text box.**

10. **Make sure that the Convert Ruler Data to Ruler Layer and the Create Panel Ruler from Ruler Data check boxes are both deselected.**

11. **Click OK.**

 12. **On the Layers palette, hide the Panel Ruler layer by clicking the eye icon to the left of its name.**

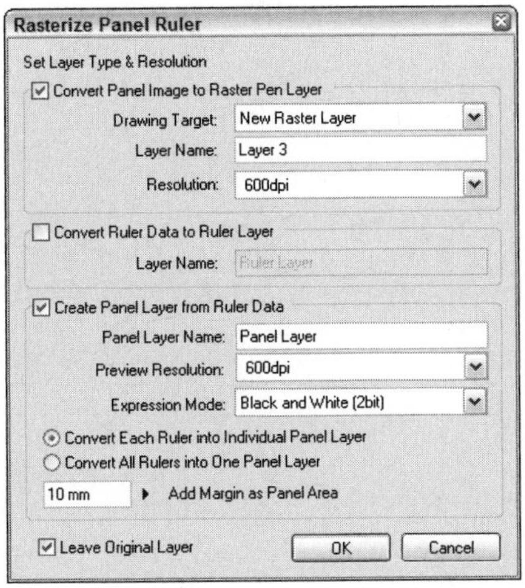

Figure 3-12:
The
Rasterize
Panel Ruler
dialog box.

Rasterize Panel Ruler

Set Layer Type & Resolution

☑ Convert Panel Image to Raster Pen Layer

Drawing Target: New Raster Layer

Layer Name: Layer 3

Resolution: 600dpi

☐ Convert Ruler Data to Ruler Layer

Layer Name: Ruler Layer

☑ Create Panel Layer from Ruler Data

Panel Layer Name: Panel Layer

Preview Resolution: 600dpi

Expression Mode: Black and White (2bit)

◉ Convert Each Ruler into Individual Panel Layer
○ Convert All Rulers into One Panel Layer

10 mm   ▶   Add Margin as Panel Area

☑ Leave Original Layer   OK   Cancel

And there you go! You should now see something much like what I created in Figure 3-13. Not only are the borders created, but the *gutters* (the space in between the panels) are all filled with white — so all the art outside the panels has automatically been trimmed.

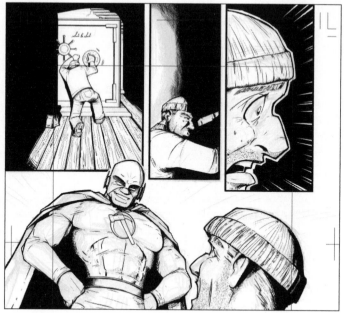

Figure 3-13:
A new layer
is created,
with your
completed
panel
borders and
excess
artwork
trimmed.

Adding Screentones

As a staple of many of your favorite manga, screentones help give your page that extra *pop,* for lack of a better term. Tones help to add color (rather, grays) to your black-and-white drawing. These can help add depth to your work and give you the ability to add effects you may not be able to do with inks alone.

To add tones to your page, follow these steps:

1. **If it isn't already open, click the Tones palette button on the Main tool-bar.**

2. **On the Tools palette, select the Lasso tool. (Or hold the button down for a few seconds and select the Polygonal Lasso tool.)**

3. **Using the Lasso tool, select an area on your drawing to paste the tone, as shown in Figure 3-14.**

   When you paste the tone onto your page, it's prudent to select the area you'd like to place the tone. Otherwise, any tone you paste will take up the entire page, and you'll just spend time erasing all the excess tone.

   Now that you've made your selection, you can choose the tone you'd like to use. Looking at the Tones palette, you'll see two folders, named Basic and Computones. (If you don't see them, click the Default folder in the Folder tree in the left pane).

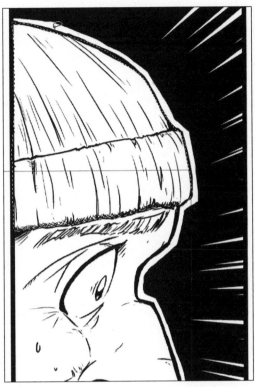

Figure 3-14:
The Lasso tool helps you select the area you'd like to paste the tone into.

For this exercise, I suggest using a tone from the Basic folder.

4. **Double-click the Basic➪Screen➪Dot➪35L folders.**

   Each of the sub-folders within the Dot folder represents tones with a set number of lines per inch. I explain this in Chapter 11, but the short version is that smaller numbers mean fewer lines, while larger numbers mean more lines. The 35L tones are a good middle ground.

5. **Click the 35L 25% tone sample.**

   The percentage represents how dark the tone is. The higher the percentage, the darker the tone.

6. **Click the Paste Tone button in the upper-left corner of the Tones palette.**

   If you check out the page, you see that the tone is now placed in your selection, as shown in Figure 3-15. Congratulations! Repeat the steps with different tone types, and you'll soon have your basic "colors" set on your page.

Figure 3-15:
After you add some tone, your selection really pops out from the rest of the page!

If you want to get trickier, you can overlap and erase your tones to create some more depth and dimensionality to the page. Check out Chapter 11 for more information and tips on how to do that.

 Each tone pasted on the page becomes its own layer. If you have multiple sections of the page that happen to use the same type of tone, you don't need to paste a brand-new one each time. Just make sure that the tone you want to use is highlighted on the Layers palette. Now, when you select an area, you can use the Fill tool to fill in the screentone.

Adding Text

Pictures are only one half of the equation when it comes to comics and manga. Whether it's for character dialogue or narration, the text of the story can be just as important as the images on the page. (See Figure 3-16.)

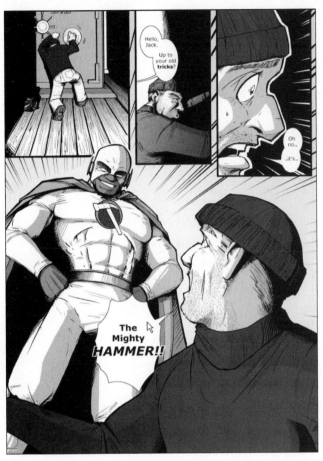

Figure 3-16:
It can be easier to understand a scene with word balloons.

I go over how to use the text in conjunction with word balloons in Chapter 12. For this exercise, you can use the Text tool to get a feel for how to add text to the page.

1. **On the Tools palette, click the Text button.**

2. **Find an area on your page where you'd like to place the dialogue and click it with your mouse or stylus.**

   You see the Layer Properties palette open with a new text tab selected, as shown in Figure 3-17. Here's where you're going to add your dialogue.

   Most comics and manga like to have their text center-aligned. You can do the same here.

Figure 3-17:
The Text
Properties
tab.

3. **Click the Align drop-down list and select Align Center.**

4. **Click the large text area and type whatever you'd like.**

   Be sure to add a couple of line breaks (press the Enter/Return key) every now and then to keep from creating one long sentence. It makes it easier to wrap a word balloon around the text.

5. **Click OK.**

Saving Your Work

There's nothing more frustrating than putting a lot of effort into a page and then losing it all because you forgot to save your work. Here's my friendly reminder to save . . . and save . . . and save. Save often. And then save again.

To save your new page in Manga Studio, follow these steps:

1. **From the main menu, choose File⇨Save.**

If this is the first time you're saving this page, the Save As dialog box opens, as shown in Figure 3-18.

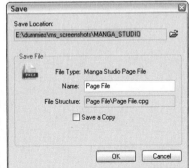

Figure 3-18:
The Save
dialog box.

2. To select where you'd like to save the file, click the folder icon next to the Save Location text box.

The Browse for Folder dialog box opens, as shown in Figure 3-19. Choose the folder you'd like to save the page in and click OK.

Figure 3-19:
(Windows)
Using the
Browse for
Folder
dialog box
helps you
place the
new page
where you
want it.

3. Enter the name of the page file in the Name text box.

As you change the name of the file, the filename, and corresponding folder name change in the next text box. This is because all the pertinent information for this page (along with the page file itself) is saved in its respective folder.

4. Click OK.

Reopening Your Work

Hopefully you remember where you saved your file, because it's pretty hard to reopen it otherwise. At least that's the only hard part of opening a Manga Studio file.

If you want to open a file you've recently worked on, you can reach it pretty quickly from the main menu. If you select File➪Recent Files, you'll see a list of the last few files you worked on. Select the file you want, and you're ready to go.

To open your Manga Studio file, follow these steps:

1. **From the main menu, choose File➪Open.**

    You should now see the Open File dialog box that goes with your particular flavor of operating system.

2. **Navigate to where you placed your Manga Studio Page File.**

    When the page was initially saved, it was placed in a folder of the same name as what you entered in Step 3 of the "Saving Your Work" section. So when you're looking for it, be sure to look inside that folder.

3. **Select the page file and click OK.**

Exporting to an Image File

If you're looking to save a copy of your work to use in another program, or if you want to create a file to send to a professional printer, Manga Studio has that covered. The Export function lets you create a file in many common formats at any size you'd like. Here, you get the option to choose what parts of the page are exported (such as inks, tones, or text), and which are ignored (such as roughs or the print guide). I explain these options in-depth in Chapter 5.

For this example, you can try exporting the page into a Web site-friendly format.

1. **From the main menu, choose File➪Export➪Export Image by Pixel Specification.**

    Notice in the Export menu that you actually have two ways you can export your file. If you know the exact size in inches or centimeters you'd like to export the file to, you would choose Export Image by Size Specification. But because this exercise is all about exporting for the Web, you'll want to export by pixel size. (I explain why pixels matter with Web applications in Chapter 13.)

    You now see the Export Image dialog box, as shown in Figure 3-20.

2. **Enter a width of** 700 **pixels in the Width text box.**

   The aspect ratio of the page is locked. This means that regardless of what size you set the width, the height automatically adjusts so that the page retains the same general shape. So when you adjust the width in the text box, the height is automatically adjusted as well.

   The average user has her computer monitor set at a resolution of 1024 pixels wide by 768 pixels high, with some still going as low as 800 by 600. Having an image of about 600–750 pixels is a safe size to cover every potential computer resolution you can run into, while still keeping some sense of readability.

3. **From the Resolution drop-down list, select 72 dpi.**

   72 dpi is the resolution that a computer monitor best approximates the physical size of the image. So anything beyond that, even though you'd be shrinking the image down to 700 pixels regardless, is overkill. Stick with 72 dpi if all you need is an image for the World Wide Web.

4. **In the Output area, select the Image Within Print Guide radio button.**

   Much like when the printer cuts off the trim area of your page for the final product, you want to do the same type of thing for your Web image. It's good to stay in the mindset that what really matters is the area of the page within the print guide and that anything in the trim area is expendable.

5. **In the Output Color Depth area, select the RGB Color radio button.**

   When you're exporting to such a small file, using a monochrome setting results in poor quality line work, and a moiré effect on your screentones (for those unfamiliar with the moiré effect, I discuss that in Chapter 11). Setting the image to RGB adds enough anti-aliasing to keep the integrity and general feel of the line art intact.

6. **In the Output Data Settings area, make sure that the Output Finished Image, Output Text, and Output Tone check boxes are the only ones selected.**

   Any layers you designated as Sketch layers (check out the "Roughing Your Page" section earlier in this chapter to set up your Sketch layers) are ignored when the file is exported, which is exactly what you want — because the only part you're interested in showing off is the final line work, tones, and text.

   The rest of the check boxes you see in the dialog box are irrelevant for exporting a Web-ready image, so they can remain unselected. But if you want to find more information on what exactly those other boxes do, you can check out Chapter 13, where I go over each and every one of them.

7. **Click OK.**

   What you see now is the Save As dialog box corresponding to your particular operating system.

8. **Enter the name of the file in the File Name text box.**

9. **Select JPEG from the Save As Type drop-down list.**

   JPEG files are probably the most well-known and often-used file format on the Web, as they produce a fine combination of image quality and file size. Odds are, every single graphical browser created can read a JPEG file, so you may as well stick with what works.

You're done! You now have a page that is all set for you to upload to your Web site of choice.

Printing a Hard Copy

"You mean it's not just File➪Print?"

It can be. But what if you want to print only the line art, without any screentones? Setting up your page for printing gives you the chance to be as specific as you want regarding what is printed and what is ignored. Then, when you're ready to print, you'll know that you're going to get exactly what you want.

For this example, you can set up the page to include the final artwork, the bleed area, and the print guide, should you decide to put together your book yourself or send off to a professional printer.

Follow these steps to set up your page for printing:

1. **From the main menu, select File⇨Print Setup.**

   The first thing that appears, at least the first time, is the Printer Setup dialog box. You can go through and change those settings however you want, depending on your printer type and your operating system.

2. **Click OK in the Printer Setup dialog box.**

   The Print Setup dialog box appears, as shown in Figure 3-21. This is where you can get as specific as you want, regarding what is printed and what is left behind.

3. **In the Print Size area, select Actual Size radio button.**

   This is going to depend on dimensions of the page file, but if you want to avoid any potential moiré effect in your screentones (see Chapter 11), it's best to print your work at actual size.

   If you're not able to print at the actual size, then you can choose to shrink the image down to fit the page by selecting the Adapt to the Page Format radio button.

4. **In the Print area, select the Entire Page radio button.**

   This makes sure that all the art you've drawn is printed, including the parts that you'll trim off later.

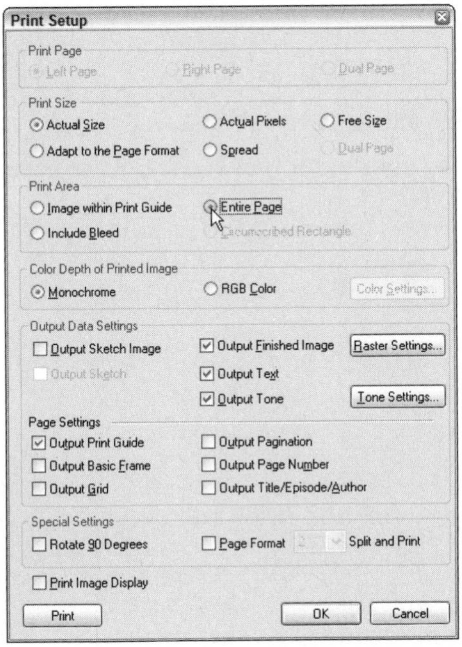

Figure 3-21: The Print Setup dialog box.

5. **In the Color Depth of Printed Image area, select the Monochrome radio button.**

   Unlike in the "Exporting to an Image File" section of this chapter, where you switch to RGB to maintain quality during image shrinking, keeping the image in monochrome when printing it works just fine. This helps maintain the sharpness of the line art and tones, without any chance of potential anti-aliasing happening.

6. **In the Output Data Settings area, select the check boxes that refer to the parts of your artwork that you want to print.**

   I go over this in much more detail in Chapter 13, but basically this section helps you pick and choose what parts of the image you want printed out.

   For example, if you wanted to print out only the line art and text, you would check the Output Finished Image and Output Text check boxes, and deselect all of the other ones in this section.

   For layers that you have as sketches and finished art, whatever gets printed will depend on how you've designated the layers. Check out the "Roughing Your Page Out" section of this chapter to find out how you can set the layer as Sketch or Finish.

7. **In the Page Settings area, select the Output Print Guide check boxes.**

   Printing the guide can help you later when you trim the bleed off the paper. All the other check boxes are irrelevant for this exercise (although I go over them all in Chapter 13).

8. **Click Print.**

   This brings you back to the Printer dialog box.

9. **Click OK in the Printer dialog box.**

   You're done! Check out your printer, and you should see your page, hot off the press.

Part II
Roughing It

The 5th Wave   By Rich Tennant

"How's it going? You get a handle on that Lasso function yet?"

In this part . . .

Before you dive headfirst into Manga Studio, it's a good idea to get a basic understanding of the program. You'll find it pretty difficult to start creating the next Great American Manga if you don't know how to set up your pages properly, or scan in your artwork, or get the drawing tools set up if you're planning on going the all-digital route.

This part of the book covers all the basics you need to get your page ready, from concept to finished pencils. Chapter 4 is all about properly setting up your page and story files so that they're at the proper dimensions you want to work in. Chapter 5 covers how to scan in your work and get it adjusted properly on the page. If you're looking to use a drawing tablet to clean up the scanned-in artwork — or possibly even create all your work digitally — the chapter also covers how to use the Pencil and Eraser tools, as well as how to work with the page as though it's a real piece of paper.

Chapter 6 helps you take advantage of the digital realm, with discussion of the various layers you can add to your page and how you can quickly adjust the layers' settings on-the-fly, if need be. Chapter 7 goes over how you can divide your page into panel layers that you can work on separate from the rest of the page, as well as how to quickly create nice, clean panel borders using the panel ruler layer.

Chapter 8 talks about how you can use Manga Studio's exclusive virtual ruler feature to create all kinds of rulers and guides to assist you in your technical drawing. Finally, Chapter 9 explains how you can use selections to make tweaks to your roughs without having to erase and start over, as well as using selection layers to save your selections for future use.

Chapter 4

Your New Page Awaits

*W*hen I first started drawing comics, I was pretty sure I understood how the system worked: I would draw all my art and word balloons within the borders of my 11-x-17-inch piece of bristol board and then send my stack of pages away to be printed. No problem! It wasn't until I first saw my work in a book that I realized I did something drastically wrong. Panels were cut off! Important pieces of art were nowhere to be seen! What happened?

It was then that I discovered terminology that would be vital if I ever wanted to see my artwork in print — terms such as *bleed, trim,* and *safe area.* Confusing? Totally! I had no idea that printing comics would be so . . . technical!

Fortunately for you, Manga Studio helps with this very important step as soon as you open a new document. In this chapter, I show you how to set up your pages so that you don't have to learn the hard way where your pages will be trimmed at the printer, and so on . . . like I did.

Creating a New Page

Before you can draw the first line in Manga Studio, you need to open a new page. Admittedly, not a big surprise. To do this, choose File⇨New⇨Page on the main menu or press Ctrl+N (⌘+N on the Mac).

Instead of a blank canvas suddenly appearing, you see a New Page dialog Box with two tabs: Custom Page and Page Templates. If you're interested in setting up your own page, read on. If, however, you're impatiently saying, "But I want to start drawing *now*," skip ahead to the "Selecting page templates a la carte" section.

Setting up a custom page: As you like it

The Custom Page tab of the New Page dialog box, shown in Figure 4-1, is where you'll select the size of the paper you wish to work with, as well as its resolution, finish frame, basic frame, and bleed width.

Open a new, custom page by following these steps:

1. **Choose File⇨New⇨Page. Alternatively, click the New Page icon on the toolbar (it's the leftmost icon) or press Ctrl+N (⌘+N on the Mac).**

   A New Page dialog box appears. Notice the settings area on the left side of the dialog box and a preview area on the right. Changes you make on the left side are reflected in the right side preview.

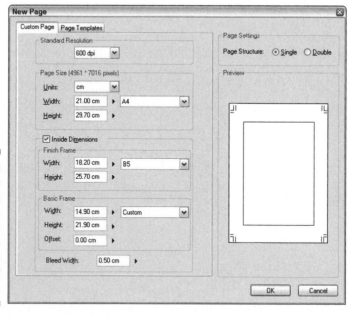

Figure 4-1:
The Custom Page tab allows you to create your own page however you'd like.

2. **To set up a customized page, make sure the Custom Page tab is active and then select the options you want.**

   The options on the Custom Page tab are as follows:

   - *Standard Resolution (dpi):* The technical definition of *dpi* (dots per inch) is the number of dots that a printer can print within a one-inch line. What this means for you is simple: The higher the resolution chosen for your page, the crisper the line art and tone work will be when it's printed.

   The drawback to working at a higher resolution is that it results in a bigger page, and therefore a large file size. Larger pages (like, say, an 11-x-16-inch piece of paper at 1200 dpi) can be more taxing on your computer, especially if the computer is more than a few years old or you have a small amount of memory available. So, if Manga Studio seems to be running sluggishly, try the same size paper at a lower resolution and see if that improves things.

   - *Page Size:* This refers to the physical dimensions of your page. From here, you can select your units of measurement (inches, centimeters, millimeters, or pixels) and adjust the width and height as small or as large as you'd like. If you prefer a preset size, the drop-down list on the right provides a list of page dimensions to choose from. (I break down what each of the sizes are in Table 4-1.)

   The size of the page has limits. You can't create a page larger than 42 x 42 centimeters (approximately 16.5 x 16.5 inches) or smaller than 3 x 3 centimeters (approximately 1.1 x 1.1 inches).

3. **Select the Inside Dimensions check box to display a collection of blue lines in the preview pane.**

   The blue lines are printing guides that assist you if you're planning on having your work printed and bound. You can adjust the settings of each frame to what you need. These guides are:

   - *Finish Frame:* Also known as the *trim*. This is the absolute boundary for your page. Anything drawn beyond these borders won't be visible when printed.

   - *Basic Frame:* Also known as the *safe* or *live area*. This is where all the important pieces of art and dialogue go. Anything within this frame won't be cut off by the printer. You can offset this frame by however far to the left or right you would like it.

   - *Bleed Width:* Sometimes an artist wants to extend the art to the absolute edge of the page. To prevent any possible white edges showing in the final print, a bleed extending past the finish frame is set. Make sure there is nothing important you want shown in the bleed area, or it will be lost!

It's always better to err on the side of caution when it comes to the bleed width of your page. If you're planning on having your manga professionally printed, it's much better to have too much bleed than not enough. This is because the settings on copiers and paper cutters can vary from printing service to printing service. If you aren't careful, your full-bleed artwork may have white streaks along the edge!

4. **When you've finished adjusting your settings, click OK.**

Selecting page templates a la carte

If you don't feel like setting up your own page, just switch to the Page Templates tab, as shown in Figure 4-2, and you have a large variety of predefined templates at your disposal. All of the necessary page dimensions have been planned out for you, so all you need to do is choose your resolution and start working!

Looking at the list of templates can be a bit daunting, especially if you aren't familiar with the terminology of paper sizes or what the difference between Submission paper and Dojinshi paper. (Don't feel bad. I didn't really know when I first started making comics either!) Table 4-1 breaks down the various page sizes into centimeters and inches.

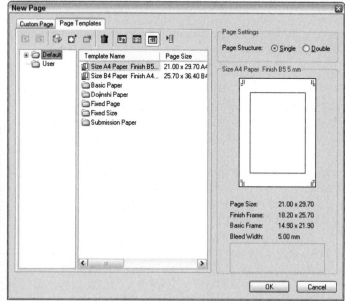

Figure 4-2:
The Page Templates tab gives you plenty of predefined pages to choose from.

Table 4-1	Common Paper Sizes for Manga	
Paper	*Size in cm*	*Size in Inches*
A3	29.7 x 42.0 cm	11.7 x 16.5 inches
A4	21 x 29.7 cm	8.3 x 11.7 inches
A5	14.8 x 21 cm	5.8 x 8.3 inches
A6	10.5 x 14.8 cm	4.1 x 5.8 inches
B4	25.7 x 36.4 cm	10.1 x 14.3 inches
B5	18.2 x 25.7 cm	7.2 x 10.1 inches
B6	12.8 x 18.2 cm	5 x 7.2 inches
B7	9.1 x 12.8 cm	3.6 x 5 inches
Japanese postcard	10.0 cm x 14.8 cm	3.9 x 5.8 inches

So, when you see a template with the title Basic Page A6 Finish B7 5mm, it's telling you that you'll be working on a 10.5-x-14.8-centimeter piece of paper with a finish frame of 9.1 x 12.8 centimeters and a bleed width of 5 millimeters.

The page templates are shown in centimeters. So keep that in mind when you select your template. If you aren't careful, that piece of paper you think is 10 x 15 inches will turn out to be 4 x 6 inches! I've made that mistake on more than one occasion, so I speak from experience.

Now that I've covered the sizes, you can tackle the various template types that are available to you:

- ✔ **Basic Paper:** As its name implies, these are basic templates with various sizes for the canvas as well as its bleed, finish, and basic frames. These templates are available in both 600 and 1200 dpi.

- ✔ **Dojinshi Paper:** *Dojinshi* is a Japanese term used for independently produced/distributed manga. These are fan comics that are made outside the system and are sold through mail order or other means, instead of in book and comic stores.

- ✔ **Fixed Page:** This is the same as the basic paper types, with a larger variety of sizes and resolutions.

- ✔ **Fixed Size:** These are templates that are formatted in inches or pixels. They don't have any printing frames associated with them; they're just blank pages. The pages formatted by pixels are at a much lower resolution than any of the other templates (72 and 150 dpi).

- ✔ **Submission Paper:** These are templates typically used for various Japanese magazines.

Just like on the Custom Page tab, you can select a single page or a two-page spread.

Now for the moment you've been waiting for: selecting your template!

1. **From the main menu, choose File⇨New⇨Page.**

2. **Select the Page Templates tab on the New Page dialog box.**

3. **Choose your template from the Default folder on the left side of the window.**

   Click the folder of the paper type you'd like to work from.

4. **If there are a group of folders organized by resolution, choose the folder of the resolution you'd like to work in.**

5. **Choose the template size you'd like to work on from the list on the center window.**

6. **In the Page Settings section (located above the page preview on the right side of the window), select the Single option button if you'd like only one page, or you can select the Double option button if you'd like to work on a two-page spread.**

7. **When you're set, click the OK button.**

   You're now ready to start drawing!

Creating your own page templates

Say you've looked through the list of page templates but don't see what you need to work with. Or perhaps you've created a custom page but you don't want to change the settings every time you want to create a new page (or worse, forget what your settings originally were!). Fortunately, Manga Studio allows you to design your own template. Now, you can create and come back to your custom page whenever you want, and not worry about having to change any settings!

If you skipped the "Setting up a custom page: As you like it" section earlier, now is your chance to go back and review how that section works, because the New Template dialog box works exactly the same way.

To create your own template, follow these steps:

1. **Choose File⇨New⇨Page.**

   Alternatively, you can click the New Page icon or press Ctrl+N (⌘+N on a Mac).

2. **In the New Page dialog box that appears, click the Page Templates tab.**

3. **Click the New Template button on the Page Templates menu.**

   The Page Template Settings dialog box appears, which is almost identical to the Custom Page tab you see when creating a new page. (Refer to Figure 4-1.)

4. **Make sure the User folder is highlighted in the left pane of the Page Templates tab.**

   You can create a custom template only in that folder.

5. **Like the Custom Page tab, you select your resolution, finish frame size, basic frame size, and bleed width.**

   (See the earlier section, "Setting up a custom page: As you like it," for details on these settings.)

6. **Enter a name for your template in the Template Name text box.**

7. **(Optional) Type any notes or reminders you may wish to include in the Memo text box.**

8. **Save your template by clicking the OK button.**

   When you save the template, the resolution and page size become fixed. You can't go back and change them. So, be sure that this is the size you wish to work with!

That's not to say that everything is locked up on your new template! You can still edit the size of the basic frame, finish frame, and bleed area at any time. Follow these steps to view your new template's properties and make any adjustments (or view the properties of the preinstalled templates):

1. **When in the New Page Window, double-click the user-created template you want to adjust.**

   The New Template dialog box pops up.

2. **Now you can adjust the template's frames, bleed area, title, and memo.**

   (With the preinstalled templates, you can select only the units of measurement. It doesn't change any dimensions but at least helps you if you're used to metric or imperial units.)

If you've made a mistake in your template creation, no problem! On the page template menu, there's a Trash Can icon. Just highlight the page you wish to remove and click the Trash Can, as shown in the margin. That's all!

You can adjust the properties of the page you're currently working on at any time by double-clicking the Print Guide and Basic Frame Layer on the Layers palette. You'll see a properties tab appear similar to the page template properties. From here, you can adjust the Finish Frame, Basic Frame, and Bleed width. You won't be able to adjust the page's resolution or physical size.

Save As Template: On-the-fly template creation

As you work on your page, you may find that the template settings you created (or opened from one of the default templates) aren't quite working like you originally expected. So, you make your adjustments to the print guide, add and adjust a few layers (I cover how to do this in Chapter 6), and you're all set to go. If you're planning on using these settings for future pages or stories, however, you don't want to have to readjust the settings all over again, do you? (Especially because the New Template dialog box doesn't give you the option to add and adjust layer settings.)

Manga Studio provides the option to save a new template at this stage.

1. **Choose File⇨Save As Template from the main menu.**

   A window pops up, just like the one used for creating new templates.

2. **Enter a descriptive name for your template in the Template Name text box.**

3. **Make any final adjustments to the print guide dimensions.**

4. **(Optional) Add a memo in the Memo text box.**

   (Or remove them altogether, if you'd like.)

5. **Click the OK button, and your template is now saved in the User folder of your page templates, ready to be reused again and again!**

Just like when you use an existing template, you can't adjust the physical size of the page. So, if you're working on an 8-x-10-inch page, it will remain that size when you save your new template.

Creating a New Story

Manga Studio provides a great organizational tool for those who may be working on a book (or a chapter of a book). Creating a new story allows you to have as many pages as you need in one convenient place. Now, instead of opening an individual page to work on, you can open a story, select your page from a list, add and delete pages as needed, create two-page spreads, and preview how consecutive pages may look when placed together.

To create a new story, follow these steps:

1. **From the main menu, choose File⇨New⇨Story.**

Alternatively, click the New Story Icon on the toolbar (second from the left), or you can press Ctrl+Alt+N (⌘+Option+N on the Mac) on your keyboard.

The New Story dialog box pops up, as shown in Figure 4-3. It's just like the one used for creating a new page (custom pages or page templates), except that there is a new group of settings available called Page Settings:

- *Pages:* This is where you enter the number of pages you want for your story or chapter. The drop-down list provides a selection of choices, or you can enter your own number.

- *Closing Position:* This setting depends on how you would like the book to be read. If you're going for an authentic manga style, where the reader reads from right to left, choose Right. If you'd like the reader to read from left to right, choose Left.

- *Starting Page:* This determines what the starting position for the first page of your book will be. If you'd like the first page to start on the right side, choose Right; for the left side, choose Left.

- *Page Structure:* This gives you the option of either keeping each page in the story separate (Single) or joining them together by twos, so you can spread your art over two pages (Double).

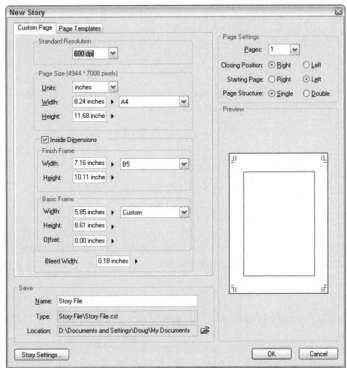

Figure 4-3:
The New Story dialog box helps you set up your multi-page story file.

2. **After you've adjusted your page settings, create or select your page size and print guides.**

   (Check out the "Setting up a custom page: As you like it" and "Selecting page templates a la carte" sections in this chapter.)

3. **Enter the name of your story in the Name text box, located in the Save section at the bottom of the dialog box.**

4. **Click the Location button to select the place on your computer you'd like the files saved.**

5. **When that's all set, click the OK button.**

A new window appears, containing thumbnails of all the pages you've created for your story. All you need to do now is double-click your mouse on the page (or pages, if it's a two-page spread) you'd like to work on, and it opens in a new window!

What happens if you're working on your story and you realize that you have too many pages (or not enough)? Manga Studio has that covered as well!

1. **Choose Story⇨Insert Page.**

   Alternatively, right-click (Control+click on the Mac) a story page and select Insert Page. Or click the Show Menu button on the toolbar and select Insert Page.

   The Insert Page window pops up. You can't choose a page size different from what you already selected for your story, but you can choose the number of pages you wish to add.

   a. *Enter the number of pages you wish to add in the Insert Page combo box (or select a number from the list provided).*

   b. *Select whether you want to add these pages before or after the current page.*

2. **If you want to delete a page, select Delete Page.**

3. **When you're done, click the OK button.**

From the Story Window, you can adjust the single/double page settings on a page-by-page basis. To do this, click the page you wish to combine or separate and choose either Story⇨Match Pages to combine them or Story⇨Unmatch Pages to split them up.

Adding author and page information

Having your pages centrally located in one story file is certainly a convenient means of keeping your story together. But what if you want to include some additional clerical information to the file, such as story file or author name?

Manga Studio gives you that ability with the Change Story Settings dialog box. This dialog box gives you the option to add items like the author or story name, page number placement and format, and so on. Even more, you can choose to add that info to only one page, or to all the pages in the story file at once.

For this example, you can use the included story file (labeled, simply enough, Story File), located in the Author/Chapter 4 folder of the CD-ROM.

To use the Change Story Settings function, follow these steps:

1. **Open the story file, and make sure that you are in the Story window.**

2. **Choose Story⇨Change Story Settings from the Main menu.**

   With the Change Story Settings dialog box open (see Figure 4-4), you can now insert the following information onto the story file.

   - *Story Info:* Inserts the story's title, episode number, and subtitle to the page. Additionally, you can choose the placement of the information (lower left, center, or right) on the page.

   - *Author Info:* Inserts the author's name to the page. Additionally, you can choose to place the author's name on the bottom left, bottom center, or bottom right of the page.

   - *Page Number:* Sets the placement of the page number on the page. You can choose to place it on the bottom left, bottom center, or bottom right of the page.

   - *Pagination Settings:* When selected, the page number is placed and formatted within the print guide of the page.

     You can add a prefix or suffix to the page number, set the starting page number, and set its placement on the page (bottom left, bottom center, or bottom right of the basic frame).

   - *Apply Settings to All Pages:* When selected, all the information (and placement of that info on the page) you added to this dialog box will be saved to all the pages in the file. You can choose to save both the content and placement together, just the content, or just the content placement.

     Left unchecked, the info and positioning you entered will be saved to the currently selected page.

3. **Click OK to add your selected elements to the page.**

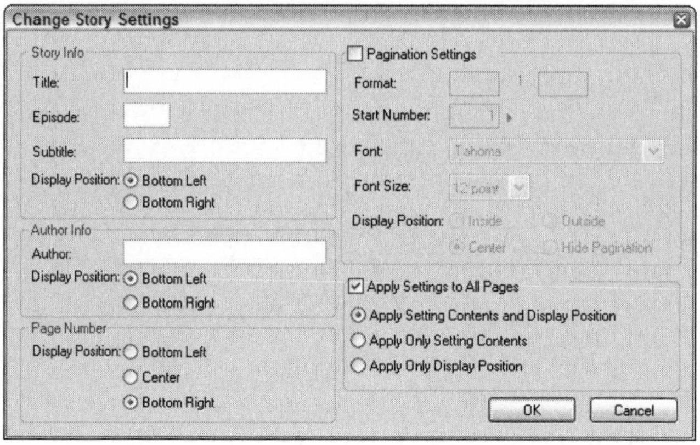

Figure 4-4:
The Change
Story
Settings
dialog box
helps you
add the title
and author
name.

Change Story Settings

Story Info
Title:
Episode:
Subtitle:
Display Position: ⦿ Bottom Left
○ Bottom Right

Author Info
Author:
Display Position: ⦿ Bottom Left
○ Bottom Right

Page Number
Display Position: ○ Bottom Left
○ Center
⦿ Bottom Right

☐ Pagination Settings
Format:
Start Number: 1 ▸
Font: Tahoma
Font Size: 12 point
Display Position: Inside   Outside
⦿ Center   ○ Hide Pagination

☑ Apply Settings to All Pages
⦿ Apply Setting Contents and Display Position
○ Apply Only Setting Contents
○ Apply Only Display Position

OK   Cancel

The Save Button: A Vital Tool

After you create/open your new page or story, you see a new blank page
ready for you to draw away to your heart's content. Before you get too
far along, though, it would probably be wise to know how to save your
newly-created work.

You can save your work in three ways:

✔ Click the Save button on the main toolbar.

✔ Choose File⇨Save.

✔ Press Ctrl+S (⌘+S on the Mac).

By default, saving a new document immediately brings you to a Save As
dialog box. Here, you can name the page (or story), choose where on your
computer you'd like to save it, and choose to save a separate copy of
your work (if you want to save different versions of your art, for example).

Saving frequently is the most important thing you can do in Manga Studio.
Your computer or program can crash unexpectedly, taking your art along
with it. It can be very frustrating to work on an intricate piece of art, forget
to save, and then watch it vanish because of a system crash or power outage.
So save frequently! You'll thank yourself in the long run.

Chapter 5

Importing and Penciling Your Rough Draft

In This Chapter

▶ Importing art from a scanner or an image file

▶ Adjusting the imported art for the page

▶ Drawing digitally with the Pencil tool

▶ Choosing the size of your Pencil and Eraser tools

▶ Moving around the canvas as you work

*I*t's funny; when I sat down to write this chapter, I couldn't think what to write for the introduction. Then it hit me . . . that's probably the fundamental thing you need before you can start working on a project — a place to start. When you don't have a starting point, you've got *nothing*.

For the purposes of Manga Studio, the starting point is your rough draft. It can be a quick sketch done on a sticky note, or it can be a blank canvas waiting for you to apply your first strokes on your tablet with the Pencil tool.

In this chapter, I explain how to import art into Manga Studio using your scanner, as well as how to import art files you may already have on your computer. If you plan on penciling digitally or you just want to touch up your imported roughs, I explain the ins and outs of your two new Manga Studio friends, the Pencil and Eraser tools. Finally, I explain how you can easily treat this digital canvas like it's a physical piece of paper with the Hand, Rotate, and Zoom tools.

Time to Import Some Art!

Maybe you're like me, and you're raring to use your mouse or drawing tablet and start sketching away with the different tools Manga Studio offers. However, you may prefer to get your hands dirty with graphite and/or ink, and you'd simply like to know how to import your scanned work into Manga Studio. The following sections show you how to import your work from a scanner or from an electronic art file.

TIP

Scanning tips and tricks

If you're new to the world of scanning, it can be a bit tricky to import your image into Manga Studio properly. Here are a few tips to help make sure you get the best-quality scan possible. Doing so will certainly help you when it comes time to ink and/or screentone your page.

✔ Make sure that the scanner glass is free from dust and smudges.

✔ Check your paper to make sure it's properly aligned with the glass. (Unless you sketched your drawing crooked. In that case, you can align the paper however you'd like.)

✔ Use the Brightness and Contrast to adjust the image optimally. You have the option of using your scanner's settings, or using Manga Studio's Brightness and Contrast filters. Try each of these out to see which will produce the best result. (Heck, you may find that using both will help!)

✔ If your computer can handle it, try to scan your drawing at 300 dpi or greater resolution. It's a lot easier to ink your work from crisp pencils than blurry ones. Scanning at a higher resolution and scaling it down to fit the page helps. I go over scaling in the "Adjusting the image size" section, later in this chapter.

Using your scanner

Manga Studio offers several options for importing your work into the program. The most direct method is to scan in your artwork.

Before you can scan anything, you need to let Manga Studio know where your scanner is. To do so, follow these steps:

1. **From the main menu, choose File➪Import➪Select TWAIN Device.**

   The Select Source dialog box opens with a selection of peripheral devices it believes could be your scanner. (See Figure 5-1.)

Figure 5-1:
The Select
Source
dialog box.

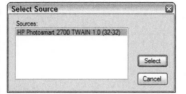

2. **Select the device from the list and click the Select button.**

Now you can scan in your art! Follow these steps to scan and import your artwork:

1. **From the main menu, choose File⇨Import⇨TWAIN.**

   The scanning dialog box for your scanner appears.

2. **Follow the directions for your particular scanner.**

   Each scanner has a different window for scanning and adjusting your image. As such, it's nearly impossible for me to possibly cover all of them. So, I simply suggest that you follow along with whatever your scanning program would like you to do.

3. **Click the OK (or Scan) button when you're happy with the scan preview.**

Importing an image file

Perhaps you've already scanned your work into your computer through a different program. Or maybe you've used a digital sketching program to create your roughs. In that case, the Import Image File function best suits your needs.

Follow these steps to import an existing art file into Manga Studio:

1. **From the main menu, choose File⇨Import⇨Image File.**

2. **When the Open File dialog box opens, navigate to wherever you've stored your image file, select it, and click OK.**

You see the Import Images dialog box. If the imported image is set how you want it to be on the page, click OK. If not, the next section helps you tweak the image's settings until it's exactly the way you want it displayed on the page.

With Manga Studio Debut, you have the option of importing a JPEG (.JPG) or bitmap (.BMP) image. If you have Manga Studio EX, you can also import PNG (.PNG) and Targa (.TGA) files. If your artwork is not in one of those formats, Manga Studio won't be able to find it!

What Happened?! (The Image Looks All Wonky)

So you imported your image into Manga Studio, but things don't seem right when you view it on the page? The image size is completely wrong! And why is the color all gone? (That is, if your drawing was in color.) Or worse, why can't you see (or only barely see) the pencil work you just scanned in?! Check out Figure 5-2 — which is what I think would be a worst-case scenario.

It's okay. Your image is really there, and it's a cinch to tweak the settings so you can see your art, as well as resize, rotate, and position it so that you can get right to work.

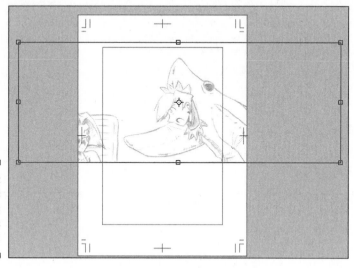

Figure 5-2:
Ack! What's wrong with this picture?!

ON THE CD

I've included a sample image on the CD (look in the Author/Chapter 5 folder) so you can see what happens when you import an image larger than the page you're working on. It's a good way to practice and experiment with the various image properties and transformations.

Adjusting the image layer settings

The first order of business is to adjust the settings so you can see your roughs. Here's how to do that:

1. **If you haven't done this already, import the image.**

   See the earlier section, "Importing an image file," for instructions.

   The Import Images window opens.

2. **If it isn't already active, click the Layer Settings tab (shown in Figure 5-3).**

3. **Enter or change the name of the image in the Layer Name text box.**

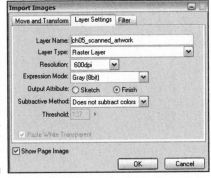

Figure 5-3:
Change
your
imported
image's
layer
settings.

4. **Choose an option from the Layer Type drop-down list:**

    • If you're using the image as a reference for inking and you aren't planning on making any changes to it, select Sketch Layer from the Layer Type drop-down list.

    This creates a layer on the page that you can't modify. The rest of the layer settings are grayed out at this stage, so you're now done changing your layer settings. If you need to fix the imported image's size, skip ahead to the next section, "Adjusting the image size."

    • If you're planning on making additional tweaks to the image after importing it, select Raster Layer from the Layer Type drop-down list.

5. **Select the image resolution you'd like the image to be from the Resolution drop-down list.**

    The higher the resolution you choose, the smoother your lines are when working on this image. This choice is a matter of preference, so feel free to experiment.

6. **The Expression Mode drop-down list sets the amount of grayscale you want in your image. You can choose among Black (1bit), Black and White (2bit), or Gray (8bit).**

    If you're trying to import pencils, I suggest choosing the 8Bit (256 Shades of Gray) option because it produces a better-quality image. However, you can always experiment and see what works best for you. You can see the differences among the various resolutions in Figure 5-4.

8Bit Does Not Convert to Gray

2Bit Threshold (27)

Figure 5-4:
The same
image
shown in
various
resolutions.

2Bit Dither

2Bit Diffusion

7. Choose whether your image is a sketch or finished layer from the Output Attribute radio buttons.

This is useful later on when you're exporting or printing your image. I go into further detail about the output attributes in Chapter 13.

8. If you select either 1Bit (Black Only) or 2Bit (Black and White) from the Expression Mode drop-down list, select how you want the *intermediate colors* (the shades of gray between black and white) displayed in the Subtractive Method drop-down list. The following options are available:

- *Threshold:* Depending on the shade, any grays become either black or transparent (or black and white, if you selected the 2Bit (Black and White option). (Refer to Figure 5-4.) How the colors are divided depend on the threshold level you enter in the Threshold text box.

- *Dither:* This option converts the grays into a collection of one-pixel black dots of various densities (depending on the shade of gray). (Refer to Figure 5-4.)

- *Diffusion:* Much like dithering, the Diffusion option converts the grays into a series of one-pixel black dots of varying densities. Diffusion goes into a greater level of detail than dithering. (Refer to Figure 5-4.)

9. **If you've chosen the Threshold subtractive method, enter the threshold level in the Threshold text box.**

   This helps Manga Studio decide how to split up the shades of gray between black and transparent/white. Each shade of gray has a value between 0 and 255. If you chose a threshold value of 100, any shade of gray with a value below 100 will become black, while anything above 100 will become transparent or white. Check out Figure 5-5 for some examples of various threshold levels.

10. **If you don't need to adjust the image's size or position, click OK. If you *do* need to adjust the image's size or position, skip ahead to the next section, "Adjusting the image size."**

Dither and Diffusion do not preview properly in Manga Studio. You will see only the changes made to the imported image when you click OK.

Now that you can see your image properly, you can focus on getting the darn thing to fit on the page!

Threshold: 27

Threshold: 50

Figure 5-5:
Examples of
threshold
levels.

Threshold: 100

Adjusting the image size

When you import an image, it sometimes appears much larger or smaller than you expected. (Refer to Figure 5-2.) If your imported image is too large or too small, you can correct the problem by following these steps:

1. **Import your image (see the "Importing an image file" section), and when you arrive at the Import Images dialog box, click the Move and Transform tab, shown in Figure 5-6.**

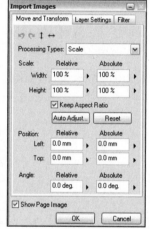

Figure 5-6:
The Move
and
Transform
tab.

2. **Make sure the Keep Aspect Ratio check box is selected.**

   This helps maintain the original *aspect ratio* (the ratio of the width and height) of your image. In other words, it ensures that your image isn't squashed, stretched, or distorted when you resize it.

3. **Click the Auto Adjust button.**

   A new dialog box, shown in Figure 5-7, opens with these options:

   • *Position:* This drop-down list enables you to adjust the image relative to the page, print guide, or basic frame by selecting among the Page, Outside Print Guide, Inside Print Guide, or Basic Frame. (The latter three options are applicable only if you're using the print guide and basic frame.)

   • *Page:* If you're using a double page, you use this drop-down list to select whether to position the image on the left or right page by selecting the Left Page or the Right Page option.

   • *Direction:* Selecting the Up, Left, Right, or Down option button positions and sizes the page relative to either the top, left, right, or bottom of the page.

- *Pixel Ratio to the Original Image:* This is an optional drop-down list that resizes the page according to the percentage you select, from 100% to 800%. You *can't* add your own percentage to this drop-down list.

- *Align to the Previously Loaded Position:* This button pretty much works only if you have previously imported and resized an image. Clicking this button adjusts the position and size of the image exactly like the previously imported image. The aspect ratio of the image is ignored, so this choice will squash or stretch your image.

Figure 5-7:
Auto
adjusting
the image is
a snap!

4. **The Auto Adjust dialog box doesn't have an OK or Cancel button. To exit this dialog box, just click your mouse on the Import Images dialog box.**

5. **Click one of the boxes along the edges of the preview pane and drag the box to resize the image.**

   If you look carefully at the image in the preview pane, you'll notice that it's surrounded by a thin border with tiny boxes along the corners and sides. The boxes are where you can grab and resize with your mouse. Using one of the boxes along the perimeter, drag the image in and out until it fits approximately within the borders of the finish frame.

   Resizing the image may move it out of the page. If that happens, just click the image and drag the image to the center of the page, and continue to resize until the image is where you want it to be.

   If the image was scanned in crooked, you can use the Rotate tool until it lines up properly to the page. In the Import Images dialog box, select Rotate from the Processing Types drop-down list. Then, just like scaling, use your mouse to grab the image (or use the angle's absolute/relative values) and rotate until it looks right.

   To manually position the image, just click your mouse anywhere within the black border and move the image to your desired place.

If you don't wish to use the mouse to resize, position, or rotate the image, you can enter the values in the Scale, Position, and Angle text boxes in the Import Images dialog box.

6. If you're happy with the settings, click OK.

If you're feeling experimental, you can use some of the other options from the Processing Type drop-down list, such as Distort, Perspective, or Free Transform. These options can create effects you may not have thought of before, so have fun and play around. If you don't like what you see, you can always start over!

It's possible that you may have imported your image and clicked OK in the Import Images dialog box before you adjusted anything. The best thing to do in this instance is to undo the action by pressing Ctrl+Z (⌘+Z on the Mac) and import the image again.

Regarding color

Manga Studio is first and foremost a black-and-white program, so any color image you import into the system automatically becomes grayscale (at least initially — there are options for adding color later on in the production process). I cover color options in Chapters 6 and 14.

The Pencil and Eraser Tools: Your New Best Friends

As a person who likes to consider himself a penciler above all else, I find the Pencil and Eraser tools to be the items I absolutely, positively need to have. They give me the freedom I want to just go crazy with my roughs like I would with a traditional pencil and paper. The kicker is, with Manga Studio's Pencil and Eraser tools, I don't waste paper as I struggle to figure out exactly what I want to draw. (Believe me, that happens more often than not!)

However, these tools aren't just for those who have decided to make the total digital leap. If you're still well-grounded in the traditional tools of the trade and primarily use Manga Studio for inking and/or screen toning, you'll still find the Pencil and Eraser tools useful. It's a snap to clean up your scan, remove or tighten up a few lines here and there, or strengthen the outline around your characters to help them stick out just a bit more.

If you're drawing digitally or just cleaning up your scanned-in artwork, I'm sure the more you use the Pencil and Eraser tools in Manga Studio, the more you'll discover how indispensable they truly are.

Laying down the line: The Pencil tool

There are two ways to access the Pencil tool:

- ✔ On the Tools palette, select the Pencil tool, as shown in Figure 5-8.
- ✔ On the keyboard, press the P key until the Pencil tool is selected.

  Some tools in Manga Studio share the same shortcut key. In this case, the P key is shared by the Pencil, Pen, and Magic Marker tools. Pressing the P key multiple times will cycle through each of the three tools.

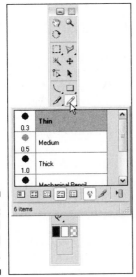

Figure 5-8:
The Pencil
tool and
cursor.

When you've selected the Pencil tool, the cursor changes to what looks like a tiny pencil when you hover it over the page. All you need to do next is . . . draw! Draw like you normally would with a real pencil.

Whoops: The Eraser tool

I'd love to meet the artist who can do his or her work without the need for an eraser, because I could certainly learn a thing or two from this superhuman. For the rest us, Manga Studio provides a wide variety of erasers. You access the Eraser tool in two ways:

- ✔ On the Tools palette, select the Eraser tool.
- ✔ On the keyboard, press E.

When you choose the Eraser tool, the mouse cursor changes to a small eraser icon when you hover it over the page. Then, just like the pencil tool, you just need to draw over the offending piece of art and watch it disappear forever (unless you want to Undo the erasing, of course)!

If you have a drawing tablet with an eraser tip, there's a third option for you: Just turn the pen over and erase away. Unlike the Eraser tool, which you can set to any size you need (I explain how to do that in the next section), the size the eraser tip uses depends on the size of the drawing tool you're currently using. So, if you're using the pencil with a 0.5 mm tip, the eraser will also be 0.5 mm.

Pencils and erasers of all shapes and sizes

While initially, it may look like there's only one size pencil and eraser to work with, you actually have a large selection to choose from! Manga Studio comes with a prebuilt selection of pencils and erasers to use, which you can select and tweak however you'd like. Taking into account the myriad options you can adjust, tweak, and modify, you have a near-infinite number of tools at your disposal. Try carrying *that* number of pencils and erasers around in your toolbox.

You can access the tool selections in two ways:

✔ On the Tools palette, click and hold your mouse on the Pencil or Eraser tool.

A menu appears with a selection of different sizes and styles for that tool. For tools such as the Pencil and Pen, the menu provides different tips you can choose to draw with. (Refer to Figure 5-8 to see the menu for the Pencil tool.) Just select your option from the list and draw (or erase) away.

✔ Open the Tool Options palette (shown in Figure 5-9) by pressing F3 on your keyboard.

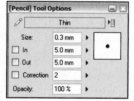

Figure 5-9:
The Tool
Options
palette.

✔ Here's where you really get to have fun, as you tweak your tool settings as you see fit. Here are your options:

- *Tool Settings Menu:* Right at the top of the palette, you'll see the name of the tool you currently have selected. (For example, you may see Medium for the Pencil tool.) Click the name, and a drop-down list appears, like the one shown on the Tools palette, with your selection of pencils and erasers. Click the tool option you wish to use.

- *Size:* All the tool sizes in Manga Studio are measured in millimeters. You can enter the size you'd like to use in the Size text box, or you can click the black arrow and drag the slider that appears to select your desired size.

- *Affect Display Size (Eraser Only):* Selecting this option adjusts the size of the eraser, depending on how far you've zoomed in or out on the page. The further you zoom in, the smaller the eraser becomes, and vice versa.

  If you're changing the Eraser settings, your options end here, but if you're changing the pencil settings, keep reading.

- *In/Out:* This option is very useful if you're drawing with a mouse or a tablet with no pressure sensitivity. These two options add a taper to the lines you draw at either the beginning (In) or end (Out). Enter the value you'd like for the tapered length in the text box. You can also click the black arrow and use the slider to select your desired taper length.

- *Correction:* Sometimes (especially when you're drawing from a smaller zoom size) you'll notice that the lines come out crooked or jittery as you draw. Selecting the Correction check box helps alleviate that problem by correcting the jitter. You can manually enter the amount of jitter correction in the Correction text box or use the slider to select your desired value.

- *Opacity:* This adjusts the transparency of your pencil lines. Enter the percentage you'd like to work at in the Opacity text box or use the slider to select your desired level.

To quickly adjust the size of your drawing tool, just click the [(left square bracket) key to reduce it — or the] (right square bracket) key to enlarge it. If that weren't enough, there are even *more* options to fine-tune your pencil and eraser, such as tweaking the pressure sensitivity, thickness, and angle of your drawing tool (covered in Chapter 14).

Treat Your Canvas Like You Would in the Real World — and Then Some!

Over the years, I've used many programs while searching for that Holy Grail of drawing: the ability to manipulate the canvas as though it were a physical piece of paper on a drawing table. Fortunately, Manga Studio does just that. In fact, it was its ease of moving, rotating, and zooming the canvas that convinced me to initially purchase this program (among other features, but I get to those soon enough).

Why would I be excited about something like this? Let me explain each of the functions, and I'll let you be the judge.

The Zoom tool

A staple of many art programs, the Zoom tool does exactly what it says — it allows you to zoom as far in or out as you'd like on the page. That way, you can get a full view of the entire page (or an individual panel) on your screen, or you can get that "closer than you can get your face to a real piece of paper" view, when you need to work on an intricate design.

You can adjust the zoom in several ways:

✔ On the Tools palette, click the Zoom button.

Using the Zoom button changes your mouse cursor into a magnifying glass whenever it hovers over the page. All you need to do now is hover over the section you'd like to zoom in, and click the mouse. If you want to zoom out, hold down the Alt key (Option key on the Mac) while you click the mouse.

If you'd like to zoom in to a specific area of the page, just click and drag the mouse over the area. When you release the mouse, the page automatically zooms to the selected area.

✔ Use the Zoom In/Zoom Out buttons on the Page toolbar.

If you don't want to switch tools for the purpose of zooming, you can always just use the Page toolbar Zoom buttons. These buttons use the same percentages as the Zoom tool.

✔ Use the Zoom sliding bar or manually enter your own value on the Page toolbar, shown in Figure 5-10.

If you have a specific zoom value in mind, you can always enter it manually. Just input your value in the Zoom text box on the toolbar and press Enter. Or if you click the arrow to the right of the text box, a slider bar appears, which you can see in Figure 5-10. Use your mouse and slide the value up and down until you reach your desired level.

✔ Use the keyboard shortcuts.

- To use the Zoom tool, press / (the backslash key, near the right-hand Shift key).

- To zoom in (whether you have the Zoom tool selected or not), press Ctrl++ (⌘++ on the Mac) — that's the + key on your keyboard's number pad.

- To zoom out (whether you have the Zoom tool selected or not), press Ctrl+- (⌘+- on the Mac) — that's the - key on your keyboard's number pad.

There's always the possibility that you'll be so focused on your work, the very idea of using the toolbar or the Zoom tool would be a waste of time. I know I'm like that. So, I like to use the keyboard shortcuts.

If you're like me and you work on a laptop, you don't have access to a number pad. (Well, you do . . . but it's a bit cumbersome to switch the keys around while you're working.) Fortunately, if you own Manga Studio EX, you can change the keyboard shortcuts to keys you're more comfortable with.

The Hand tool

Another staple of art programs, the Hand tool enables you to grab the page and effortlessly move it as you shift your focus from one area to another. The Hand tool also allows you to move the page beyond its edges, so if you need to focus your attention to an area on the corner of the page, you can bring that corner to the center of your screen if you want to.

You can access the Hand tool in two ways:

✔ On the Tools palette, click the Hand button.

The mouse cursor changes to a hand when you hover it over the page. All you need to do now is click the page and drag around to your heart's content.

✔ Use the keyboard shortcuts.

There are actually two shortcuts you'll need to know, one of which you may find yourself using more than the other:

- To use the Hand tool, press H.

- To use the Hand tool *temporarily*, hold down the spacebar while you click and drag the mouse. This is the function I like to use more often than not. I find it almost becomes second nature to draw, hold the spacebar, and move to the next section I'm working on — and then release the spacebar to draw some more.

The Rotate tool

While many art programs have a Zoom and Hand tool, very few have a rotate page function. Like I mention earlier, this vital function was a dealmaker for me when I decided to buy Manga Studio. When you try it out, you'll find yourself wondering how you ever got along without it!

You can access the Rotate tool in a few ways:

✔ On the Tools palette, select the Rotate tool.

The mouse cursor turns into a curved line with arrows on either end of it. All you need to do now is click the page and drag (or draw circles) until the page is at the angle you want to work at.

✔ Use the Rotate slider or manually enter your own value in the Rotate text box on the Page toolbar. (You can enter values from –180 to +180, or from 0 to 360). Much like the Zoom slider and text box, these functions allow you to more accurately dial in the exact angle you would like.

✔ Use the keyboard shortcuts:

- To access the Rotate tool, press R.

- To access the Rotate tool temporarily, hold down Shift+spacebar.

Just like with the temporary Hand tool function, pressing Shift+spacebar allows you to turn your page without having to switch back and forth from your drawing tool to the Rotate tool. Now, you can draw, quickly rotate, and draw some more with the same ease that you would have with a regular paper and pencil.

If you have a drawing tablet with programmable keys on the pen, consider assigning them to the temporary Rotate tool and Hand tool functions (Shift+spacebar and spacebar, respectively). You'll be surprised how intuitive it feels to just click those buttons as you're drawing along.

Chapter 6

Layers, Layers, Layers!

*I*f you've used other art programs — such as Corel Painter or Adobe Photoshop — you're probably familiar with the concept of using layers. Maybe you can even use, manipulate, and create all kinds of effects with layers without breaking a sweat while doing it. You'll be happy to know that layers are an integral part of Manga Studio — possibly even more so than in the other art programs out there.

If you aren't so familiar with drawing programs, you might think layers are just something that onions and cakes have. Trust me, when you get to know and understand how layers work — as well as how you can use them to your maximum benefit — you'll wonder how you ever did your work without them.

The Benefits of Using Layers

I like to think of the layers feature as an all-in-one solution while drawing digitally. Now, I know that people tend to throw the term *all-in-one* around quite a bit, sometimes incorrectly. In the case of Manga Studio, however, I feel it's apropos; using the layers feature allows you to have all kinds of drawing space, tools, guides, and so forth . . . all in one convenient place.

For drawing, layers are like a near-infinite stack of tracing paper. On one layer, you can work on your pencil roughs, while on another you can have your inked line work. On another layer you have your various screentones, and on yet another, you have all your various effects, such as speed or focus lines.

Manga Studio takes the layers concept one step further than other drawing programs. In addition to pencil, ink, and screentone layers, the program provides layers for many of your drawing aids. You can have masking and selection areas (discussed in Chapter 9), rulers and guides (Chapter 8), individual panels (Chapter 7), perspective and other effect lines and rulers (Chapter 8), and a printing guide (Chapter 1), each on its own layer! (See Figure 6-1.)

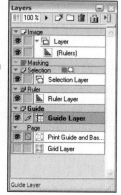

Figure 6-1:
You can place multiple drawing aids on their own layers.

The layers feature can also be a means to increase efficiency. For example, if you work with traditional tools, you might be aware of a few schools of thought regarding how you pencil and ink your work:

✔ You use your trusty 2B pencil to rough your work, ink directly over your roughs, and erase the pencil marks when the inks are dry.

✔ You use a blueline pencil to rough your work, ink over your roughs, and send the page(s) to the publisher, who will then remove the blueline marks. (Or you scan the art and remove the blueline marks yourself using a program like Photoshop.)

✔ You pencil your work on one sheet of paper and then use either tracing paper or a lightboard to ink over the pencils on a separate sheet.

Each option has its advantages and disadvantages. With the first two options, you lose your original pencil roughs, but you have only one sheet of paper to keep track of. With the last option, you keep your pencil work, but now you have two sheets of paper (or possibly more if you make a copy of your inks to screentone on), which can clutter up your workspace quite a bit over time. Not to mention, if you happen to use blueline and don't happen to own a copy of Photoshop, you'll be spending hours cleaning up your line art by digitally erasing all the roughs.

Working with layers in Manga Studio gives you the best option. You can scan in (or digitally draw) your pencil roughs on one layer, change the pencil color to blue (or any other color you'd like) and then ink on a new layer. (See

Figure 6-2.) If you happen to notice a mistake in the roughs while inking, just go back to the roughs layer, erase and correct as need be, and go right back to the inks layer to finish the work.

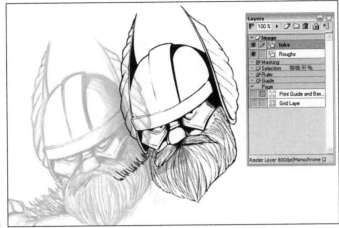

Figure 6-2:
You can place your roughs and inks on separate layers in Manga Studio.

This way, not only do you have the ability to ink over your pencils like they were on one sheet of paper, you can keep the two steps separate, just like you were using tracing paper. Plus, you save the time spent erasing your roughs by simply hiding that layer, leaving the inks visible for you to continue on to the next stage of your work.

Getting to Know Your Layer Types

Manga Studio provides a selection of layer types to use in your work. You're going to see them a lot over the next few chapters, so now is a good time to get to know them.

- ✔ **Raster Layer:** This is the basic drawing layer that you use for roughing and inking your work, as well as adding various effects, like speed lines. Most of the drawing tools can be used on this layer.

- ✔ **Vector Layer:** An option available to Manga Studio EX users, this layer is used primarily for inking. Unlike a raster layer, a vector layer can be printed at any size without any loss of image quality. Only the Pen and Marker — and (for EX users) Gradation tools — can be used on this layer. I explain the pros and cons of using vector versus raster layers in Bonus Chapter 1 on the CD.

- ✔ **Reverse Layer:** Placed on top of raster or vector layer, the reverse layer reverses the colors of the lower layer.

✔ **Layer Folder and Text Folder:** As you can probably guess, these aren't layers. These are folders that group and store your layers. It's a good way to keep your background drawings in one folder and your character drawings in another folder. Or with text folders, it helps to keep your dialogue layers in one place.

✔ **Selection Layer:** This can keep any circular, rectangular, or polygonal selections you may wish to reuse later in the finishing process. (I discuss this further in Chapter 9.)

✔ **Ruler Layer:** This can contain the drawing rulers and guides you create to assist in your technical or background drawings (which I discuss further in Chapter 8). You can place as many rulers and guides as you'd like on this layer.

✔ **Panel Ruler Layer:** This can be used to create the individual panels and gutters for your page (which I discuss further in Chapter 7).

✔ **Guide Layer:** This can be used as a repository for your vertical and horizontal drawing guide lines (which I discuss further in Chapter 8).

✔ **Masking Layer:** Much like selection layers, this keeps a collection of masks that you may wish to reuse later in the production of your comic page. Unlike the selection layer, the masking layer selects areas that you wish to cut off from the final work. You can use this layer only within a panel layer, which I go over in Chapter 9.

✔ **Tone Layer:** This choice is available only when you're going to adjust an existing layer. This changes the layer into one that lets you create and adjust a screentone (which I discuss further in Chapter 11).

Over the course of this chapter, I use the term *image layers* pretty frequently. That's my shorthand term for raster, vector, reverse, and/or tone layers. I get to type less when I write *image layers* instead of all that — which makes me happy.

Creating a New Layer

To create a new layer on your page, follow these steps:

1. **Create the new layer by either**

    • Pressing Ctrl+Shift+N (⌘+Shift+N on the Mac) on your keyboard

    or

    • Clicking the New Layer button on the Layers palette. (Press F4 on your keyboard if the Layers palette isn't visible.)

    The New Layer dialog box appears.

2. **Enter the name of the layer in the New Layer text box.**

3. **Choose the type of layer you wish to create from the Layer Type drop-down list.**

   The previous section, "Getting to Know Your Layer Types," describes the different types of layers you can choose from.

   If you're choosing a non-image layer (ruler, selection, guide, panel, panel ruler, or print guide), all the other options are grayed out, so click the OK button.

   Note that you can select a masking layer only when you're within a panel layer. (Chapter 7 is devoted entirely to panel layers and panel rulers, so be sure to check that out.)

4. **Select the resolution you wish to use with the Resolution drop-down list.**

5. **Select whether you want a Black (1bit), Black and White (2bit), or Gray (8bit) layer from the Expression Mode drop-down list.**

6. **Beside Output Attribute, choose either the Sketch or the Finish option button.**

   Aside from keeping your sketch layers and finish layers organized, this option is most useful for deciding which layers are printed and which are omitted when you're ready to print or export your finished work — only layers with the Finish option selected are exported or printed. Check out Chapter 13 for more information on printing and exporting your work.

7. **If you've chosen an 8-bit expression mode, select your subtractive method (Does Not Subtract Colors, Threshold, Dither, or Convert to Tone) from the Subtractive Method drop-down list.**

   I explain the differences in the various modes in Chapter 5.

8. **If you've selected the Threshold method, enter its level in the Threshold text box. Or use the slider bar (activated by clicking the black arrow to the right of the text box) and adjust it until you've reached the desired threshold level.**

   I explain what the threshold level is a bit more in Chapter 3. To summarize, adjusting the threshold level tells the program how to treat any grayscale drawing (below the level converts to black, while anything at or above will be ignored). Admittedly, if you're working on roughs, the threshold method probably won't be useful to you, so you won't need to worry about this selection when you're working on roughs.

Picking the right layer for your work

I talk a bit about resolution and expression mode in Chapter 5, but here is a good place to discuss what types may work out best for you, depending on what you're working on.

✔ When you're working on roughs, it's really a matter of preference. If you prefer to draw very loose roughs purely to guide your inking process and you aren't planning on keeping them afterwards, I'd suggest using a lower resolution at 150 dpi or so, with a 1-bit or 2-bit expression mode. Using a low resolution and expression uses less memory, reduces the file size, and is a bit easier on the processor than, say, using a 1200 dpi 8-bit layer that doesn't subtract colors. And because you're not planning on keeping the roughs in the end, it's overkill to go higher than you really need to.

✔ If you're like me and you prefer to work on very tight pencils to ink later on (or export to a file to send to your inker), you want the highest-quality layer for your roughs. Choose the highest possible resolution relative to your page — that is, if you're working on a 600 dpi page, create a 600 dpi layer to work from.

Picking the expression mode is a bit more subjective because your choice really boils down to your comfort level. You may find that drawing on a 1- or 2-bit layer feels more natural, or that an 8-bit layer set to dither is more what you're looking for. My suggestion is to experiment to find the right combination that produces what you're looking for.

✔ When inking, the choice gets easier — pick the highest resolution available relative to your page's resolution, with a 1-bit or 2-bit expression. You want to have the smoothest lines possible when you're inking, and that's possible only with a high resolution. If you use too low of a resolution, the lines will look jagged when you print or export them, and your publisher won't be terribly pleased.

For Manga Studio EX users, you get the additional option of using a vector layer for your inks. You have a bit more freedom regarding resolution (because vectors are resolution independent), which means you could theoretically work on a smaller page if you wanted. (The benefit is a smaller file, which may be good if you're working on an older computer.) Even if you go this route, I suggest working on a higher-resolution page for best results when you print or export your inks.

Adjusting a Layer's Settings

So you may be asking, "Well, I created a new layer, but it isn't exactly what I meant to select. Can I adjust a layer after I create it?" The short answer is, "It depends."

One thing you'll come to know as you use this program is that most of the settings are not set in stone. It's definitely an advantage to working digitally — if the settings on a layer are not to your liking, change them! You can do this in a couple of ways in Manga Studio, which I discuss in the following subsections.

Untitled is a dirty word

It sounds like a trite thing to do, but you'd be amazed how a simple thing like naming your layers can help organize your work, as well as help you keep track of exactly what layer you're working on. I figure at the very least, by writing this down, maybe it'll help remind me to actually practice what I'm about to preach.

If you aren't worried about labeling layers for yourself, consider this: If you're just penciling your work and planning to send the file to your inker (or if you're inking and sending it to your screentoner), consider that the other person is going to have no clue what each layer is supposed to be and which layers she should actually focus on.

You can lose a lot of time and energy when you find yourself drawing on the wrong layer. While I won't say that naming your layers will absolve you of such headaches in the future, it may help to cut down on the amount of aspirin you'd be taking otherwise.

The Properties palette

With all of the layer types, you can view a layer's properties in two ways:

- ✔ Pressing F7 on your keyboard.
- ✔ Clicking the Properties button on the main toolbar.

When the Properties palette is open, you'll notice that there are a few options to adjust, but most of them are grayed out. That's because, for the most part, the options on a new layer are locked, and the palette reminds you about the settings you created with the new layer. You really only have the option to rename your layer from this level.

If you're working on an image layer (raster, vector, reverse, and/or tone) or selection layer, you may notice two additional check boxes for ruler settings: the Convert to Layer and the Hide check boxes. Use these check boxes for any layer-specific rulers and guides you may choose to work with. I explain this further in Chapter 8.

In any case, these are the only options available to you to adjust on the Layer Properties palette . . . unless you click the Advanced View button. Normally, I would suggest checking out Part IV: Advanced Tips and Tricks, but in this instance, I think it's useful right now to go over the advanced features that you can do with a layer.

When you have the Advanced View open (shown in Figure 6-3), you have the following options available:

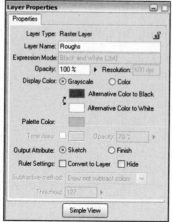

Figure 6-3:
The
Advanced
View of a
raster layer
in the Layer
Properties
palette.

✔ **Opacity:** As the name implies, this function allows you to adjust how opaque or transparent you'd like the layer to be. You may find it useful to adjust the opacity when creating effects for your page. If you're like me and tend to have very heavy and sloppy pencil roughs, you may adjust the opacity of a layer to lighten up your roughs during the inking stage.

Another way to use this function is to adjust the opacity on a ruler layer so that you can see the guides just enough to use them.

The great thing about adjusting the opacity is that it doesn't affect your work on the layer in the slightest. You can adjust the opacity as much or as little as you'd like. If you want to revert or adjust it further, feel free! (Incidentally, this function is available with all layer types.)

To adjust the opacity, enter a value between 0% and 100% in the Opacity text box, or you can use the slider (activated by clicking the black arrow next to the text box) to adjust with your mouse or stylus until you've reached your desired level. Figure 6-4 shows the same image on two layers; the image that appears lighter is on a layer with a lower opacity.

✔ **Display Color:** I mention at the beginning of this book that Manga Studio is primarily used as a black-and-white program. It is, but that doesn't mean you can't use color if you want to. The Display Color function allows you to change the black (and/or white) colors to whatever colors you'd like. This is especially helpful to pencilers who prefer to work with a blue (or *any* color) pencil. Just select your color, and you have yourself a colored layer to pencil on!

To activate this function on an image layer, make sure you have the Layer Properties palette open for the layer, and then follow these steps:

1. Select the Color radio button.

If you already have line art down, you'll see that it changes to the default color.

2. **With your mouse or stylus, double-click the Alternative Color to Black color box.**

   This brings up the Color Settings dialog box shown in Figure 6-5.

3. **Select your new color from the Default Color Set list.**

   If you don't see a color you like, you can use the color picker area (to the right of the Default Color Set) and select the exact color you would like with your stylus or mouse.

4. **When you've picked your color, click OK.**

Figure 6-4:
You can set
an image
layer to any
opacity.

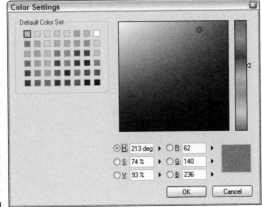

Figure 6-5:
Adjust your
layer colors
with the
Color
Settings
dialog box.

5. **If you want to change the White color, double-click the Alternative Color to White color box, and repeat Steps 3 and 4.**

6. **If you'd like to change your layer back to black and white, click the Grayscale radio button.**

While I'm explaining how to change the colors on an image layer, keep in mind that the same rules apply to all of the other layer types. Each layer type has a different name for its primary and secondary colors, but you can adjust them all in the same way.

✔ **Palette Color:** This function doesn't affect the layer so much as it does the Layers palette. All changing the palette color does is change the display color of the layer within the Layers palette. This is good if you have a large number of layers and wish to organize them via color-coding.

✔ **Tone Area:** Applicable to the tone layer only, this function assists you in the placement of your screentone on the page.

There have been many times when I've zoomed in close to place a screentone on a part of a character, only to zoom out and discover more than a few glaring areas that I've missed. Setting the tone area color helps fix that problem by laying down a flat color in addition to your screentone. It'll be pretty obvious from the get-go what areas are covered and which still need to be touched up.

To activate the tone area color, click the Tone Area check box. Adjusting the area color and opacity works the same way as adjusting the layer colors and opacity, so you can follow the steps provided earlier in this list.

✔ **Output Attribute:** As I mention earlier, setting a sketch or finish layer helps keep you mentally aware of which layer is which. It's also integral to determining which layers will be used when you decide to print or export your work.

✔ **Ruler Settings:** As I mention earlier, these settings allow you to create a layer-specific group of rulers and guides for an image layer. I explain how these work in Chapter 8.

✔ **Subtractive Method:** Used only with 8-bit layers, you can adjust how the line art is displayed (Does Not Subtract Colors, Threshold, Dither, and Convert to Tone). I explain each of these subtractive methods in Chapter 3.

Changing the layer type

For most of the layer types you create, you're pretty much stuck with what you make. You can change the name, color, and opacity of the layer, but that's pretty much it.

Image layers provide a little bit more flexibility than other layer types. If you use the Change Layer Type function, you can take your image layer and convert it to a completely different layer type! (Well, within reason. It would seem awfully silly to convert your image file to a print guide or grid layer.)

To change your image layer type, either

- Press Ctrl+Alt+E (⌘+Option+E on the Mac)

  or

- Choose Layer⇨Change Layer Type.

The Change Layer Type dialog box opens. If you created a new layer, this should look very familiar to you; it's exactly the same as the New Layer dialog box. I go over the options in more detail in "Creating a New Layer" earlier in this chapter, but to summarize:

1. **Enter the name of your layer in the Layer Name text box.**

2. **Select the layer type you wish to convert to from the Layer Type drop-down list.**

   Your selection of layer types is more limited here. You can convert to only a raster, vector (if you have Manga Studio EX), tone, or selection layer.

3. **Select the layer's resolution from the Resolution drop-down list.**

4. **Select Black (1bit), Black and White (2bit), or Gray (8bit) from the Expression Mode drop-down list.**

5. **Select either the Sketch or the Finish option button to determine the output attribute for the layer.**

6. **If you've chosen an 8-bit expression mode, select the subtractive method you wish to use (Does Not Subtract, Threshold, Dither, or Convert to Tone) from the Subtractive Method drop-down list.**

   If you've chosen the Threshold subtractive method, enter the threshold level in the Threshold text box, or you can activate the slider bar by clicking the black triangle to the right of the text box and adjust until you've reached your desired level.

7. **If you wish to keep a copy of the original layer in addition to the converted layer, select the Leave Original Layer check box.**

8. **When you're satisfied with the settings, click OK.**

Keep in mind that while you can convert an image layer to a selection layer, you can't do the reverse. If you're looking to convert a selection layer to an image layer, the best solution I can come up with is to select your selection layer and use the Fill tool to fill the selection on a new image layer.

Using Simple Layer Functions

Knowing how to create and adjust layers is only the beginning of what you can do with them. As always, you need to crawl before you can walk, so the following sections show some of the basic functions you can do with your layers.

Copying layers

I really like to use the Undo button when I'm working on a drawing. The only problem is that Manga Studio allows a limited number of undos. So every now and then, I make a copy of the layer I'm working on as my safety net. Then, if I don't like where the drawing is going, I can scrap that layer and work from the backup layer.

Another reason to create a copy (or multiple copies) of a layer is to make duplicates of a character or object that doesn't change much from panel to panel. Or you can use a copy of a layer to thicken up your ink work. As you work with Manga Studio, you might even come up with ways of using copies of layers that no one else has thought of.

Follow these steps to copy a layer:

1. **With your stylus or mouse, highlight the layer you wish to copy.**

2. **Create a copy of the layer by using one of the following methods:**

    - Drag the layer to the New Layer button located at the top of the Layers palette.

    - Press Ctrl+Shift+C (⌘+Option+C on the Mac).

    - Choose Layer➪Duplicate Layer.

    The layer copy appears above the original in the Layers palette, with "Copy" affixed to the end of the original layer's name, as shown in Figure 6-6.

Figure 6-6:
Your new layer copy appears above the old one on the Layers palette.

Locking layers

Here's something that has happened to me on *many* occasions, especially if I don't change the color or opacity of my roughs: I get a good amount of ink work done on a drawing, only to discover that the layer I thought was my ink layer is in fact my *roughs* layer! The Undo button can only undo so much, so I'm stuck either erasing all the pencil lines from the layer or starting the inking process all over.

If this has never happened to you, I'll be in touch because I need to find out your secrets. Otherwise, I suggest taking advantage of the Lock Layer function to save yourself a lot of time and frustration. Locking the layer allows you to view the layer, but you can't write, erase, or do anything to it. It's a very simple yet extremely important step to prevent what can be costly mistakes.

To lock and unlock a layer, follow these steps:

1. **Using your mouse or stylus, select the layer on the Layers palette. (Press F4 if the Layers palette isn't currently visible.)**

2. **Lock the layer by using one of the following methods:**

   - Click the Lock icon.
   - Press Ctrl+L (⌘+L on the Mac).
   - Choose Layer⇨Lock Layer.

   You now see a small lock icon next to the name of your layer. (Or it disappears if you're unlocking the layer.)

Locking a layer doesn't have to apply to just an image layer — you can lock each layer type. You'll find this helpful when you want to make sure that a ruler or a selection layer isn't accidentally altered, for example.

Deleting and hiding layers

There comes a time when you decide that a drawing just isn't working for you, and you decide to part ways with it. I know it's happened to me; I've scrapped entire pages because it was easier to start from scratch than to fight tooth and nail with the abomination that was staring at me.

So, you could use the eraser tool and take your time erasing all the lines from the layer . . . or you could just get rid of the layer altogether. I happen to like the latter; there's something cathartic about doing a virtual "crumpling up the paper and throwing it in the trash."

Follow these steps to delete a layer:

1. **Using your mouse or stylus select the layer from the Layers palette. (Press F4 if it isn't currently visible.)**

2. **Delete the layer by using one of the following methods:**

   - Drag the layer to the Trash icon at the top of the Layers palette.

   - Click the Trash icon. When the dialog box asks if you're sure you want to delete the layer, click OK.

   - Choose Layer⇨Delete Layer. When the dialog box appears and asks if you're sure you want to delete the layer, click OK.

 If you want to *temporarily* remove a layer from sight, you can simply hide it. To do this, just click the eyeball icon in the Layers palette to make the layer disappear and reappear. It's a great way to see how your inks are coming along by hiding your pencil roughs.

Organizing Related Layers

At the beginning of this chapter, I talk about how layers are a great way to organize your work within Manga Studio. But, what happens if you're working with so many layers that things become . . . well, cluttered? If you happen to be using multiple layers for your roughs, inks, tones, rulers, and so on, it can get very confusing to remember which layers are for what (naming your layers can only go so far) — or frustrating having to move each related layer around individually (or hide them one at a time just to see how other layers look).

Manga Studio provides three ways to help reduce layer clutter and confusion. You can organize layers by placing them in layer folders, by grouping layers, and by merging multiple layers into a single layer. These methods help you to not only keep the layers in their respective places, but also to move them around (or hide/show them) as a group. Small things like this can help save you lots of time in the long term.

Layer folders

Layer folders are the simplest means of organizing related layers into one place. All you have to do is move the layers into the folder, and that's it. You can dig into the folder and work on each layer individually, or you can use the folder to move the layers around, hide or show them, or adjust opacity all at once.

To create a Layer folder and add layers to it, follow these steps:

1. **On the Layers palette, click the New Folder button.**

   A new folder appears in the Layers palette. You can rename it by entering the new name in the Layer Name text box on the Layer Properties palette. (Double-click the folder if the Properties palette isn't visible.)

2. **Using your mouse or stylus, highlight the layer you wish to add to the folder and drag the layer into the folder.**

   You'll know the layer is in the folder because the layer icon located is slightly indented in relation to the folder icon. (Check out Figure 6-7 to see what I mean.)

Figure 6-7:
Placing layers in a folder is a simple way to group layers together.

To select multiple layers to move to a folder, hold down the Ctrl key (⌘ on the Mac), and click on each layer you want to move with your mouse or stylus. If you want to highlight many layers at once, click the top layer you want to move, hold the Shift key down, and click the final layer in the list that you want.

Grouping layers

Depending on how you do it, grouping your layers is a great way to temporarily merge layers together — or add them to a Panel Layer, where you can work on them in an independent space. (I explain how Panel Layers work in Chapter 7.)

A benefit of grouping layers, especially if you're working on an older machine, is that it can save on your system resources. When you're working on a file with lots of layers, it can increase in file size and use more RAM on your system. Grouping the layers is a good way to alleviate pressure on your machine, so to speak.

Follow these steps to group your layers together:

1. **Ctrl+click (⌘+click on the Mac) the layers you wish to group.**

2. **Group the selected layers by using one of the following methods:**

   • Press Ctrl+G (⌘+G on the Mac).

   • Choose Layer⇨Group Layers.

   The Group Layers dialog box appears. Here, you can set the group properties, as shown in Figure 6-8.

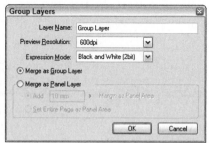

Figure 6-8:
The Group
Layers
dialog box.

3. **Enter the name of the layer group in the Layer Name text box.**

4. **Select the group's resolution from the Preview Resolution drop-down list.**

5. **Select whether you want Black and White (2bit), Grayscale (16bit), or Color (32bit) preview expression from the Expression Mode drop-down list.**

   This setting affects how the group will look, resolution and expression-wise, on the page. All of the individual layers that have been grouped retain all of their original information, including their respective resolutions and expression modes.

6. **Select whether you want to merge into a Group Layer or a Panel Layer.**

   Group layers are good if you plan to have this group as just a read-only reference — or if this is a temporary repository for your layers and you intend to ungroup them later.

7. **If you're merging into a Panel Layer, either select the Add option button and type the size into the Margin as Panel Area text box or select the Set Entire Page as Panel Area option button.**

8. **Click OK.**

When you're done, the selected layers appear as one group or panel with the name you entered.

Unlike layers within a folder, you can't draw on a group layer. If the group is a panel layer, you can access the layers to draw on by double-clicking the panel layer on the Layers palette, by right-clicking (Control+click on the Mac) and choosing Open Panel Layer from the menu, or by selecting Layer⇨Open Panel Layer from the Main Menu.

Merging layers

Merging layers is a way to permanently (unless you Undo, of course) group all of your related layers into one layer. This is a good solution if you wish to flatten all of your inks or roughs onto one layer, for example. Unlike with layer folders and grouped layers, you can draw and edit directly on a merged layer.

To merge one or more layers together, follow these steps:

1. **Ctrl+click (⌘+click on the Mac) the layers you wish to group.**

2. **Merge the selected layers by using one of the following methods:**

   • Press Ctrl+Shift+E (⌘+Shift+E on the Mac).

   • Choose Layer⇨Merge Layers.

   The Merge Layers dialog box appears, enabling you to set the new layer properties, as shown in Figure 6-9.

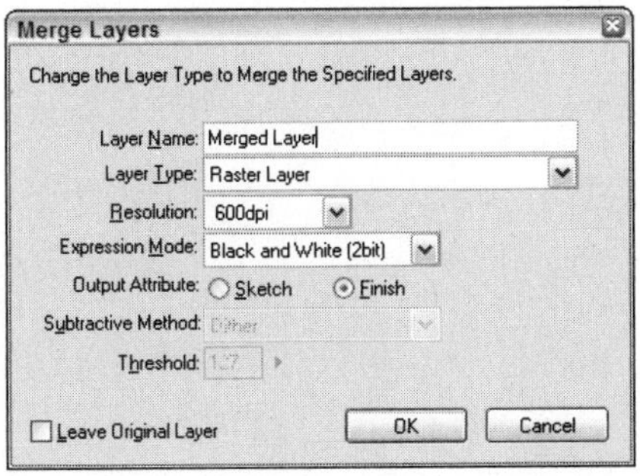

Figure 6-9:
The Merge
Layers
dialog box.

3. **Enter the name of the new layer in the Layer Name text box.**

4. **(Manga Studio EX only) Select the type of layer you'd like from the Layer Type drop-down list.**

   This applies only if you have Manga Studio EX, where you can choose either a raster layer or a vector layer. In Manga Studio Debut, raster layer is the only option available.

5. **Select the resolution from the Resolution drop-down list.**

While this is a matter of preference, my suggestion is to select the highest resolution of the layers you've selected. I think it's best to work from a higher resolution rather than lose the quality of your high-res linework to a low-res layer.

6. **Select Black (1bit), Black and White (2bit), or Gray (8bit) expression from the Expression Mode drop-down list.**

7. **Choose whether you want this to be a sketch or finish layer by selecting the appropriate option button beside Output Attribute.**

8. **If you've chosen a Gray (8bit) layer, select the subtractive method of your grayscale from the Subtractive Method drop-down list.**

9. **If you chose the Threshold subtractive method, enter the threshold level (0 to 255) in the Threshold text box.**

10. **If you want to keep a copy of the original layers, select the Leave Original Layer check box.**

11. **Click OK when you're done.**

When the layer merge is complete, you have a brand-new merged layer with the name you specified, ready to be drawn and edited on.

In addition to merging image layers, you can also merge ruler, selection, and guide layers.

Chapter 7

Panel Layers and Rulers

. . . .

. . . .

I've never owned a very large scanner. So trying to scan an 11-x-17-inch comic page was problematic at best. Usually what I ended up doing (before eventually giving it up and going all digital) was to draw each panel on a separate sheet of paper, scan those in, and then piece all the panels together in Photoshop. (Other webcomic artists employ this same technique — or at least something very similar.)

What I liked about this technique was that I could go crazy on a page, rendering the scene out as much as I wanted, and then just crop out the area I thought would work for the page. It was probably a bit of a waste of ink and paper, but it helped me to make sure that everything looked as it should. The drawback? I used lots and lots of paper.

Interestingly enough, Manga Studio incorporates the same kind of idea. Imagine the ability to work from several sheets of paper containing a single panel each, so you can fully work out a complex scene without fear that you may run into and ruin another panel. Then, you can crop out all but the part you want for the panel. Now imagine keeping all those sheets of paper in one convenient place.

That's how panel layers work.

The Idea Behind Panel Layers

You can think of a panel layer in Manga Studio as a page within a page. Each panel layer acts as its own page file, with the ability for multiple image layers, just like the main page. Rulers, guides, and other tools that you would use on the main page can all be used within a panel layer.

Only the section of the page covered in the panel layer can be shown at any time. This helps focus your attention on the one part of the page. What's more, each panel layer is independent of other panel layers. So, anything you work on can overlap onto a different panel layer, and the other panel layer isn't affected by it. You may see the scribblings from the other panel layer, but the art on the current one is untouched.

The idea here is to give you the freedom to really go crazy with your drawing. Need to draw the entire body of a character in a scene to make sure the half that will be seen looks correct? No problem. Anything you draw that you don't want to show can be easily masked off; that way, the final piece will contain only the artwork you want everyone to see.

Using panel layers is a great way to give you that little extra freedom to make sure your work looks just how you want it, without being constrained by the borders of the comic panel.

Creating a Panel Layer

There are few ways you can create a panel layer in Manga Studio. Some of them are good to create panel layers on the fly very quickly. Others allow some customization of settings while creating them. Whichever type you use probably just depends on the situation, as well as plain-old personal preference.

Converting a selection to a panel layer

The easiest way to create a panel layer is to simply use your selection tool (Lasso or Polyline), create a selection on the page (I explain how to create selections in Chapter 9), and convert it into a panel layer. You can create any size or shape selection, and Manga Studio converts the rectangular size around the selection into a new panel layer.

To create a panel layer from a selection, follow these steps:

1. **From the Tools palette, select either the Marquee (rectangle, circle, or polygon) or Lasso (freeform or polyline) tool.**

2. **Create your selection on the page (see Figure 7-1 for an example) with the selection tool of your choice.**

3. **From the main menu, choose Selection⇨Convert Selection to Panel Layer.**

   Manga Studio converts the selection into a panel layer. If the selection is a nonrectangular shape, Manga Studio boxes the selection into a rectangle and creates the panel layer from that rectangular area, as shown in Figure 7-2.

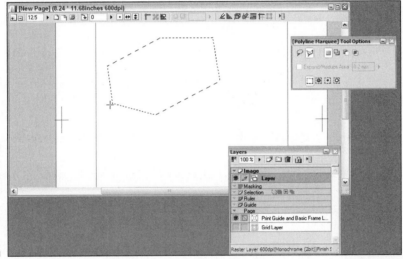

Figure 7-1:
Make a selection to change into a panel layer.

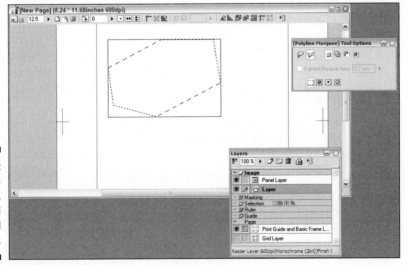

Figure 7-2:
The polyline selection, converted into a panel layer.

That's all! It's an effectively simple way to create your panel layers wherever you'd like. The only drawback is that you don't get control over either the panel layer resolution or expression mode for preview. (See the sidebar "Previewing your panel layer" for more about the preview mode.)

The Panel Maker tool

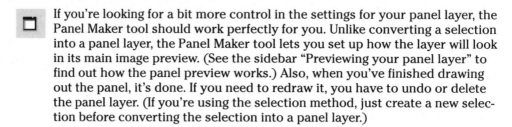 If you're looking for a bit more control in the settings for your panel layer, the Panel Maker tool should work perfectly for you. Unlike converting a selection into a panel layer, the Panel Maker tool lets you set up how the layer will look in its main image preview. (See the sidebar "Previewing your panel layer" to find out how the panel preview works.) Also, when you've finished drawing out the panel, it's done. If you need to redraw it, you have to undo or delete the panel layer. (If you're using the selection method, just create a new selection before converting the selection into a panel layer.)

Follow these steps to use the Panel Maker tool to create a new panel layer:

1. **Select the Panel Maker from the Tools palette with your mouse or stylus.**

2. **If it isn't open already, open the Tool Properties palette by pressing F3 on your keyboard.**

   Initially there are only two options available for the Panel Maker. This is because the options are in Simple Mode.

 3. **At the top of the Tool Options palette, click the Show Menu button and select Advanced Settings Mode.**

4. **The Tool Options palette expands, as shown in Figure 7-3.**

   Here's how the Tool Options break down for the Panel Maker:

   - *Shapes:* The panel layer you create can be any shape you'd like. So, you're given the option to create a rectangular, circular, polygonal, polyline, or freeform panel. Each of the nonrectangular panel layer types are automatically masked off to maintain the final form of the shape you create.

   - *Line Size:* This refers to the size of the border created with the panel layer. You can enter a value from 0.1mm to 10mm in the Line Size text box.

   - *Sides:* If you're creating a polygonal panel layer, you can choose the number of sides created, from 3 to 32.

   - *Brush Shape Thickness:* Adjusting this changes the shape of the borders created. For example, creating a thin brush shape results in thin vertical borders and wide horizontal borders.

   - *Direction:* Adjust the direction of the brush when you create borders.

Previewing your panel layer

When you're on the main page looking at a panel layer, the artwork you see isn't necessarily what it will look like in print. That's because each panel layer provides a read-only preview of the contained artwork. Because of the possibility of multiple image layers within each panel layer, it's easier to simply show a static image of all the visible layers at once. (Besides, it's significantly easier on the program and your system to do that, as opposed to displaying every separate layer from every panel layer at the same time).

When you first create a new panel layer using the Panel Maker tool, you have the option to open the Tool Options palette and select the preview resolution from the Preview Resolution drop-down list (from 150 dpi to your page file resolution) and select an expression mode (the way the line art will be presented) from the Expression Mode drop-down list. Deciding which option to select from the Expression Mode drop-down list depends on personal preference:

✔ **Select Black and White (2bit)** from the Expression Mode drop-down list for the simplest type of preview. This mode is great for showing off your finished ink work. However, the preview will look fairly poor at low resolutions, and things may look jumbled if you forgot to hide your pencil work and it gets mixed up with your ink work.

✔ **Select Gray (16bit) or Color (32bit)** from the Expression Mode drop-down list for a richer preview. These options work really well to preview your pencil work. The two expression modes are essentially the same — the difference is that only 32-bit layers can display colors in the preview; 16-bit layers are limited to grayscale.

Keep in mind that you're stuck with the resolution and expression mode you pick for that panel layer — you get only one shot at this (unless you just delete the panel layer before you draw anything and start over, I guess).

- *Keep Aspect Ratio:* Used by the rectangular, circular, and polygonal shapes, this maintains a general shape of the panel layer you're creating. You can adjust the ratio by entering values from 0.1 to 20 in the corresponding Width and Height text boxes.

- *Start From Center:* The panel layer you create starts from the center and works its way out however you drag it along the canvas. (If you leave this check box deselected, the panel starts from a corner.)

- *Rotate After Size is Decided:* Useful for any last-second tweaks, this option allows you to adjust the angle of the created panel layer. You also have the additional option of locking the rotation to intervals of 45 degrees by selecting the Rotate at 45 Degree Intervals check box).

- *Lock at 45 Degree Angles:* Used by the polyline shape, this locks the lines created to intervals of 45 degrees.

- *Convert to Curve:* Instead of creating straight lines, the panel maker (when you select the polyline shape option) creates curved lines. The curve is set by the placement of the polyline endpoints on the page. When completed, the border will be the curved shape, with everything outside the shape masked off.

- *Fill Inside:* The shape created is automatically created with a masking layer. The mask is filled in the shape you create.

- *Draw on Mask Only:* Used by all but the lasso shape, this replaces the border with a masked off area.

- *Panel Name:* This is the name of the panel you're creating.

- *Preview Resolution:* Ranging from 150 dpi to the page file's resolution, you select the resolution of the panel layer when previewed on the main page.

- *Expression Mode:* Along with the Preview Resolution, the values in this drop-down list help set up how the panel layer looks when previewed on the main page. You can select from Black and White (2bit), Gray (16bit), and Color (32bit). (See the sidebar, "Previewing your panel layer," for more information).

Figure 7-3:
The Panel
Maker
Options in
Advanced
Mode.

Working with Your Panel Layer

A very important thing to remember with panel layers is that you can't work on them from the main page. Panel layers work much like group layers (discussed in Chapter 6), in which all layers within the panel layer are set to read-only. So what you see on the main page is only a preview of the contents of a panel layer.

It's only when you open the panel layer in its own window that you can do any drawing or editing within it. Once opened, you can work on it just like you would work on the main page, This means you can add and remove image layers, draw your roughs and inks, add screen tones, work with rulers, and so on.

So, before you can do anything with your newly created panel layer, you need to open it up.

Opening a panel layer

Open your panel layer for editing by double-clicking the panel layer in the Layers palette. (Press F4 if the Layers palette isn't open.)

The panel layer opens. The view actually doesn't look any different than if you were looking at the main page; the only difference is that the panel is now localized to the area of the page you sectioned off with the Panel Maker tool. The rest of the page is grayed out and inaccessible until you close the panel you're currently working on. (See Figure 7-4.) Other than that, the panel layer works just like the main page; image layers, rulers, guides and practically everything else can be used exactly the same way.

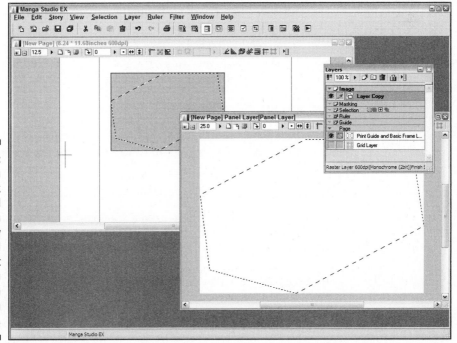

Figure 7-4:
When you double-click on a Panel Layer, you can draw and add layers on it like you would on the main page.

Adding layers

Adding an image layer within a panel layer works exactly the same way as if you were adding one to the main page. Chapter 6 is all about layers (in case you skipped it to get to this chapter), so I recommend checking it out if you're not familiar with how layers work. Here's a quick recap on how to create a new image layer.

- ✔ From the main menu, choose Layer⇨New Layer

   or

- ✔ Press Ctrl+Shift+N (⌘+Shift+N on the Mac).

Like the main page, you can add as many new image layers as you need to work with.

Masking off areas

If you've ever painted your house, I'm sure you've had to block off parts of a wall (such as electrical sockets or windows) so you wouldn't accidentally paint over them. Usually, you cover the area(s) with some blue painter's tape to protect it. Then, when you're all done painting, you simply remove the tape, and all the places you want protected come out clean.

Masking in panel layers work the same way. The idea here is that you mask off areas of the panel layer that you want to protect. This way, you can work out your drawing as much as you want. Then, when you close the panel layer, everything that's masked off simply disappears from the main page.

To create a mask for your panel layer, follow these steps:

1. **Open the panel layer you want to work on by opening the Layers palette (F4 on your keyboard), and double-clicking the layer.**

   The panel layer opens in its own window.

2. **Create a new masking layer in either of the following ways:**

   - Click the icon next to the masking title on the Layers palette. When the dialog box pops up, click OK. (You can't change any of the settings anyway.)

   - Or you can create a masking layer from the main menu by choosing Layer⇨New Layer. In the New Layer dialog box that appears, select Masking Layer from the Layer Type drop-down list (all the other options except for the Name will gray out) and click OK.

3. **Select either the Lasso/Polyline or Marquee tool.**

   You can use most any kind of drawing or selection tool on a mask layer if you want to, but the Marquee or Lasso tools work best if you want to mask off large sections.

4. **Select the Fill tool from the Tools palette.**

5. **Click the selection you created.**

   You see a light red/pink color filled into the selection.

6. **Repeat Steps 3-5 as necessary until all the areas you want masked off are filled in.**

If you want to create a masked panel layer from the main page, you can select the Draw on Mask Only option. Now, when you create a panel layer, a mask layer will be created that covers the area outside the shape you created.

You won't see anything on the main page, because there is no border draw. It's only when you open the panel layer that you'll see the masked-off area.

You can have only one masking layer per panel layer.

Closing a panel layer

Closing a panel layer is exactly the same as closing a complete page:

- ✔ From the main menu, choose File⇨Close

   or

- ✔ Press Ctrl+W (⌘+W on the Mac) on your keyboard.

When you close the panel layer, you go right back to your main page, as shown at the bottom of Figure 7-5. Only this time, the artwork you just created in the panel layer is displayed at the preview settings you made when you first created the panel. Anything you drew that was in a masked area doesn't show up (represented by the darker areas in the top of Figure 7-5), which is exactly what it's supposed to do.

What you see in the preview on the main page isn't what the final drawing will look like. That will look like what you had drawn in the panel layer itself.

Figure 7-5:
With the
panel layer
(top) closed,
you can see
its preview
on the main
page
(bottom).

Manipulating Your Panel Layers

When working, there's always the possibility that something you initially set up won't work as you thought it would, and you need to readjust it to fit with the new plan. In the case of panel layers, you could find that the size or placement on the page isn't working for you. Or maybe you need to delete the panel layer altogether. The following sections describe how to do these tasks.

Scaling

You might find the panel area you assigned isn't large enough to work on. Fortunately, you can adjust the size of the panel layer pretty easily.

Follow these steps to scale the panel layer up or down:

1. **From the Layers palette, select the panel layer you want to adjust.**

2. **From the main menu, choose Layer⇨Scale Panel Layer.**

   The panel layer displays four adjustment points, as shown in Figure 7-6.

3. **With your mouse or stylus, click one of the adjustment points and drag along the canvas to resize.**

4. **Repeat as necessary with the other adjustment points.**

5. **When you're happy with the new size of the panel layer, press Enter/Return.**

   Manga Studio adjusts the panel layer, and the adjustment points disappear, as shown in Figure 7-7.

Figure 7-6:
When you choose to scale the panel layer, four adjustment points appear.

Figure 7-7:
Your panel layer is now adjusted to how you want it.

If you're scaling down a panel layer, keep in mind that the image layers within it won't scale. Scaling affects only the canvas size of the panel layer. Any layers within it are just cropped down. Don't worry that you could lose any information, though; anything cropped is restored if you scale up the panel layer.

Moving

Moving a panel layer works the same way as if you were moving any other layer type. Follow these steps to move a panel layer:

1. **On the Tools palette, select the Move Layer tool.**
2. **On the Layers palette, highlight the panel layer you wish to move.**
3. **Using your mouse or stylus, click the panel layer and drag along the canvas to your desired placement.**

Deleting

If you realize the panel layer you created is just not going to work for you, you can simply delete it. Delete a panel layer by following these steps:

1. **On the Layers palette, highlight the panel layer you wish to delete.**
2. **At the top of the Layers palette, click the Trash icon.**
3. **When prompted, click Yes to confirm.**

The Panel Ruler Layer

If you're looking for a quick-and-easy means to create panel borders (or even panel layers) in Manga Studio, the panel ruler layer may be just the thing for you. As the name implies, the panel ruler layer creates rulers that you then divide, combine, and adjust to fit what you've roughed out. You can then convert these rulers however you'd like — from a new ink layer with fresh clean borders to a series of panel layers all ready for you to open and work on individually.

You can create a new panel ruler layer in two ways:

✔ From the main menu, choose Layer⇨New Layer. In the New Layer dialog box, select Panel Ruler Layer from the Layer Type drop-down list and then click OK. (See Figure 7-8.)

✔ On the Layers palette, click the icon next to the Rulers title. This brings up a simpler version of the New Layer dialog box, shown in Figure 7-9.

In the Layer Type drop-down list, select Panel Ruler Layer and click OK.

Whichever method you choose, you see a thick blue line outlining the safe area of your page. That's your new panel ruler layer, and that's what you shape into your new panels.

In order to shape the panel ruler layer, the first order of business is to cut it up. For that, you need the Panel Cutter tool, located on the Tools palette.

Using the Panel Ruler Cutter is much like using the regular Line tool on an image layer: You click one endpoint, drag across the canvas, and release. This time, however, the line you create bisects the panel rulers you cross, as you can see in Figure 7-10.

Figure 7-8:
The New Layer dialog box.

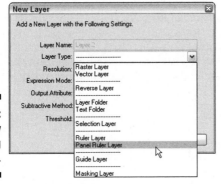

Figure 7-9:
The New Ruler Layer dialog box.

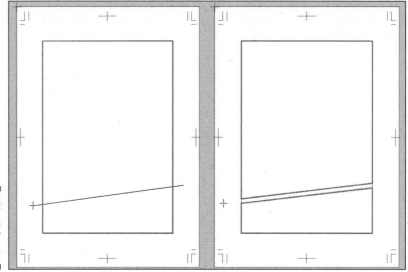

Figure 7-10:
Using the
Panel Ruler
Cutter.

If you hold down the Shift key while dragging the Panel Ruler Cutter, you draw a perfectly horizontal or vertical line.

The panels that you rough out may be larger than the panel ruler layer. That's perfectly okay; at this stage, you're really focused only on approximating the panel shapes. The following section is all about shaping the rulers to fit what you've drawn.

Manipulating the Panel Rulers

Cutting the panel ruler into smaller panels helps to approximate the panels you roughed out. However, it *is* still just an approximation. You may find that the rulers still don't quite match up with what you intended. You may need to shift the rulers around until you really are happy with both placement and size. The following sections show you how to refine your panels.

Adjusting panel rulers with the Object Selector tool

You have several means to adjust panel rulers in Manga Studio, and a good amount of them involve the Object Selector tool, located on the Tools palette. Just like if you were using it for regular rulers and guides in the program (see Chapter 8), the Object Selector allows you to select and manipulate the panel rulers however you'd like. In fact, even though I explain some other functions you can use to adjust things easily, you really could get by using only the Panel Cutter and Object Selector tools.

You can use the Object Selector to adjust a panel ruler in several ways. If you select a corner, as shown in Figure 7-11, you can drag it practically any place on or off the canvas with your mouse or stylus, and the rulers adjust accordingly. This can result in some unique panel shapes, if you're feeling artistically adventurous.

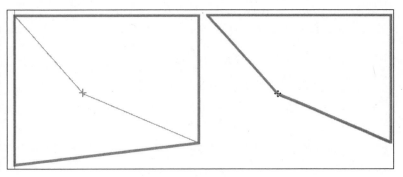

Figure 7-11: Selecting a panel ruler corner can help you create some interesting shapes.

Selecting and adjusting a panel ruler side (see Figure 7-12) helps you adjust the size of the panel, while still maintaining the general shape you originally created.

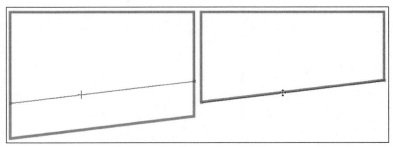

Figure 7-12: Selecting a panel ruler side helps keep the panel's general shape while resizing.

If you're looking to take advantage of Manga Studio's automatic functions, which I describe in the following sections, you usually need to first select a whole panel or group panels. You can select an entire panel in two ways:

✔ Ctrl+click (⌘+click on the Mac) the panel with the Object Selector tool

  or

✔ Open the Tool Options palette (press F3) and select the Select All Continuous Points on Ruler check box so that you can simply click a panel to select the whole thing.

Merging panels

If you find that two panels you initially created might work out better as one large panel, you can take advantage of Manga Studio's Merge function.

The Merge function works only when the two panels share sides of the same length and those sides are parallel to each other.

Follow these steps to use this function:

1. **From the Tools palette, click the Object Selector tool.**

2. **Select the two panels you wish to merge by holding down the Shift key while clicking the panels.**

   Alternatively, you can click your mouse or stylus and drag across the panels.

3. **From the main menu, choose Ruler➪Panel Ruler➪Merge Two.**

   You see one large panel instead of the two smaller ones you selected. (See Figure 7-13.)

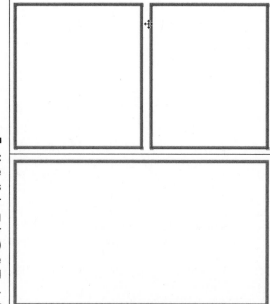

Figure 7-13:
The Merge function is good for combining two smaller panels (top) into one large panel (bottom).

If you're looking to combine several panels at once, you're out of luck — the Merge function works with only two panels at a time. You need to perform a series of merges for multiple panels.

Dividing panel rulers evenly

The Parallel Division function takes a selected panel ruler and divides it evenly as many times as you want. You can create vertical divisions, horizontal divisions, or both.

To create parallel divisions of a panel ruler, follow these steps:

1. **Select the Object Selector from the Tools palette and make sure that the Select All Continuous Points on Ruler check box is selected on the Tool Options palette.**

2. **On the panel ruler layer, click the panel you wish to divide.**

3. **From the main menu, choose Ruler⇨Panel Ruler⇨Split By Interval.**

   The Panel Ruler Split by Interval dialog box appears, as shown in Figure 7-14.

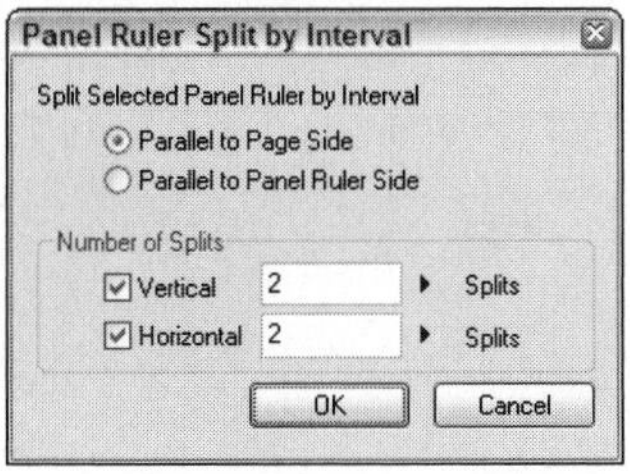

Figure 7-14:
The Panel Ruler Split By Interval dialog box.

4. **Decide how you want the panels split by selecting one of the radio buttons under Split Selected Ruler By Interval.**

   You're given two choices on how to split the panels:

   • *Parallel to Page Side:* This option produces panels where the borders are at 90 degree angles, as shown in the middle in Figure 7-15.

   • *Parallel to Panel Ruler Side:* Choosing this option creates panels in which the borders are parallel to the panel rulers surrounding it, which you can see in the bottom in Figure 7-15.

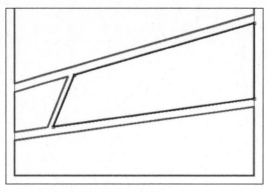

Original panel

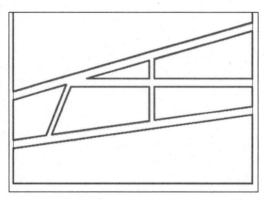

Panel split parallel to page sides

Figure 7-15:
You can
divide a
panel ruler
parallel to
the page
(middle) or
to the
surrounding
panel rulers
(bottom).

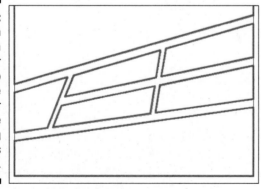

Panel split parallel to panel ruler sides

5. **If you want the panel ruler divided vertically, select the Vertical check box and enter the number of splits in its corresponding text box.**

6. **If you want the panel ruler divided horizontally, select the Horizontal check box and enter the number of splits in its corresponding text box.**

   Note that you can split a panel both vertically and horizontally if you wish.

7. **Click OK when you're done.**

Expanding panels

A recurring trend in comics and manga is expanding the artwork of a panel all the way to the edge of the page. It's a seemingly little trick, but it's really an effective tool if you want to bring the reader a little further into the scene you're looking to establish.

Follow these steps to expand a panel to the edge of the page:

1. **Select the Object Selector from the Tools palette and make sure that the Select All Continuous Points on Ruler check box is selected on the Tool Options palette.**

2. **On the panel ruler layer, click the Panel you wish to expand.**

3. **From the main menu, choose Ruler⇨Panel Ruler⇨Expand.**

   The Expand Panel Ruler dialog box appears, as shown in Figure 7-16.

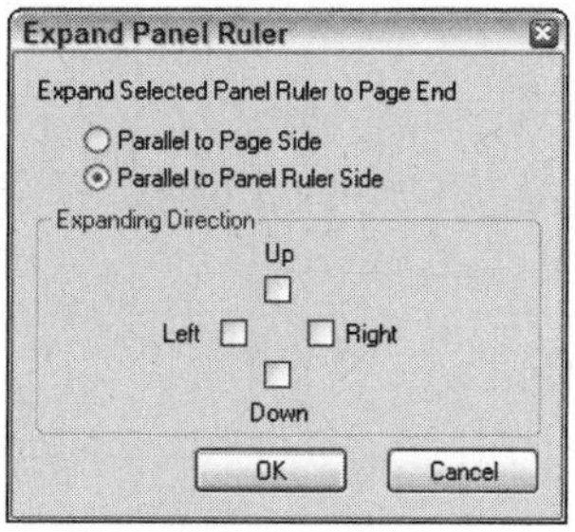

Figure 7-16:
The Expand
Panel Ruler
dialog box.

4. **Choose how you would like the panel borders to look after expansion by selecting one of the radio buttons under Expand Panel Ruler to Page End.**

   Like when you use the Parallel Division function, you're offered two options here:

   • *Parallel to Page Side:* The expanded panel borders become parallel to the page at 90 degree angles, as shown in the middle in Figure 7-17.

• *Parallel to Panel Ruler Side:* The expanded panel borders remain parallel to the panel borders surrounding it, as shown in the bottom in Figure 7-17.

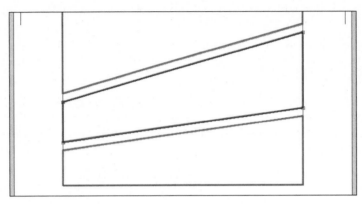

Original panel

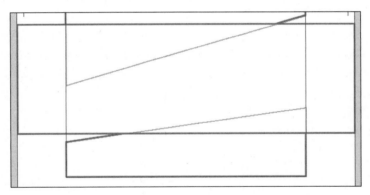

Panel expanded parallel to page sides

Figure 7-17:
You can
expand the
panel ruler
parallel to
the page
(middle) or
to the
surrounding
panel rulers
(bottom).

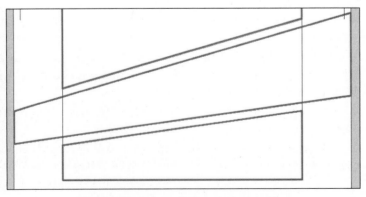

Panel expanded parallel to panel ruler sides

5. **Choose the directions you wish to expand the borders from the check boxes under Expanding Direction.**

   This is your opportunity to specify how you want the panel to expand. For example, if you're just looking to expand the left and right sides of the panel, select the Left and Right check boxes. You can choose any (or all) of the four directions.

6. **Click OK when you're done.**

Deleting points from a panel ruler

If you want to simplify the shape of a panel, you can remove points from the ruler.

Follow these steps to delete points from a panel layer:

1. **Choose the Object Selector from the Tools palette.**

   You don't need to select an entire panel for this function, so make sure you deselect the Select All Continuous Points on Ruler check box from the Tool Options palette, if it isn't already deselected.

2. **Select the point you wish to remove from the panel ruler.**

   You can see two selected points on the left in Figure 7-18.

3. **From the main menu, choose Ruler⇨Delete Selected Points.**

   Alternatively, you can use Ctrl+Alt+D on your keyboard (⌘+Option+D on the Mac).

That's all you need to do. The panel ruler adjusts to match the new number of points, which you can see on the right in Figure 7-18.

Figure 7-18:
Deleting
points from
a panel ruler
helps
simplify the
shape.

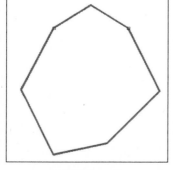
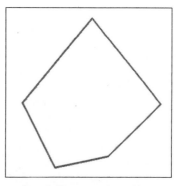

Original panel   Panel after removing points

Adding points to a panel ruler

Adding points to a panel ruler adds articulation; it's an extra joint (or joints) you can use to create complex panel designs. It's certainly a good way to break out of your typical square panel boundaries.

To add points to your panel ruler, follow these steps:

1. **Choose the Object Selector from the Tools palette.**

   You need to select only one side of the panel to add a point, so you need to deselect the Select All Continuous Points on Ruler check box from the Tool Options palette, if it isn't already deselected.

2. **Click the side of the panel you wish to add a point to.**

3. **From the main menu, choose Ruler⇨Add Points to Selected Sides. Or can press Ctrl+Alt+A (⌘+Option+A on the Mac).**

   You see a new point located in the middle of the panel side.

4. **Using the Object Selector, click the new point and drag it around until you've created your desired shape. (See Figure 7-19.)**

   You can repeat this process as many times as you'd like to as many sides as you like.

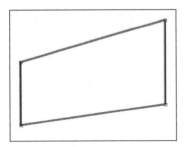

Original panel

Figure 7-19:
Adding
points to a
panel ruler
can result in
more
complex
panel
designs.

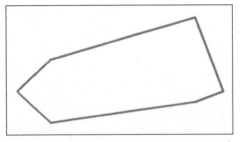

Panel after adding points

Converting Panel Ruler Layers

So after you've cut up, merged, squashed, and stretched the panel ruler — and moved it all over the place — everything matches the panels you intended to create. Now what?

You actually have several options for what to do with your panel rulers, and all of them involve the Rasterize function. Rasterizing your panel rulers allows you to create a series of panel layers, a set of rulers to draw your own borders, or let Manga Studio create the borders for you. What's even better is that you aren't limited to only one choice; you can pick and choose which of the three you want to use. If you want, you can even use all three!

Follow these steps to use the Rasterize function:

1. **Make sure the panel ruler layer is selected on the Layers palette.**

2. **From the main menu, choose Ruler⇨Panel Ruler⇨Rasterize.**

   The Rasterize Panel Ruler dialog box appears, as shown in Figure 7-20. There are three check boxes that you can pick from regarding your panel ruler conversion.

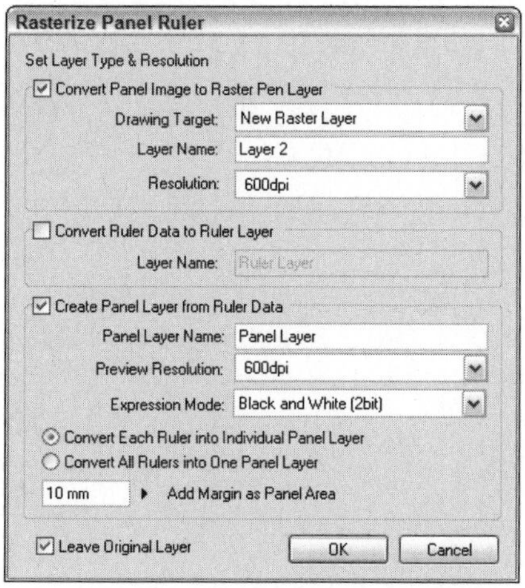

Figure 7-20:
The
Rasterize
Panel Ruler
dialog box.

3. **For a simple panel creation, select the Convert Panel Image to Raster Pen Layer check box.**

   This creates an image layer with panel borders. The panels themselves are transparent, while the area outside the panels are filled with white ink. This helps cut off any of your artwork beyond the panel borders, while not damaging the artwork itself.

- *If you're using Manga Studio EX, you can choose whether you want to create a raster or vector image layer by choosing from the Drawing Target drop-down list.*

  Manga Studio Debut users can create only raster layers, so there isn't a Drawing Target drop-down list.

- *To change the name of the image layer, enter a name in the Layer Name text box.*

- *To choose the resolution of the image layer, select a value from the Resolution drop-down list.*

  The resolutions available range from 150 dpi up to the resolution of your page file. Keep in mind that the lower the resolution, the more jagged the borders may turn out if you created non-square panels.

4. **To convert the panel ruler layer into a series of normal rulers, select the Convert Ruler Data to Ruler Layer check box.**

   This is a good option to use if you're looking to add a bit of personal flair to the panel borders, instead of the generic borders the program creates in Step 3.

5. **To create a series of panel layers from the panel rulers, select the Create Panel Layer from Ruler Data check box.**

   Here's your solution to automatically create all the panel layers you need for your page. All the steps are taken care of here: Not only are the panel layers created, but they're also labeled, masked off, and previewed at the resolution you want, all in one fell swoop.

   - *To change the name of the panel layers, enter a value in the Panel Layer Name text box.*

     All of the panels are named the same, but numbered individually to tell them apart. You may need to re-label each panel layer later on in the Layer Properties palette if you need further differentiation.

   - *To adjust the preview resolution, select a value from the Preview Resolution drop-down list.*

   - *To choose the preview expression mode, select a value from the Expression Mode drop-down list.*

     Each of the various expression modes are broken down in the "Previewing your panel layer" sidebar earlier in this chapter. If you're not sure which to use, be sure to check out the sidebar.

   - *If you want to create a panel layer for each panel ruler, select the Convert Each Ruler into Individual Panel Layer radio button.*

   - *If you want to create one panel layer that houses all the individual panels, select the Convert All Rulers into One Panel Layer radio button.*

- *To set the* buffer area *(that is, extra drawing space) around the panel layers, enter a value in the Add Margin as Panel Area text box, or you can select the black triangle to the right of the text box and use the slider to adjust to your desired value.*

  Each of the panel layers created uses the same margin. Remember that each of the panel layers are independent of each other, so you can select as large an area as you'd like to draw on, and they won't interfere with any of the others.

6. **Check the Leave Original Layer checkbox if you want to keep the Panel Ruler Layer after it has been rasterized.**

   This will be useful if you're planning on re-using the Panel Ruler Layer at some point in the future. If you don't need it anymore, de-selecting the checkbox will remove the Panel Ruler Layer after it's been rasterized.

Chapter 8

You Can't Draw a Straight Line without a (Virtual) Ruler

A few extremely talented artists may be able to draw a cityscape or pickup truck perfectly without using some kind of a straightedge or curved tool. The rest of us use rulers, French curves, and all sorts of other drawing tools to make those lines and curves look as good as possible on the page.

If you draw digitally, though, it's a different story. With some drawing programs, you might have a rudimentary straightedge tool to work with. If you're really lucky, you might have a curve tool available. For the most part, however, you're pretty much stuck with no kind of a freeform drawing guide to assist in any kind of perspective or technical drawing. Until now, that is.

A major feature of Manga Studio is the ability to create a near-infinite number of freeform rulers, curves, and shapes that you can work with just as easily as the real thing. Not having a virtual ruler or guide has caused me a lot of frustration in the past, and it was the only thing that held me back from going 100 percent digital until Manga Studio came out. Trust me when I say that once you use the rulers in Manga Studio, you'll wonder how you got along without them.

What's the Big Deal about Rulers?

A problem I see with whatever straightedge tool that other drawing programs use is that all the lines created look exactly the same; about the only variation between lines is their length. There's usually no character to the simple, fixed-width lines drawn. I feel the idea of using a virtual ruler while working is a very big thing. It gives you that much more feeling like you're working with real-world tools in a virtual space because you can treat the rulers just like you would with the real thing. Actually, you can do even more with virtual rulers — you can squash, stretch, grow, and shrink them to fit your needs. Most importantly, you can create any type of line you want with virtual rulers. Dotted or dashed, thin or thick (or all of the above!), you have the control to create the lines you want on the page, instead of settling for the ones the program gives you.

Keeping It Simple: Using the Line and Shape Tools

Before you start using the ruler tools, you should first become familiar with the simplest method to create lines and curves in Manga Studio: the Line and Shape tools.

Okay, okay, I *know* I just spent a half a page raving about how you don't need to use these tools when you can just create your own rulers. However, learning and understanding how these tools work can help you later when it comes time to create rulers, because you create your virtual rulers using the Line and Shape tools.

The Line tool

If you aren't looking for anything special in the lines you want for your technical and background work, using the Line/Curve/Polyline tool (Line tool, for short) is the simplest method. The Line tool (and its variant Curve and Polyline functions) puts down a basic, no-frills line, curve, or freeform polygonal shape at any length or size you need.

 To use this, click the Line tool icon, located on the Tools palette. To change the default options, use the Tool Options palette, shown in Figure 8-1. (If the Tool Options palette isn't open, you can open it by pressing F3.)

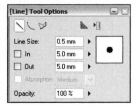

Figure 8-1:
The Line
Tool Options
palette in
Basic mode.

Basic line tools

Here's how the basic Line tool options break down:

- ✔ **Shape:** This is where you can choose whether you want to create a line, curve, or polyline shape. To switch from one tool to another, click the tool's corresponding icon. Alternatively, you can adjust the type of Line tool you want to use by holding down the Line tool button for a few seconds until the curve and polyline options pop up.

- ✔ **Create Rulers on Current Layer:** When you activate this button, anything you draw with this tool draws rulers instead of inked lines. (I explain this option in the "Rulers on an image layer" section, later in this chapter.)

- ✔ **Line Size:** This sets the thickness of the line you create.

- ✔ **(Taper) In:** This sets how much the starting point tapers out to the main thickness of the line. You can enter a value in the text box from 0 to 20 mm, or you can use the slider bar (activated by clicking the black triangle to the right of the text box) and adjusting that until you reach your desired taper length.

- ✔ **(Taper) Out:** This sets how much the line created tapers to its endpoint. You can enter a value in the text box from 0 to 20 mm, or you can use the slider bar (activated by clicking the black triangle to the right of the text box) and adjusting that until you reach your desired taper length.

- ✔ **Opacity:** This adjusts how transparent the line is when you draw it. You can enter a value between 0% (completely transparent) and 100% (completely opaque) in its text box, or you can use the slider bar (activated by clicking the black triangle to the right of the text box) and adjusting that until you reach your desired opacity.

- ✔ **Absorption:** Used on a Vector Layer, the endpoints of the lines or curves become "magnetized," in which they join any other lines or shapes in close proximity. You can adjust the absorption strength (Weak, Medium, or Strong) by selecting from the Absorption dropdown list.

Advanced Line tool options

Clicking the Open Menu Icon at the top of the Tool Options palette and selecting Advanced Options brings up an additional group of settings to adjust, which you can see in Figure 8-2.

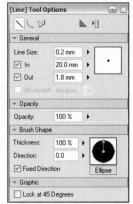

Figure 8-2:
The Line
Tool Options
palette in
Advanced
mode.

Here's how the Advanced Options break down:

✔ **Thickness:** You can adjust the roundness or flatness of the line shape by entering a value between 0 and 100 percent in the Thickness text box.

✔ **Direction:** Entering a value between 0 and 360degrees in the Direction text box sets the angle the brush will lay at. This is useful only if you've changed the thickness of the line shape in any way.

✔ **Fixed Direction:** Selecting this option keeps the line angle fixed, regardless of the angle you start drawing the line.

✔ **Lock at 45 Degrees:** Selecting this option keeps the lines created locked within 45 degree intervals.

The Shape tool

Like the Line tool, the Rectangle/Circle/Polygon tool (what I call the Shape tool for short — it's much easier to type) creates a simple, no-frills shape to an image layer. If you aren't looking to add anything special to the line work, this is a very easy and quick means to add whatever shapes you need.

If you want to use the Shape tool, click its button on the Tools palette. When you activate the Tool Options (F3 on your keyboard) you see something similar to Figure 8-3.

Basic shape tools

Here's how the basic Shape tool options break down:

✔ **Shape:** You can choose whether you want to create a rectangle, ellipse, or polygon here. To switch to a different shape, click its corresponding icon.

▼ 🗗 Ruler

- ✓ **Create Rulers on Current Layer:** When you activate this button, anything you draw with the Shape tool draws rulers on the image layer instead of inked lines. (See the "Rulers on an image layer" section, later in this chapter.)

- ✓ **Line Size:** This sets the thickness of the line you create.

- ✓ **Absorption:** Used on a Vector Layer, rectangle or elliptical tool becomes "magnetized," in which it joins to any other lines or shapes in close proximity. You can adjust the absorption strength (Weak, Medium, or Strong) by selecting from the Absorption drop-down list.

- ✓ **Opacity:** This adjusts how transparent the line is when you draw it. You can enter a value between 1% (totally transparent) and 100% (completely opaque) in its text box, or you can use the slider bar (activated by clicking the black triangle to the right of the text box) and adjusting that until you reach the desired opacity.

Advanced Shape tool options

Clicking the Open Menu Icon at the top of the Tool Options palette and selecting Advanced Options brings up an additional group of settings to adjust, as shown in Figure 8-3.

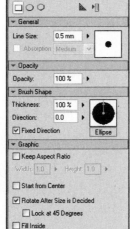

Figure 8-3:
The Shape
Tool Options
palette in
Advanced
mode.

Here's how the Advanced Options break down:

- ✓ **Thickness:** You can adjust the roundness or flatness of the line shape by entering a value between 1 and 100 percent in the Thickness text box.

- ✓ **Direction:** Entering a value between 0 and 360 degrees in the Direction text box sets the angle the line will lay at. This is useful only if you've changed the thickness of the line shape in any way.

- ✔ **Fixed Direction:** Selecting this option keeps the brush angle fixed, regardless of the angle you start drawing the shape.

- ✔ **Keep Aspect Ratio:** This option helps you keep a specific width-height ratio, regardless of how you draw the shape. Enter the ratio in the corresponding Width and Height text boxes.

- ✔ **Start from Center:** If selected, any shape you draw starts from the center, as opposed to a corner, of the shape.

- ✔ **Rotate after Size is Decided:** If you select this option, you can choose to rotate it along its center point, after you draw the shape. Additionally, you can choose to lock the rotations at iterations of 45 degrees by selecting the Lock at 45 Degrees check box.

- ✔ **Fill Inside:** Selecting this check box fills the entire shape with the foreground color.

Drawing a line or shape

Drawing with either the Line or Shape tool is all about endpoints; specifying where the line or shape begins and ends on the canvas is all you need to do.

To get started, follow these steps:

1. **Select either the Line or Shape tool from the Tools palette.**

2. **Create a starting point with your mouse or stylus on the canvas.**

3. **Drag the mouse or stylus to the ending point and release to create the line or shape.**

   If you're drawing a curve, you need to set the bend by dragging the line until you reach the desired point and then click the canvas.

   If you're working with the Polyline tool, continue dragging and clicking endpoints. To complete a shape, simply click the starting point again.

   To create a perfectly circular, square, or polygonal shape, hold down the Shift key when using the Shape tool.

You Can't Use Rulers until You Make Rulers

It would probably be difficult to work with the virtual rulers of Manga Studio if you don't exactly know how to *create* them. Here's some good news — creating rulers is very easy to do. All you need to do is decide whether you want the rulers localized to one image layer, or on their own ruler layer, which can be used by all image and selection layers on the page.

The ruler layer

If you're looking to create rulers that all the image layers on your page will use, place them on a ruler layer. Like image layers, you can create as many ruler layers as you want. So, if you'd like to work with one layer containing nothing but ellipses, another with straightedges, and another with your oddly-shaped rulers, you can.

There are two ways you can create a new ruler layer:

⌐ From the main menu, choose Layer⇨New Layer.

   When the New Layer dialog box pops up, choose Ruler Layer from the Layer Type drop-down list. All the other options will become unavailable (except for the Layer Name text box, should you decide to rename the new layer).

⌐ On the Layers palette, click the icon next to the Rulers header.

   Clicking that brings up the New Layer dialog box with Ruler Layer already selected. You can enter the name of the ruler layer in the Layer Name text box and click the OK button to finish.

Rulers on an image layer

If you're looking to limit the rulers to a particular image layer, thereby keeping them limited to the layer you're working with, you can do that in Manga Studio. You can place them on a localized ruler layer, or you can use them directly on the image layer itself. Both do exactly the same thing — it's really a matter of taste regarding which method you like to use.

To set up your localized rulers for an image layer, highlight the image layer you want to add rulers to. (If the Layers palette isn't showing, press F4 to bring it up.)

From here, you have two ways you can lay down your rulers:

⌐ If you'd like to have the rulers on their own layer, you set that on the Layer Properties palette. (Press F7 to bring up the Layer Properties palette). Simply select the Convert to Layer check box. Now, when you look at the Layers palette, you see a ruler layer directly underneath the image layers, as shown in Figure 8-4.

Figure 8-4:
Selecting
Convert to
Layer on the
Layer
Properties
palette
creates a
localized
ruler layer.

Unlike working with normal ruler layers, where you can create as many layers as you want, you're limited to only one ruler layer per image layer.

✔ If you don't care about creating a separate layer for your rulers, you can create them directly on the image layer. All you need to do is click the Create Rulers on Current Layer button on the Line or Shape Tool Options palette. (Press F3 to make this palette appear.)

The Line or Shape tools can now draw rulers on an image layer. You can create all the rulers you want on that layer. If you want to hide them, simply click Hide on the Properties palette for that image layer.

 ✔ To hide a localized rulers layer, simply click the Eye icon located to the left of the layer on the Layers palette.

Creating rulers with the Line and Shape tools

Here's where figuring out how the Line and Shape tools work (discussed earlier in this chapter) pays off. These are the tools you use to create the rulers. In fact, they're the *only* ones you can use on a ruler layer, because none of the other drawing tools will work.

Follow these steps to create rulers with these tools:

1. **Create a starting point with your mouse or stylus on the canvas.**

2. **Drag the mouse or stylus to the ending point of your ruler and release.**

   If you're drawing a curve, you need to set the bend by dragging the line until you reach the desired point and then clicking the canvas.

   If you're working with the Polyline tool, continue dragging and clicking endpoints, finishing the shape by clicking the starting point.

The only thing limiting your ability to create rulers is your imagination. Just like you would use the Line and Shape tools to create any kind of line or shape you want, you can use them to draw up any kind of ruler you need. Check out Figure 8-5 for some examples of the various types of rulers you can make.

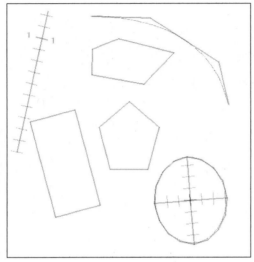

Figure 8-5:
You can create all kinds of shapes to use as rulers.

Deleting rulers

One of the best things about creating and working with any type of ruler you want is that you can simply delete them when you're done!

To delete a ruler, follow these steps:

1. **Select the Object Selector tool from the Tools palette.**

2. **Holding down the Ctrl key (⌘ on the Mac), click the ruler with your mouse or stylus.**

3. **Press Ctrl+Alt+D on your keyboard (⌘+Option+D on the Mac). Alternatively, you can use the main menu and choose Ruler⇨Delete Selected Points.**

Adjusting and Transforming Rulers

You're going to need to become very familiar with two tools vital to working with rulers in Manga Studio: the Object Selector and the Ruler Manipulator.

These tools are the ones you'll need to use to make any kind of adjustments or transformations to your rulers.

The Object Selector

Any kind of specific adjustments you want to make to rulers involves using the Object Selector tool, located on the Tools palette. (Chapter 7 discusses the Object Selector in depth.) You use the Object Selector to manipulate the endpoints and sides of a panel ruler. The same idea applies here as well — you use the Object Selector to select and move around the endpoints and sides of your ruler until it matches exactly what you need.

Using the Object Selector is easy enough. All it involves is selecting a side or endpoint with your mouse or stylus and then dragging that selection across the canvas until you're happy with the new shape, as shown in Figure 8-6. Then, repeat with another endpoint or side as necessary.

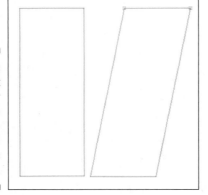

Figure 8-6:
The Object Selector helps to make specific adjustments to a ruler.

The Ruler Manipulator

The Ruler Manipulator is a great all-in-one tool to work with your rulers; you use it to scale, move, or rotate a ruler however you'd like. Actually, you can use this on as many rulers (or an entire ruler layer) as you want, all at once!

To use the Ruler Manipulator, choose Ruler➪Show Ruler Manipulator from the main menu. Or you can press Ctrl+Shift+1 (one) on your keyboard (⌘+Shift+1 [one] for the Mac). You should now see the tool as well as a small cross on your workspace, as shown in Figure 8-7.

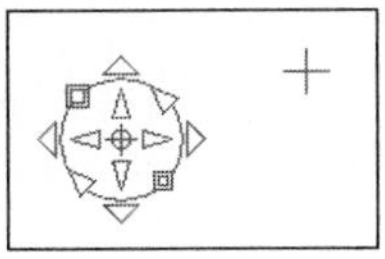

Figure 8-7:
The Ruler
Manipulator
tool and
focal point.

As you can see from the figure, each part of the Ruler Manipulator performs a specific task for adjusting your rulers.

The cross serves as the focal point for the Ruler Manipulator. All rulers rotate and scale in relation to wherever you place the focal point.

For example, say you're using a ruler to draw focal points on a panel. If you were working on a regular piece of paper, you would draw a small dot, or place a pin in the middle of the panel to use as your focal point for your ruler. Using the Ruler Manipulator's focal point works the same way. Using the focus lines example again, you place the focal point in the middle of the panel and place the ruler upon it just like you would on paper. Then, when you use the Ruler Manipulator, the ruler rotates around the focal point.

Keyboard shortcuts

If you don't want to use the Ruler Manipulator to adjust the rulers, Manga Studio provides a series of keyboard shortcuts that perform the same functions. You still need to use the Object Selector to initially select the ruler or rulers you want to adjust.

The keyboard shortcuts are listed in Table 8-1.

Table 8-1	Keyboard Shortcuts for Adjusting Rulers
Shortcut Key	*Function*
Q	Place focal point (where cursor is on page).
X	Reduce ruler size.
Z	Enlarge ruler size.
A	Rotate ruler counterclockwise.
S	Rotate ruler clockwise.

Adding points

Inserting additional points to a ruler is much like taking a drinking straw and bending it, eventually creating a crease in it. Creasing it once allows you to bend the straw a couple of ways. Add a few more creases, and you can bend the straw in more ways. The more creases you make, the more ways you can shape the straw.

Adding more points to a ruler not only allows for more intricate shapes, but it can also change the bend of a curved ruler as well, which you can see in Figure 8-8. The additional points help you to bend the curve in ways that you couldn't do before. This is a great way to create one long ruler that fits what you want to draw, instead of moving and adjusting the ruler to fit each part as necessary.

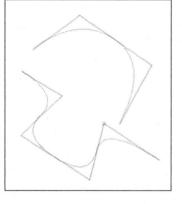

Figure 8-8:
The more points you add, the greater the ruler articulation.

To add points to a ruler side, follow these steps:

1. **Click the Object Selector, located on the Tools palette.**

2. **Make sure that the Select All Continuous Points on Ruler check box on the Tool Options palette is deselected.**

3. **Click the ruler side you wish to add a point to.**

   If you're adding points to multiple sides of a guide, hold down the Shift key as you select each side you want selected. If you want to add points to the entire guide, hold down the Ctrl key (⌘ on the Mac) as you click on the object.

4. **From the main menu, choose Ruler➪Add Points to Selected Sides. Alternatively, you can press Ctrl+Alt+A (⌘+Option+A on the Mac).**

   You see a new point in the middle of the selected ruler's side. All you need to do now is use the Object Selector to move that endpoint around until you get the ruler exactly how you want it. If it still isn't quite right, simply add another point!

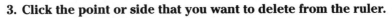

Deleting points

If you find that the ruler you're working on has more endpoints (or curve adjustment points) or sides than you need, you can simplify things by deleting them from the ruler. Just follow these steps:

1. **Click the Object Selector, located on the Tools palette.**

2. **If you want to select only one point or side, make sure that the Select All Continuous Points on Ruler check box on the Tool Options palette is deselected.**

   If you want to delete the entire ruler, make sure that the Continuous Points check box is selected.

3. **Click the point or side that you want to delete from the ruler.**

   The selected portion of the ruler turns red.

4. **From the main menu, choose Ruler⇨Delete Selected Points. Alternatively, press Ctrl+Alt+D (⌘+Option+D on the Mac).**

   The selected point(s) on the ruler are deleted, as shown in Figure 8-9.

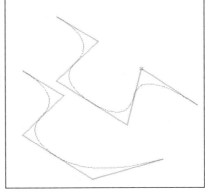

Figure 8-9:
Deleting points or sides from a ruler is easy to do.

A ruler must have more than two points in order to remove any of them. Manga Studio doesn't allow you to delete anything from a ruler with only two points (because then you'd be left with only one point, and that would be just *impractical* to use!).

Aligning rulers

If you're working with multiple rulers, you may find you need to line them up in either a certain direction or position. Manga Studio has a few functions you can use to rotate and adjust your rulers to whatever position, spacing, or angle you need.

Verticalize

The Verticalize function takes your selected rulers and adjusts them until they're all at a 90-degree angle, which you can see in Figure 8-10. The sizes and general positions of the rulers remain the same.

Figure 8-10:
The Verticalize function quickly aligns your rulers at 90 degrees.

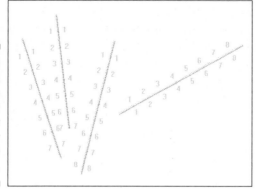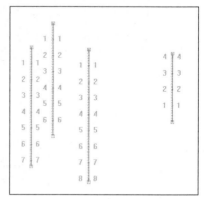

To make your rulers vertical, follow these steps:

1. **Use the Object Selector to choose the rulers you want to verticalize.**

2. **From the main menu, choose Rulers⇨Verticalize.**

That's all you need to do! The rulers instantly rotate to a vertical position.

Horizontalize

The Horizontalize function takes your selected rulers and adjusts them until they're all in a horizontal position, while maintaining their size and location on the canvas. Check out Figure 8-11 for an example of this.

Figure 8-11:
Use the Horizontalize function to lay selected rulers at 0 degrees.

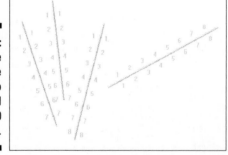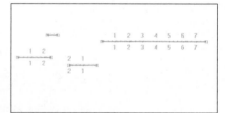

To make your rulers horizontal, follow these steps:

1. **Use the Object Selector to choose the rulers you want to verticalize.**

2. **From the main menu, choose Rulers⇨Horizontalize.**

Pretty simple, eh? Your selected rulers are all lying horizontally on the page.

Align sides

Useful for aligning ruler shapes, the Align Sides function takes your selected ruler sides (if the rulers are rectangular or polygonal) or ellipses and moves or transforms them until they line up on the same axis. (See Figure 8-12.)

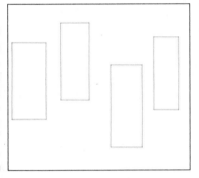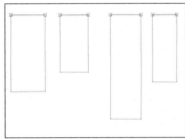

Figure 8-12: The Align Sides function lines up the rulers along the axis of your choice.

To align the sides of your rulers, follow these steps:

1. **Use the Object Selector to select the ruler sides or ellipses you want to align.**

2. **From the main menu, choose Ruler⇨Align Sides.**

   The Align Sides dialog box appears, as shown in Figure 8-13. The rulers line up according to the default settings.

Figure 8-13: The Align Sides dialog box.

3. **If you're aligning elliptical rulers, select whether you want to align them by their long or short axes by selecting the appropriate Ellipse Ruler Settings option button.**

4. **Select which ruler you want to use as the reference point for alignment by clicking the Swap Base with Moving Line button.**

Each click on the button cycles through each ruler and aligns the other selected rulers accordingly.

5. Click OK when you're done.

Parallel by interval

The Parallel by Interval function allows you to quickly horizontalize or verticalize your rulers a set distance apart from each other, as shown in Figure 8-14.

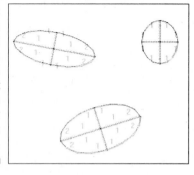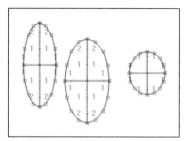

Figure 8-14:
The Parallel by Interval function aligns and spaces out your rulers at whatever amount you like.

To make your rulers parallel by interval, follow these steps:

1. Use the Object Selector to select the rulers you want to align.

2. From the main menu, choose Ruler⇨Parallel by Interval.

The Parallel by Interval dialog box appears, as shown in Figure 8-15. The rulers align according to the default settings.

Figure 8-15:
The Parallel by Interval dialog box.

3. Choose how you want the rulers aligned (either vertically or horizontally) by selecting the appropriate Aligning Direction radio button.

4. **Choose the amount of spacing between the rulers by selecting an option from the Interval radio buttons.**

   You have three options to choose from in this section:

   • *Horizontal Interval:* This sets a spacing interval based on the default Horizontal Interval value. You can't change this value in this dialog box.

   • *Vertical Interval:* This sets a spacing interval based on the default Vertical Interval value. You can't change this value in this dialog box.

   • *Set Interval:* This is a custom spacing interval you can use by either entering a value between 0 and 200 mm in its text box, or you can use the slider bar (activated by clicking the black triangle to the right of the text box) to adjust until you find your desired value.

5. **If you're aligning elliptical rulers, select whether you want to align them by their long or short axes by selecting the appropriate Ellipse Ruler Settings radio button.**

6. **Select which ruler you want to use as the reference point for alignment by clicking the Swap Base with Moving Line button.**

   Each click on the button cycles through each ruler and aligns the other selected rulers accordingly.

7. **Click OK when you're done.**

 You can change the default Horizontal and Vertical Intervals in the System Preferences by choosing File➪Preferences. In the Preferences dialog box that appears, click the + next to Page to expand the list, and then select Ruler. You can then adjust the default options as you please.

Time to Start Drawing with Your Rulers!

You have your rulers all created, adjusted, and ready to go. Now, it's time to start drawing with them! Here's where the fun begins.

To draw along a ruler, you must first make sure that any lines you draw will snap to it. There are two buttons located on the Page toolbar that you need to make sure are turned on to enable snapping:

 ✔ **Snap:** Clicking the Snap button turns on and off the ability to lock what you're drawing to a drawing aid in close proximity.

 ✔ **Snap to Rulers:** Clicking the Snap Rulers button turns on and off the ability to lock what you're drawing to a ruler in close proximity.

When you've turned those two buttons on, you're all set to start using them with your pens and pencils! Simply draw along the rulers like you would with the real thing, and before you know it, you're creating perfectly straight lines and all the curves and shapes you need for your work, as shown in Figure 8-16.

Using rulers when you're drawing something with lots of straight edges (such as a building) or curves (such as a sports car) can make the difference between professional-looking work and a sub-par drawing.

Figure 8-16:
You can add your own personality to the lines you draw along your virtual rulers.

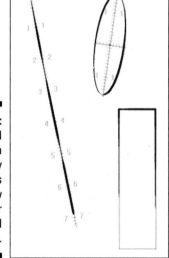

Chapter 9

Working with Selections and Selection Layers

*I*f you're new to the world of digital art programs, you might be a bit confused when I mention the term *selection tools*. However, ask a veteran digital artist about the term, and you'll find out just how important (some would even say *vital)* selection tools can be to your work.

A staple of practically every art program on the market today, selection tools are deceptively simple: You use a *selection tool* to confine a specific area of your canvas. It probably doesn't sound like much, until you find out what you can now do; namely, you can work within the selected area without worrying about ruining the rest of your work. Whether it's to add a subtle effect, fill in a sold color or screentone, or remove a piece of your drawing that just isn't working for you, only the area bound by the selection is affected. The more you use it, the more you find out how much of a timesaver it can be to your work (especially when you consider the alternative approach to filling in a section, which is to create a new layer, fill it with the color or tone, and then trim away the excess).

So, I'm sure I'll surprise no one reading this that Manga Studio includes many of the basic selection tools that other drawing programs have. (It's always good to go with what works, right?) However, Manga Studio includes an additional option that not many other art programs offer (if at all): the ability to save or create your selection on a specialized selection layer, which you can then use and reuse as many times as you want!

Piqued your curiosity yet?

In this chapter, I discuss how to first work with the basic selection tools and functions that Manga Studio provides, as well as go over examples of how to work with them on the page. Then I explain how selection layers work and how you can use them to create new selections or convert existing ones (and then convert them back to selection areas on your page).

The Basics, or Getting (Re)Acquainted with the Selection Tools

Before you can start working with selections, it would probably be a good idea to discuss exactly how to *create* them.

If you're familiar with Photoshop or Painter, you'll find that Manga Studio provides all the same selection tools that those other programs offer. That said, you should still read on, as you'll find that there are additional settings and general tweaks you can do to these tools that you can't do in either of those programs. (I've looked, trust me!)

Manga Studio provides three basic tools that you can use to create selections on the page: the Marquee tool, the Lasso tool, and the Magic Wand tool. I discuss how to use each tool in the following sections.

The Marquee tool

You can use the Marquee tool to create basic rectangular or elliptical selections on the page. It's actually very similar to the Shape tool (which I discuss in Chapter 8), with the exception that you aren't automatically committed to a filled-in or outlined shape. (See Figure 9-1.)

 To get started, either click the Marquee tool button on the Tools palette or press M. In addition, you can cycle between the rectangular and elliptical tool by either pressing and holding the Marquee tool button and selecting from the drop-down list that appears or by pressing the M key again.

If the default settings aren't to your liking, you can always change them by altering the tool options as follows:

1. **If it isn't already visible, open the Tool Options palette by choosing Window⇨Tool Options or by pressing F3 on your keyboard.**

   The Tool Options palette appears, as shown in Figure 9-2. Manga Studio EX has a few additional options on its Options palette that the Debut version doesn't offer, so I point those out later in this list.

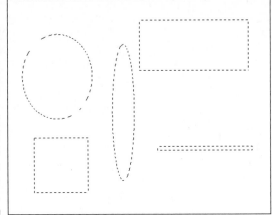

Figure 9-1:
You can
create all
kinds of
rectangular
and
elliptical
selections
with the
Marquee
tool.

Figure 9-2:
The
Marquee
Tool Options
palette.

2. **Choose the marquee shape (rectangular or elliptical) you want to work with by clicking its respective icon.**

3. **Choose the way you want to create selections by clicking one of the Selection Type buttons.**

   If you're looking to create multiple selections at once, or perhaps you want to edit an existing selection, you can alter how the Marquee tool creates them, as shown in Figure 9-3. You have four options to choose from.

   • *New Selection:* Creates a new selection each time you use it. Any previous selections are removed.

   • *Add Selection:* Adds new selections to the page, while retaining any previous selections. Selections that overlap are merged into one larger selection.

   • *Subtract Selection:* Removes any intersecting area between the current and previous selection on the page.

   • *Multiply Selection:* Any selections that are inside the new selection you're creating remains on the page, while selections residing outside the new selection are removed from the page.

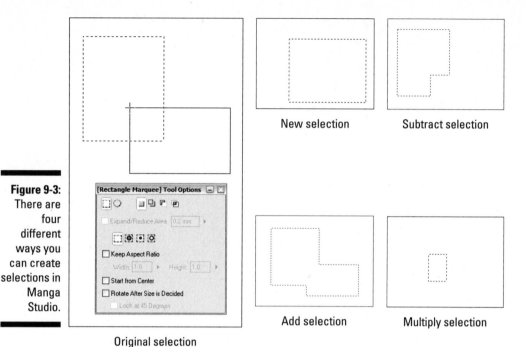

New selection   Subtract selection

Figure 9-3:
There are
four
different
ways you
can create
selections in
Manga
Studio.

[Rectangle Marquee] Tool Options

Expand/Reduce Area   0.2 mm

Keep Aspect Ratio
Width: 1.0   Height: 1.0
Start from Center
Rotate After Size is Decided
Lock at 45 Degrees

Add selection   Multiply selection

Original selection

4. **(EX only) If you want to grow or shrink the selection after it's created, click the Expand/Reduce Area check box and enter a value between -1.0 mm and 1.0 mm in its corresponding text box. The Normal Selection bounding type does not have this option.**

5. **(EX only) Select the Marquee tool's bounding type by clicking the corresponding icon.**

   When you set the bounding type, what you're doing is setting how the Marquee tool reacts when a shape is included within a selection. There are four options you can choose from, each of which are illustrated in Figure 9-4.

   • *Normal Selection (default):* Takes up the entire area created by the Marquee tool.

   • *Shrink Selection:* Shrinks to fit the enclosed shape.

   • *Inside Selection:* Shrinks to the negative space (that is, the transparent area) within the enclosed shape. The drawing lines that create the shape are ignored.

   • *Shape Selection:* Selects the drawing lines used to create the shape. Any negative space (anything that isn't a line, tone, or pattern) on the layer is ignored..

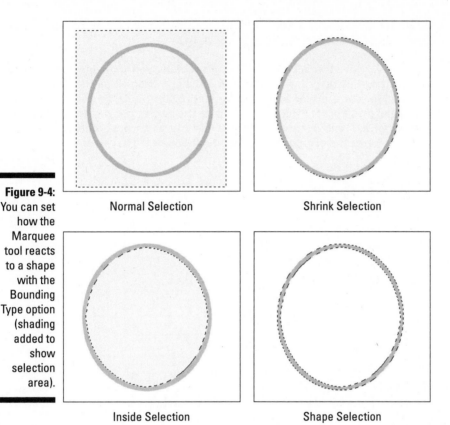

Normal Selection

Shrink Selection

Inside Selection

Shape Selection

Figure 9-4:
You can set how the Marquee tool reacts to a shape with the Bounding Type option (shading added to show selection area).

6. **If you want to force the selection to keep a specific aspect ratio, click the Keep Aspect Ratio check box and enter values between 0.1 and 20.0 in the Height and Width text boxes.**

   This option, if you want to use it, locks the shape you create to a specific height-to-width ratio, no matter how large or small you draw the shape, as shown in Figure 9-5. If you want to create a perfect square or circle, all you need to do is enter the same value (this can be any number in the range) in the height and width text boxes.

7. **Click the Start From Center check box if you want to draw the selection from the middle point of the shape outwards.**

   By default, the Marquee tool creates a selection from corner point to corner point (which I explain a bit further in the paragraph following this list). This option lets you create the selection from the middle and outwards, which can be useful during those times when you have a specific place in mind that you'd like to start the selection from.

8. **If you want to rotate the selection after it's created, click the Rotate After Size is Decided check box.**

Optionally, you can limit the shape rotation to 45-degree increments by clicking the Lock at 45 Degrees check box.

Using the Marquee tool all comes down to clicking and dragging. Specifically, you click the starting point for your selection and drag along the page until the selection is at the size you want. Depending on what you chose in the Tool Options palette, the starting point is either the center point of the selection or a corner point. (Yeah, I know — ellipses don't have corners, but the bounding box used to size the ellipse *does*.) Check out Figure 9-6 to see an example.

Figure 9-5: Setting the Aspect Ratio locks the Marquee tool to a specific shape.

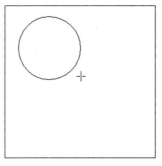 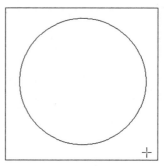

Figure 9-6: Simply click and drag the Marquee tool to create selections on the page.

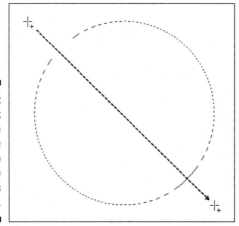

The Lasso tool

Unlike the Marquee tool, which creates a basic shape, the Lasso tool helps you create a more specific selection on the page. If you're looking to create a more complicated polygonal shape, or maybe outline a character or object on your page, this is the tool to use.

To select the Lasso tool, you can either click its icon on the Tools palette, or you can press L on your keyboard. Like the Marquee tool, you can cycle between the Lasso and Polyline tools by holding down the Lasso button until its drop-down list appears — or by pressing L again.

"What's the Polyline tool," you say? The Polyline tool takes a more connect-the-dots approach to creating a selection. While the Lasso tool allows you to free-hand your selection by drawing it out (like you're working with a pen), you use the Polyline tool to lay down points on the page. This results in a more polygonal selection compared to the more organic Lasso selection. (See Figure 9-7 to see the difference between the two.)

Figure 9-7:
The Polyline and Lasso tools allow you to create a more specific selection, compared to the Marquee tool.

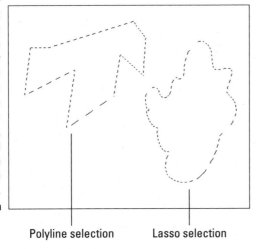

Polyline selection   Lasso selection

Which is better? Like many of the other tools you work with in Manga Studio, it boils down to personal preference. I know people that prefer the more precise selection created with the Lasso, and others who prefer the control that the Polyline tool provides. Try out each, and see which works best for you.

Like the Marquee tool, you can tweak the Lasso tool settings to your liking by using the Tool Options palette (shown in Figure 9-8) as follows:

1. **If it isn't already visible, open the Tool Options palette by choosing Window⇨Tool Options or by pressing F3 on your keyboard.**

2. **Choose the way you want to create selections by clicking one of the Selection Type buttons.**

   Check out "The Marquee tool" section, earlier in this chapter, for explanations on the various Selection Type options.

3. **If you want to grow or shrink the selection after it's created, click the Expand/Reduce Area check box and enter a value between -1.0 mm and 1.0 mm in its corresponding text box.**

4. **(EX only) Select the Marquee tool's Bounding Type.**

   See "The Marquee tool" section, earlier in this chapter, for explanations on the various Bounding Type options.

Figure 9-8:
The Lasso Tool Options palette.

The Magic Wand tool

Sometimes it's just easier to click an area of the page to select it. That's where the Magic Wand tool can help out . . . because that's all it does!

The Magic Wand is probably the easiest of all the selection tools to use in Manga Studio. You have only two steps to perform:

1. **Click the Magic Wand button on the Tools palette or press W on your keyboard.**

2. **Click the area of the page you want to select.**

That's it! No tracing. No clicking and dragging. Just click what you want selected, and you're done, as shown in Figure 9-9.

Figure 9-9:
The Magic Wand is amazingly simple to use. Just click the area you want selected, and you're done!

You aren't limited to selecting only the transparent area of the page, either. One of the reasons that all the line work in Manga Studio is aliased (jagged lines instead of smooth lines when you zoom in close) is that it makes selecting them with the Magic Wand significantly easier. So, you can choose to select an area within a piece of line work, or you can pick the line work itself if you want to.

Keep in mind that when you want to use the Magic Wand to select an area, you need to make sure that area is *fully* enclosed. While Manga Studio EX users have the option to set a gap size tolerance (more on that in the following step list), it's still good practice to make sure that the area you want is fully enclosed by a drawing line. Otherwise, you may end up selecting more than you originally planned.

To adjust the options for the Magic Wand, follow these steps:

1. **If it isn't already visible, open the Tool Options palette by choosing Window⇨Tool Options or by pressing F3 on your keyboard.**

2. **Choose the way you want to create selections by clicking one of the Selection Type icons.**

   Check out the "The Marquee tool" section earlier in the chapter for explanations on the various Selection Types.

3. **If you want to grow or shrink the selection after it's created, click the Expand/Reduce Area check box and enter a value between -1.0 mm and 1.0 mm in its corresponding text box.**

4. **(EX only) If you want to set a gap threshold, select the Close Path check box and enter a value between 0.0 mm and 1.0 mm in its text box.**

   Earlier, I mention that it's good practice to make sure that the area you want to select is fully enclosed by a drawing line. For EX users, it isn't quite as vital, if you decide to set a Close Path threshold value.

   The idea here is that the Close Path option tells the Magic Wand that if any gaps are within the value entered, treat them as if they don't exist. So, as long as the gaps in the area you want selected are no bigger than your threshold value, the Magic Wand treats it as though it's fully enclosed. (Check out Figure 9-10 to see what I mean.)

5. **Select the All Layers check box if you want use the Magic Wand to create selections from all visible layers.**

   Normally, the Magic Wand creates only selections from the active layer, ignoring any of the other visible layers on the page. When you select this option, however, all the visible layers are treated as though they're one layer. This results in different selections being created, which is illustrated in Figure 9-11.

6. **Enter a value between 0 and 99 in the Allowable Error in Color text box to set the color threshold when selecting an area.**

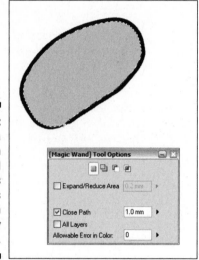

Figure 9-10:
Setting a
Close Path
threshold
treats areas
with gaps as
though
they're fully
enclosed.

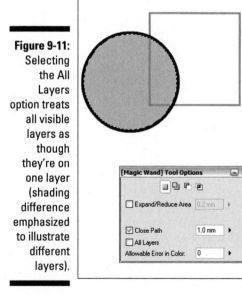
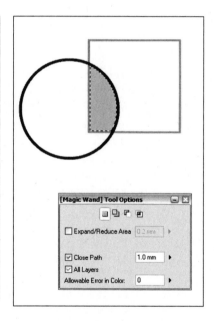

Figure 9-11:
Selecting
the All
Layers
option treats
all visible
layers as
though
they're on
one layer
(shading
difference
emphasized
to illustrate
different
layers).

Setting a threshold allows the magic wand to allow certain gray color differences between lines outlining an area you want to select. Entering a lower value increases the tolerance (meaning you can get away with a greater difference between shades of gray), while a higher value decreases the tolerance. (The magic wand ignores the lighter shades.) Figure 9-12 best illustrates what I'm talking about.

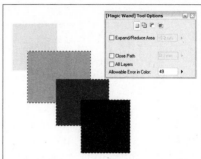

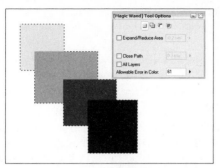

Figure 9-12:
Entering an
Allowable
Error in
Color value
sets how
the Magic
Wand treats
lines of
different
gray colors.

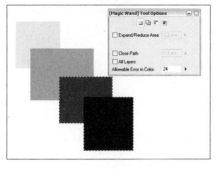

This option really works only when you're working on an 8-bit layer
that doesn't subtract colors. Other layer types won't work because they
don't produce solid lines.

7. **Click OK when you're done.**

Additional functions

The Selection tools aren't the only way to create selections on the page.
The Selection menu (located on the main menu), contains a few additional
functions that you can use to quickly make or remove selections.

You can access each of these functions by clicking the Selection menu.
Keyboard commands (if applicable) are noted in parentheses.

- **Selection⇨Select All (Ctrl+A, ⌘+A on the Mac):** A quick way to select
  the entire page at once. I personally like to use this when I want to
  quickly erase a drawing or layout that I'm not happy with at all.

- **Selection⇨Clear Selection (Ctrl+D, ⌘+D on the Mac):** This removes all
  selections on the page at once.

✔ **Selection⇨Invert Selection (Ctrl+Shift+I, ⌘+Shift+I on the Mac):** This function reverses what is selected on the page, so the opposite is now the selected region.

✔ **Selection⇨Expand Selection, Selection⇨Reduce Selection:** These are actually two separate functions, but because they work the same way, I'm lumping the explanation of how they work into this one bullet:

You can use both functions to resize selections on the page. Unlike the Expand/Reduce Area option for the various Selection tools (which automatically resizes the selection after it's created), you can use these functions to affect all the selections you may have on the page at once.

After you select one of the functions from the Selection menu, the respective dialog box appears. (See Figure 9-13.) Follow these steps to adjust the options in the Expand Selection or Reduce Selection dialog box:

1. *Select the unit of measurement you want to resize (by pixels or millimeters) from the Units drop-down list.*

2. *Enter the amount you want to resize the selection by (0.1 mm to 5.0 mm or 1 to 118 pixels) in the Width text box.*

3. *If you want the corners of the selection altered (if applicable), click the type of corner you want (square, diagonal, or rounded).*

4. *Click OK when you're done.*

✔ **Selection⇨Select By Color:** While I mention earlier that you can use the Magic Wand to select line art, this function is probably a bit easier to use (and it's definitely quicker) when you want to select the artwork of a particular color all at once.

When you choose this command, the Select by Color dialog box appears (shown in Figure 9-14). Follow these steps to adjust the options in the Select by Color dialog box:

1. *Click the type of selection you want to create (new, add, subtract, or multiply).*

   Check out "The Marquee tool" section, earlier in this chapter, for explanations on the various Selection Types you can use.

2. *Click the color you wish to select (Black, White, or Transparent).*

   By default, the foreground and background colors are black and white, but if you've changed the Display Color of the layer (located on the Layer Properties palette) from Grayscale to Color (see Chapter 6), you're going to see what you selected for the foreground (and/or background if you are on a black-and-white layer) color.

3. *Click OK when you're done.*

Figure 9-13:
The Expand and Reduce Selection functions both use the same type of dialog box.

 For 8-bit layers, the dialog box is set up differently. Instead of choosing from three color boxes, you set the color's opacity (adjusted by clicking and dragging the triangle above the bar or by entering a value between 0% and 100% in its numeric field) and threshold level (by entering a value between 0% and 100% in its numeric field).

Figure 9-14:
You can select all the artwork in the color of your choosing at once with the Select by Color function.

 Keep in mind that only the artwork on the active layer is selected. Artwork on any other layers are ignored. If you need to select anything from other layers, you need to go to each layer individually. The exception to this, of course, is when you use the Magic Wand tool with the All Layers option selected.

You've Created a Selection — Now What?

Well, the easy part's done.

Fortunately, the next step isn't all that difficult either. The important part is that the area you want to work with is now sectioned off from the rest of the page. So whether it's filling in an area, removing it, or transforming it, you can do so without worrying about ruining the rest of your art.

Filling selections

There are two ways to fill in a selection in Manga Studio:

 ✔ Select the Fill tool in the Tools palette and click the selection with your mouse or stylus

 or

 ✔ Choose Edit⇨Fill Selection.

If you choose Edit⇨Fill Selection, the Fill Selection dialog box appears, as shown in Figure 9-15. If you're using Manga Studio Debut, you see only the option to choose the color you wish to fill the selection with (foreground color, background color, or transparent — which I guess would be the equivalent to deleting the area). Click the color you want, click OK, and you're done.

Manga Studio EX users have an additional option (see the bottom of Figure 9-15), where you can choose exactly *what* parts of the selection you want to fill in by selecting the respective radio button. The following list describes the available options:

 ✔ **Fill All:** The entire selection is filled in with the color you chose.

 ✔ **Fill Closed Area:** Only shapes and other areas that are fully enclosed by a drawing line and are within the selection is filled in.

 ✔ **Protect Transparent Area:** Any area of the selection that isn't transparent (that is, an area that's drawn on with some kind of color) is filled in. The transparent area remains as it is.

 ✔ **Draw in Transparent Area:** Any transparent area in the selection is filled in. Any area drawn with some kind of color (foreground or background) remains as it is.

 ✔ **Draw in Transparent and Closed Area:** Any transparent area of an enclosed shape in the selection is filled in.

Manga Studio EX users have an additional function you can use to quickly fill in a selection with the active color you're using. To use this function, either select Edit⇨Fill Selection in Drawing Color from the main menu, or you can press Ctrl+U on your keyboard (⌘+U on the Mac).

Figure 9-15:
The Fill
Selection
dialog boxes
for Manga
Studio
Debut (top)
and EX
(bottom).

Pasting screentones into selections

Filling a selection with a solid color can (and will) be useful to you as you work, but I think that selections are most useful when you're working with screentones. I discuss screentones in much further detail in Chapter 11, but the short version of applying tone to a page is to open the Tones palette, select the tone you want to use, and then paste it in place.

Without laying down a selection beforehand, the tone is pasted on the whole page at once, and you then need to erase away all that you really don't want to use. (If you're looking for a more old-school tone technique, it's certainly the way to go.) If you place a selection on the page, though, only that area is pasted with your selected tone, as shown in Figure 9-16.

Figure 9-16:
While you
can always
fill in a
selection
with a solid
color, it's
even more
useful to
paste a
screentone
into a
specific
area.

If you're looking to do something a bit more subtle than fill in a solid color or tone, try using the airbrush or pattern brush tools to add a simple effect. Simply draw in the selection area like you normally would on the page.

Outlining selections (EX only)

Manga Studio EX users have an option to add an outline to selections of various widths and colors. (Well, only *two* colors technically, but you get what I mean). It's a good function to have when you want to create a simple border around a shape, such as a word balloon.

To create an outline, follow theses steps:

1. **Choose Edit➪Outline Selection from the main menu.**

   The Outline Selection dialog box appears, as shown in Figure 9-17.

2. **Select the color of your outline (foreground, background, or transparent) by clicking its respective Drawing Color icon.**

3. **Select one of the following radio buttons to determine how you want the outline drawn around the selection:**

   - *Draw Outside:* The outline is drawn on the outer edge of the selection border.

   - *Draw on the Border:* The outline is drawn on the middle of the selection border.

   - *Draw Inside:* The outline is drawn on the inner edge of the selection border.

   This step probably sounds a bit odd — normally, you'd think that there's only one way to draw an outline, and you'd be right. What you're really choosing is the placement of the outline in relation to the selection border. (Each of the options is illustrated in Figure 9-18.)

   I suggest trying each of the options to see which is the best fit for the selection. You can always Undo and try again if you're unhappy with how the outline comes out.

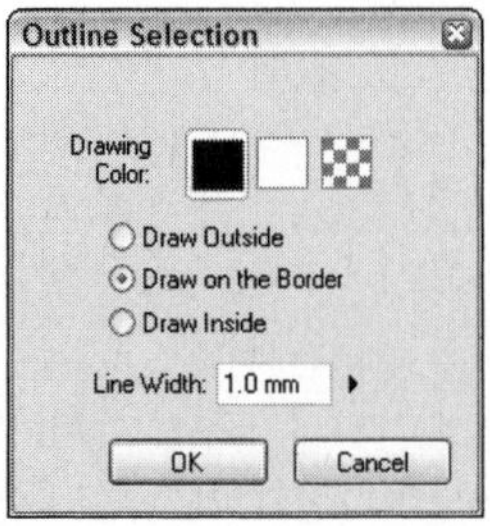

Figure 9-17:
The Outline Selection dialog box.

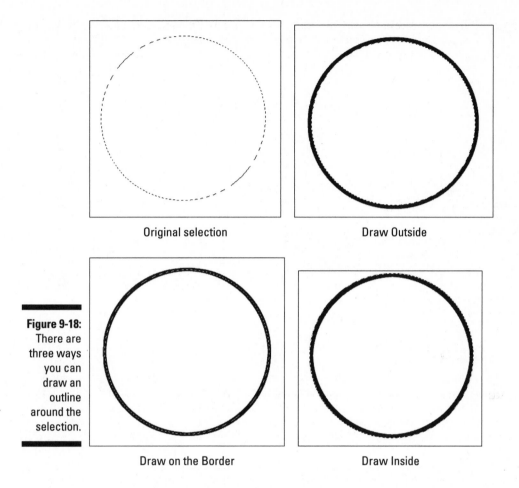

Original selection   Draw Outside

Figure 9-18:
There are
three ways
you can
draw an
outline
around the
selection.

Draw on the Border   Draw Inside

4. **Enter the size of your outline between 0.1 mm and 10.0 mm in the Line Width text box.**

5. **Click OK when you're done.**

Deleting selections

While the Eraser is an effective tool to use to remove items from a layer, it can be a bit cumbersome when you're looking to erase something specific without ruining the surrounding artwork. Conversely, you may find it too small to work with if you have a large area to remove.

That's where you may find using a selection to delete an area useful. Whether it's to select a small specific area or a large one, you'll find it a helpful alternative to quickly removing an offending object from your artwork. (See Figure 9-19.)

To delete the area within a selection, you can choose Edit⇨Clear from the main menu, or you can simply press the Delete key.

Transforming selections

In my opinion, the most important thing you can do with a selection, especially if you've selected a particular object, is transform it. The transformation can range from scaling the selection, to rotating it, to distorting it, to simply moving it around the page. Whatever you plan on using it for, you may find it a great timesaver when you make a mistake on the page.

I've lost track of the number of times I've worked on a piece of art and discover that I've drawn the head of a character too large, or an arm too long. Instead of erasing the item outright and starting over, I simply transform it until it's at the right size, angle, or whatever it is that I'm adjusting. I've used the Transform function so much, I've found myself looking for that ability when I'm working with a real pencil and paper! (Yeah . . . I need help.)

There are several transformation functions that you can choose from, and you can access all of them by selecting Edit⇨Move and Transform on the main menu. (See Figure 9-20 for examples of each.)

- **Edit⇨Move and Transform⇨Scale:** Adjusts the size of the selected area.

- **Edit⇨Move and Transform⇨Rotate:** Adjusts the angle of the selected area.

- **Edit⇨Move and Transform⇨Free Transform:** Adjusts the selected area however you want.

- ✔ **Edit⇨Move and Transform⇨Distort:** Slides and elongates the selected area in any way you choose.
- ✔ **Edit⇨Move and Transform⇨Perspective:** Warps the selected area along a perspective plane.
- ✔ **Edit⇨Move and Transform⇨Flip Horizontally:** Converts the selected area into its horizontal opposite.
- ✔ **Edit⇨Move and Transform⇨Flip Vertically:** Converts the selected area to its vertical opposite.

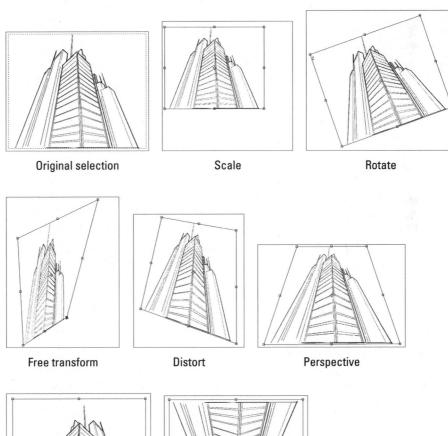

Original selection

Scale

Rotate

Free transform

Distort

Perspective

Figure 9-20:
You can
transform a
selection in
a variety of
ways.

Flip Horizontal

Flip Vertical

The Flip Horizontal and Flip Vertical functions work automatically — that means as soon as you choose Edit⇨Move and Transform⇨Flip Horizontally or Edit⇨Move and Transform⇨Flip Vertically, the selection automatically flips horizontally or vertically. When you choose any of the other commands, the Move and Transform dialog box appears. as shown in Figure 9-21.

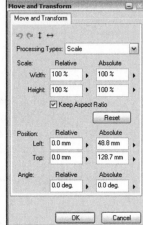

Figure 9-21:
Several transformation functions, one dialog box.

Actually, you can use all of the transformation functions (including the Flip functions) from the Move and Transform dialog box. So, you really can select *any* of the Transformation functions and you'll go to the same place. What's more, you can switch between transformation functions on the fly just by selecting from the Processing Types drop-down list.

The preview pane on the left is where you do the bulk of your transformation work, as that's where you use your mouse or stylus to directly adjust the shape, size, or angle of your selected area.

If you look closely at the preview pane, you see a rectangle surrounding the selection with small boxes along the sides and corners. Those boxes (what I call *adjustment boxes,* as I don't think they actually *have* a name) are what you use to adjust your selection. Simply click an adjustment box and drag it along the preview pane to see exactly what you can do, depending on the transformation type you selected.

For example, if you chose Edit⇨Move and Transform⇨Scale, clicking and dragging the adjustment boxes resizes the selection you made. But, if you choose Edit⇨Move and Transform⇨Distort, clicking and dragging the same adjustment boxes results in the physical shape of the selection becoming radically altered.

 Incidentally, you don't really need to select the Rotate function, as you can rotate the selection at any time with any of the functions. When you hover your cursor near an adjustment box, you see it change to a rotate cursor.

When that appears, click the page and drag across or around the preview pane to rotate the image. In addition, you can alter the point the selection will rotate around by clicking the focal point icon in the middle of the preview pane and placing it wherever you'd like.

If using the mouse isn't your thing, you can set the scale, position, and angle of the selection manually by following these steps.

1. **Open the Move and Transform dialog box by choosing Edit⇨Move and Transform⇨Scale.**

   Alternatively, you can choose any of the other commands in the Move and Transform submenu (such as Edit⇨Move and Transform⇨Rotate) to open the Move and Transform dialog box.

2. **To flip the selection horizontally, click the Flip Horizontally button.**

3. **To flip the selection vertically, click the Flip Vertically button.**

4. **To adjust the size of the selection relative to its current height and width, enter a percentage value from 50% to 200% in the Relative Width and Height text boxes.**

   After the selection is resized, the relative values reset to 100%, so you can perform a relative adjustment again if you want.

5. **To adjust the absolute width and height values, enter a value of 1% to 5000% in the Absolute Width and Height text boxes.**

   Alternatively, you can click the black triangle to the right of the text boxes, which brings up additional adjustment controls. Use the outer buttons to change the percentage value in increments of 10%. Use the inner buttons to adjust by an interval of 1%.

6. **To keep the aspect ratio of the selection intact, select the Keep Aspect Ratio check box.**

   This option keeps the basic shape of the selection intact, regardless of how large or small you scale it. In addition, this also locks the Adjustment Boxes to the aspect ratio when you use the mouse or stylus to resize.

7. **To change the selection back to it's original size, shape, and placement, click the Reset button.**

8. **To adjust the position of the selection relative to its previous position, enter a value between -50 mm and 50 mm in the Left and Top Relative text boxes.**

   Like the Relative Position text boxes, the values reset to 0 mm when the selection is moved.

9. **To adjust the absolute position of the selection on the page, enter a value between -999.0 mm and 999.0 mm in the Absolute Left and Top text boxes.**

10. **To adjust the angle of the selection relative to its previous position, enter a value between -90 degrees and 90 degrees in the Relative Angle text box.**

    When rotated, the value resets to zero, so you can relatively adjust it again if need be.

11. **To adjust the absolute angle of the selection, enter a value from -360 degrees to 360 degrees in the Absolute Angle text box.**

12. **Click OK when you're done.**

A Bit about Selection Layers and Why You'll LOVE Them!

Normally with drawing programs, if you want to reuse a selection later in the creative process, you simply redraw it with a Selection tool. It can be time-consuming (especially if the selection is particularly intricate), but it works.

But, what if you could save a selection you think you'll be coming back to later on?

That's the idea behind selection layers. Unlike creating a selection on an image layer, like you normally would, you draw one on this special layer, which you can then add to, remove from, move around, and convert to an image layer selection as many times as you want — all without having to completely redraw the selection from scratch. What's more, you don't *have* to use a Selection tool to create the selection if you don't want to. Any of the drawing tools in your toolbox can be used to outline and fill in your selection area, which can result in a myriad of effects that you can't do with the normal Selection tools.

Creating a selection layer

There are three ways you can create a selection layer in Manga Studio:

- From the main menu, choose Layer⇨New Layer; in the New Layer dialog box that appears, select Selection Layer from the Layer Type drop-down list.

- On the Layers palette, click the New Layer button, located next to the Selection header.

- If you've created a selection on an image layer, choose Selection⇨Convert Selection to Layer on the main menu.

This last option not only creates a new selection layer, but also saves your image layer selection as an area on the new layer.

Alternatively, you can use the Convert Selection to Layer button (located on the Layers palette next to the Selection title) instead of selecting the function from the main menu.

There are *technically* no limits to the number of selection layers you can create. The only real limit is your computer hardware, as having too many layers of *any* kind can hinder your computer's performance, especially if you're working on a low-end machine or don't have a lot of RAM available.

You can adjust the opacity and color of your selection layers by bringing up the Layer Properties palette. (Press F7 on your keyboard or choose Window⇨Properties from the main menu.)

Creating and editing selections on a selection layer

Working on a selection layer is just like working on an image layer. That means that you can draw and erase a selection just like you would if you were laying down some line art.

So, there are a number of ways you can lay down and edit a selection area:

- ✔ **By using any of the drawing tools (Pen, Pencil, Marker, Airbrush, or Pattern Brush tools) to outline or add effects to a selection area**
- ✔ **By using the Marquee or Lasso tool to select the area, much like you would use on an image layer**
- ✔ **By using the Fill tool to fill in the area you've outlined or selected**
- ✔ **By using the Eraser, Marquee, or Lasso tools to remove excess parts of the selection area**

What you create on the selection layer won't look exactly like a selection. In fact, it's just going to look like a green blob. (You can't easily tell in this black-and-white book, but in Figure 9-22, the character's hair is that green blob.) The idea here is that you aren't creating a selection so much as you're blocking off an area that you'll be using later on to create a image layer selection.

By creating a selection area, you can now tweak and adjust, add and remove as much or as little as you want. You can come back to it later and tweak as need be. And all of it's easier to do than if you try to do that with an image layer selection.

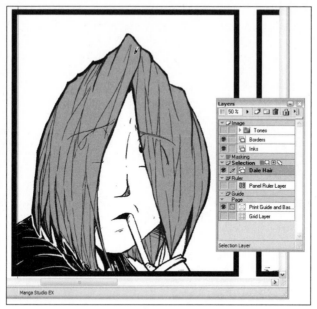

Figure 9-22:
Block off
areas on a
selection
layer that
you'll later
convert to
an image
layer
selection.

Converting selection layers to image selections

Converting an area you block off in a selection layer into an actual selection to use on an image layer is a pretty simple process. You can do it in two ways:

- ✔ Use the Magic Wand tool to select areas from the currently active layer.

- ✔ From the main menu, choose Selection⇨Convert Layer to Selection (Ctrl+F; ⌘ + F on the Mac), which converts all visible selection layers into a selection.

When converted, you see the familiar marching ants selection around the area(s) you've chosen. (See Figure 9-23.) From there, it's a matter of highlighting the image layer you want to work on from the Layers palette and doing whatever you want to with your selection!

Alternatively, you can use the Convert Layer to Selection button (located on the Layers palette next to the Selection title) instead of selecting the function from the main menu.

You can also take any visible selection layers you have and add them to or subtract them from an existing image layer selection. (See Figure 9-24.) This works like changing the Selection Type of a selection tool. (See the "Additional functions" section, earlier in this chapter, for an explanation.)

You can use either of these functions from the main menu by choosing Selection⇨Add Layer to Selection or Selection⇨Subtract Layer From Selection.

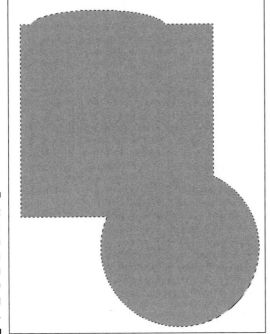

Figure 9-23: Convert a selection layer to a selection and see the marching ants.

Figure 9-24: You can convert selection layers to add to or remove from an existing image layer selection.

For EX Users: Quick Mask and Quick Select

Like many of the other exclusive features of Manga Studio EX, you can use the Quick Mask and Quick Select features to save a little bit of time and add a bit of convenience to your Manga Studio experience.

Quick Mask

The Quick Mask feature is for those of you who aren't necessarily looking to save a selection for later use, but want the ease of use that working with a selection layer can bring you.

To create a Quick Mask, follow these steps:

1. **From the main menu, choose Selection⇨Use Quick Mask. Or you can press Ctrl+M on your keyboard (⌘+M on the Mac).**

   A new Quick Mask layer appears on the Layers palette. From here, it's just like working on a selection layer.

2. **Use the Selection or Drawing tools to block off the area you want to make a selection from.**

3. **When the selection area(s) has been created, choose Selection⇨Use Quick Mask.**

   The Quick Mask disappears, and you have your image layer selection all ready to go! See Figure 9-25.

Quick Select

You use the Quick Selection feature to convert a selection layer into an image layer selection.

But wait, isn't that what the Convert Layer to Selection function is for? Yes, but unlike that function, the Quick Select command focuses on only one layer at a time. What's more, you can switch between selection layers, and the program automatically converts the active selection to match the active layer's selection area. So, you don't need to go back to the Convert Layer to Selection command every time you switch selection layers.

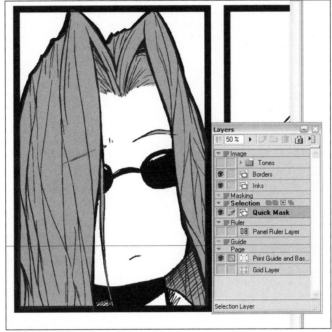

Figure 9-25:
Use the
Quick Mask
to create a
temporary
selection
area.

That's what makes it quick.

To use this function, follow these steps:

1. **Highlight the Selection layer you want to work from.**

2. **From the main menu, choose Selection⇨Use Quick Select. Or you can press Ctrl+Shift+M on your keyboard (⌘+Shift+M on the Mac).**

   All of the selection layers are turned invisible, and the current selection area is converted to an image layer selection. (See Figure 9-26.)

3. **Highlight the image layer you want to work on, and use the selection however you'd like.**

4. **If you want to use a different selection, highlight the selection layer you want to use.**

   The old selection is converted to match the active selection layer.

5. **Repeat as necessary.**

6. **When you're all done, choose Selection⇨Use Quick Select from the main menu to turn it off.**

Alternatively, you can use the Quick Mask and Quick Select buttons (located on the Layers palette next to the Selection title) to toggle the functions on and off.

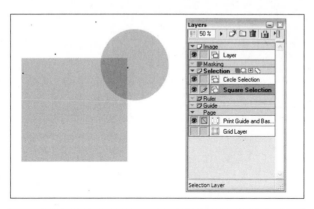

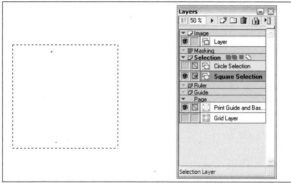

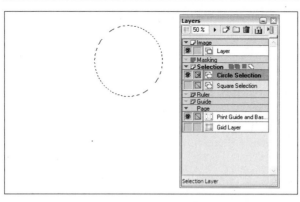

Figure 9-26: Use the Quick Select function to quickly convert and switch between selection layers.

Part III
Refining and Exporting Your Work

The 5th Wave   By Rich Tennant

In this part . . .

You have the roughs scanned in, cleaned up, and tweaked exactly how you want them on the page. Now it's time to add the finishing touches to give your work that professional look.

Chapter 10 is all about inking, whether you're planning on scanning in your inked work or you're going to use your drawing tablet to add virtual inks to your roughs. Chapter 11 covers how you can add screen tones to your work to give it that extra pop, as well as a few tricks to help add depth and dimensionality to the tones by adding shadows and highlights.

Chapter 12 helps you lay some words and sound effects down on the page so that the reader knows what's going on during that intense conversation scene, or exactly how plates crashing to the ground sounds in your world. Finally, Chapter 13 explains how you can take your completed work and prepare it for display on the Internet, print it for family and friends, or prepare it for professional printing.

Chapter 10

Inking Your Work

. . . .

. . . .

I have to admit something: When it comes to inking my work traditionally, I've never felt comfortable doing it. The thing I always like about penciling is the ability to erase and refine my lines as I go along. Not so with inking — I can get one or two do-overs before the correction fluid becomes too thick.

What I like about working digitally with a program such as Manga Studio is the ability to erase and rework my inks as much as I need to. Now, I don't have to stress over getting the inks correct the first (or second) time. If something doesn't look right, I can just remove the offending area, rework it on the pencil layer if need be, and re-ink, without the need to throw out the whole paper and start over. A pleasant side-effect is that my confidence in inking has increased, and I feel more comfortable inking traditionally. So, if you've never inked digitally (or never felt comfortable inking at all), try the tools I discuss in this chapter. You may be surprised at what you can accomplish.

In this chapter, I briefly recap how to scan in your line art, if you're planning on using the Pen tools primarily to touch up what you create with traditional tools. (For more detail on the process, check out Chapter 5.) I then cover the basics of using the three important inking tools you use in Manga Studio: the Pen, Magic Marker, and Fill tools, as well as closing any gaps in your line art with the Join Line tool. Then, I discuss some of the cool special effects that you can add to your line art with the Airbrush and Pattern Brush tools.

Why Ink at All?

Truth be told, there's nothing stopping you from using your tight pencil line art in place of inks. Some artists actually prefer using pencils, as they create a softer shade over the solid black of inks. A great example of a comic done with just pencils is Fred Gallagher's uber-popular webcomic, *MegaTokyo* (www.mega tokyo.com). If you look through some of the pages of my own webcomic (cheap plug warning), *Chibi Cheerleaders From Outer Space* (www.chibi cheerleaders.com), you'll also see many pages that are either pencil only or pencil with some grayscale shading. (Actually, there are pages of all of different styles as the story goes along. I like to experiment a lot.)

If you like the look of your pencils and are planning on coloring your work, I say go for it. However, there are a couple arguments towards using inks, at least when working on a black-and-white manga or comic:

- ✔ Inks do create crisper, darker lines than pencils and may look better in the final print form (unless, of course, you're going for the rough look). Unless you've got tight pencil line art without any need for cleanup, consider inking for a more professional look.

- ✔ If you're planning on screentoning your line art, consider that the pure black of the screentones may clash with the lighter shading of your pencils.

- ✔ If you've scanned in your roughs or you drew them at a lower resolution, the pencils may not be crisp enough for print. In that case, you either have to repencil or ink at a higher resolution anyway.

Scanning in Your Line Art

Some artists like to get their hands dirty with a good dip pen, India ink, and correction fluid and would rather just scan inked line art into Manga Studio for touch-ups and screentoning. I cover the scanning process in more detail in Chapter 5, but here's a quick run-through (and a few suggestions) for scanning your inked art preparing your new ink layer:

1. **If you haven't already set up your scanner in Manga Studio, choose File⇨Import⇨Select TWAIN Device and select your scanner in the Select Source dialog box.**

2. **Choose File⇨Import⇨TWAIN. Select Normal from the Import method dialog box. Your scanner's program opens. Follow its directions to prepare your line art.**

3. **When the Import Images dialog box opens, click the Layer Settings tab and enter the name in the Layer Name text box; select Raster Layer from the Layer Type drop-down list.**

   If the lineart is too large, check out Chapter 5 to find out how to adjust the image to fit the page.

4. **Select the highest resolution possible from the Resolution drop-down list.**

   You want to make sure you have the crispest line art possible — the higher the resolution, the smoother the lines. My suggestion is to pick the maximum resolution relative to the resolution of your page. (That is, if you have a 600 dpi page, pick the 600 dpi option from the list.)

5. **Choose 1Bit (Black Only) or 2Bit (Black and White) from the Expression Mode drop-down list; select Threshold from the Bitmap Technique drop-down list.**

   I explain why these options are the best choices in the "Why not use an 8-bit ink layer?" sidebar, elsewhere in this chapter.

6. **Adjust the threshold level by typing different values in the Threshold text box until all dirt and rough lines that may have scanned in disappear and the line art looks how you'd like it to be.**

7. **Click the Move and Transform tab and resize, reposition, and rotate your image as necessary until the image looks how you want it within the page and print guide (if applicable).**

8. **When you're happy with the settings, click OK.**

Why not use an 8-bit ink layer?

Sometimes when working on a task, the simplest solution can be the best. That principle holds true when creating an inking layer. Because the only color you need to worry about with inks is black, you ultimately need only a 1-bit layer, which just happens to be black only. If you want to add bits of white (or you happen to like the idea of using virtual correction fluid) to your ink layer, you can use a 2-bit (black and white) layer.

It isn't *bad* to use an 8-bit layer; it just isn't necessary sometimes, and it can be a bit of overkill. Using an 8-bit layer allows you to use more shades of gray than you really need for the purposes of inking your work. It also increases the size of your file more than it really needs to be.

Creating a New Layer for Inking

If you're planning on inking with a mouse or drawing tablet, the first order of business is to create a new layer above your roughs layer. This saves you hours of work, as it keeps your work organized. This is especially important because you won't need to ink directly on your roughs (and then spend a long time erasing the roughs from the final picture).

I go over layers and the various styles in Chapter 6, but here's a quick run-down on creating a new ink layer on your page:

1. **From the main menu, choose Layer⇨New Layer.**

2. **When the New Layer dialog box opens (shown in Figure 10-1) enter the name of the layer in the Layer Name text box.**

3. **Select Raster Layer from the Layer Type drop-down list.**

4. **Select the highest resolution relative to your page from the Resolution drop-down list.**

5. **Select Black (1bit) or Black and White (2bit) from the Expression Mode drop-down list.**

6. **Select Finish from the Output Attribute radio buttons.**

   (This is useful later on during the printing/exporting process, which I go over in Chapter 13.)

7. **The other options are grayed out, so just click OK.**

8. **To make sure that the new layer is above all the other Image Layers (if it isn't already), click the layer in the Layers palette and drag it to the top of the Image Layers list (just before the Layers header).**

You now have a fresh ink layer to work over your rough draft.

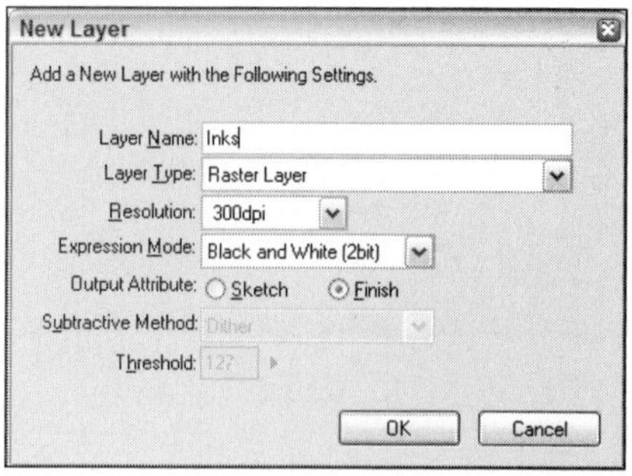

Figure 10-1:
Create a
new layer
for inks in
the New
Layer dialog
box.

Inking in the Lines

Whether you've scanned in your line art and you're just planning to touch up your art or you're inking totally within the program, Manga Studio has you covered. The program provides most of the common tools for inking a comic. And if they aren't quite to your liking, it's very simple to adjust them however you like.

If you're a traditional inker, you're going to love this: The Eraser tool works on lines or fills drawn with any of the inking tools (the Pen, Marker, and Fill tools, as well as other inking tools such as the Airbrush and Pattern Brush tools). You can use the Eraser tool to remove any unwanted inks from your drawing. No more correction fluid!

You can quickly adjust the size of all the tools I mention in the following sections using the keyboard. Just press [(the left bracket key) to decrease the tool's size, and press] (the right bracket key) to increase the size of the tool.

The Pen tool

Probably the most versatile tool for your inking, the pen can provide a wide variety of line strengths to help bring your work to life. Manga Studio provides a preset number of common pens to use.

You can access the Pen tool in two ways:

  ✔ Press P
  ✔ Click the Pen button on the Tools palette.

Holding the pen icon down for a couple of seconds brings up a list of all the pens that come preinstalled with Manga Studio, as shown in Figure 10-2. There may be some pens that feel right and others that aren't for you. I provide samples of each pen stroke in Figure 10-3. Try each and see how they feel. The nice thing is you can always erase them later.

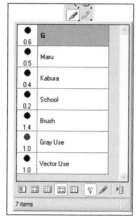

Figure 10-2:
The Pen tool button and its selection of preinstalled pens.

The different variations of the Pen tool are

- ✔ **G:** This all-purpose pen creates lines of varying thickness, depending on the amount of pressure you place on the pen (pen pressure). (Of course, if you're using a mouse, the concept of pen pressure is a moot point as it doesn't have any.)

- ✔ **Maru:** Also called a *round* pen, use this primarily used for fine lines. It can create thicker lines, although it requires a harder pen pressure than a G pen.*

- ✔ **Kabura:** Also called a *turnip* pen (because of the turnip shape of the pen), use this to create uniform lines with little variance in line weight.

- ✔ **School:** Similar to the Kabura, this pen creates uniform fine lines.

- ✔ **Brush:** This pen creates very thick (and very thin, depending on how light your stroke is if you're using a pressure-sensitive drawing tablet) lines. This can give a more organic look to your line art.

- ✔ **Gray Use:** I feel this pen is most useful if you want to add some gray shading on an 8-bit layer that's set to not subtract colors. It's essentially a G pen with the opacity set a little bit lower. (You can adjust it on the Tool Properties palette.) Using this pen on a 1- or 2-bit layer produces a dithered line, while using in on an 8-bit layer will produce a solid gray line.

If you're using Manga Studio EX, you may notice that I'm skipping over some tools, like the Vector pen. I devote Chapter 15 to all the exclusive items that Manga Studio EX has to offer, including an entire section devoted to vectors. Stay tuned!

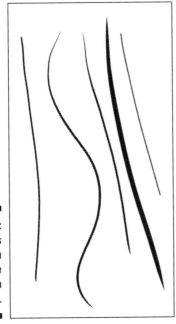

Figure 10-3:
The various
strokes you
can create
with the Pen
tool.

 Here's a semi-advanced trick for when you're working. As you're working on your line art, click the Flip Image Horizontally button on the Page toolbar. This inverts the page, so you can see how it looks backwards. You may spot a few mistakes you didn't notice while viewing it normally. Click the button again to go back to your normal view.

The Magic Marker tool

The name of this tool is a bit misleading because while you can use it to fill in a large section like you're using a magic marker, you can also use this to draw fine lines, much as if you're using Rapidograph pens. There are actually a nice variety of sizes and shapes of markers at your disposal.

To access the Marker tool, you can:

✔ Click the Marker button on the Tools palette.

✔ Press P on your keyboard until the Magic Marker is selected. (The marker shares the same shortcut as the Pencil and Pen tools. You'll be able to tell if the marker is selected if the Tools Palette is visible — the Marker button will become highlighted.)

If you hold the Marker button down for a couple of seconds, a menu with a selection of markers appears, as shown in Figure 10-4. Because the Marker tool is essentially just a simple round pen with no pressure sensitivity, you won't see the wide variety of tools compared to the Pen tool. What you do see is a group of markers of various sizes and shapes. (Examples of lines drawn with each type of marker are shown in Figure 10-5.)

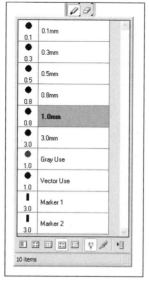

Figure 10-4:
The Magic
Marker
button and
its selection
of
preinstalled
sizes.

The options in the Marker tool's menu are

- ✔ **Round Marker:** The first six options are all the same basic round tool with sizes ranging from 0.1 millimeters to 3.0 millimeters.

- ✔ **Gray Use:** Like the Gray Use Pen tool, use this for adding a shade of gray to a layer.

- ✔ **Marker 1/Marker 2:** A cool function of Manga Studio is the ability to adjust the thickness of a drawing tool. This is best shown with these two options, which are just markers that have been adjusted to a rectangular tip, instead of a round one. You can use these markers for a calligraphic design, for example.

TIP

Much like in real life, if you're using a lighter gray marker or pen, the line drawn will not show up when drawn over a darker line. The only time a light line will show up over a dark line is when you are working on a Gray (8bit) layer and you selected the Does Not Subtract Colors option in the Expression Mode drop-down list.

Figure 10-5:
Lines drawn
with the
Marker
tool's
various
shapes and
sizes.

Customizing your pens and markers

You may find that the pens and markers Manga Studio provides aren't quite to your liking. Maybe the pressure sensitivity is too hard or too soft. Or perhaps you'd like the lines to taper more than they currently do.

Not a problem. I cover how to customize your tools in greater detail in Chapter 14, but here's a quick overview of the options you can adjust for your pen or marker with the Tool Options palette, shown in Figure 10-6. (Press F3 to activate the palette if you can't see it.) Unless mentioned otherwise, you can adjust the value of an option by entering it in its corresponding text box, or you can use the slider (which is activated by clicking the black arrow to the right of the text box), moving it up or down to your desired value.

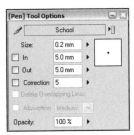

Figure 10-6:
The Options
palette for
the Pen tool.

Open the Tool Options palette (if it isn't already open) by pressing F3. Then follow these steps to customize the Pen or Marker tool:

1. **To change the size of the tool, enter a value between 0.1 mm and 10.0 mm in the Size text box.**

2. **(Pen tool only) To adjust the taper length at the beginning of a line, select the In check box, and enter a value between 0.0 mm and 20.0 mm in its numeric field.**

Using two windows while drawing

If you've ever tried to ink digitally, you either need to zoom out far enough to see the entire panel you're working on (which results in jittery lines) or zoom in close enough to focus on detail work (but lose focus of the picture as a whole). I don't know how many times I've had to go back and rework a section of a drawing because I was so focused on one piece that when I zoomed out, I discovered that the line work no longer matched the rest of the panel! The folks at Manga Studio must have taken this into account, because they incorporated a means to use two zoom levels *at the same time!*

From the main menu, choose Window➪New Window. A second window of the page you're working on appears. If you shrink the size of that window and move it to a corner of your work area, you can keep that one zoomed out while using the other window to zoom in and work at a closer level. Now you can work on your inks at a size without the worry of jitter, but close enough to work on details *and* be able to view the picture as a whole without having to constantly change the zoom! Check out the following figure to see how it works.

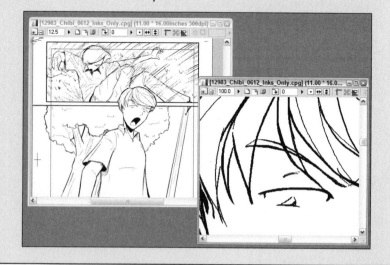

3. (Pen tool only) To adjust the taper length at the end of a line, select the Out check box, and enter a value between 0.0 mm and 20.0 mm in its numeric field

4. To adjust the amount that Manga Studio corrects a jittery line, select the Correction check box, and enter a value between 0 and 20 in its numeric field.

5. To adjust the opacity of the tool, enter a value from 0 to 100 in the Opacity text box.

Filling Large Areas with Ink

The Pen and Marker tools are great for drawing lines, but when you need to fill in a shape, why not take advantage of the digital medium you're working in? If you have a large, closed shape you want to fill with solid black, the Fill tool is just the ticket. And when you realize that your shape has a gap, you can quickly and easily close the gaps with the Join Line tool.

The Fill tool

The Fill tool is a great timesaver when you need to fill large areas of a drawing with black. Now, you accomplish in one click what would have required several passes with markers of various sizes. When you're on a bit of a deadline, you'll find that this is a nice tool to have around.

 To access the Fill tool, you can press G or click the Fill tool icon in the Tools palette. When selected, the cursor changes into a paint bucket when you hover it over the page. All you need to do now is pick a part of your drawing that's completely enclosed and click inside that area. The area is automatically filled with black.

You can adjust the settings of the Fill tool by using the Tool Options palette. (Press F3 if the palette isn't visible.) To adjust the Fill tool, follow these steps:

1. (Manga Studio EX Only) To restrict the fill to an area with gaps, select the Close Path check box and enter a value between 0.0 mm and 1.0 mm.

   Sometimes an area you want to fill isn't completely closed off. To prevent the Fill tool from going beyond what you intend to fill, use the Close Path option. The Fill tool treats any size up to the value you enter as a border and doesn't fill beyond it.

2. **To have the fill affect all visible layers, select the All Layers check box.**

   This option is useful if you happen to have multiple inking layers, as shown in Figure 10-7. The fill tool treats each layer as if there's only one. This way, you can fill any open area you want that's created by intersecting lines, regardless of what layer the lines may be on.

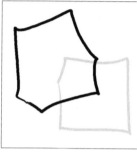 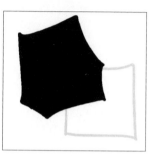 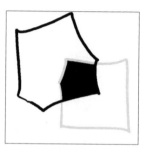

Unfilled shapes

Shapes filled with
the All Layers check
box deselected

Shapes filled with
the All Layers check
box selected

3. **(8-bit layers only) To change how the Fill tool treats gray or partially transparent lines, enter a value between 0 and 99 in the Allowable Error in Color text box.**

   By default, the fill tool treats only black lines as a border. Anything lighter than 100% opacity is filled over.

   Adjusting the Allowable Error value affects how the Fill tool treats a gray line as a border. The lower the value, the lighter the gray line can be, as shown in Figure 10-8.

The Join Line tool

A limitation to the Fill tool is that if there are gaps in what you think is an enclosed area; the tool fills beyond the area until the program finds a border without gaps. If you aren't careful, you can find yourself with a completely black page!

You could comb over the area with your pen or marker and draw in any gaps you may have missed. Or you can close all the gaps in one fell swoop with the Join Line tool. This tool goes over an area that you select and connects any gaps that it finds with a thin line. The join line may not look like much, but it restrains a fill from spilling beyond the area you intended to fill.

You can access the Join Line tool in two ways:

- ✔ Press J on your keyboard
- ✔ Click the Join Line tool button on the Tools palette.

When the Join Line tool is selected, the cursor changes into a cross when you hover it over the page. To use the Join Line tool, just click and drag a rectangular selection over the area you wish to check for gaps. When you let go of the selection, the Join tool searches for the gaps and fills them in, as shown in Figure 10-9. That's all!

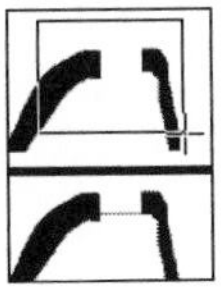

Figure 10-9:
Before and after using the Join Line tool.

The Tool Options palette gives you two options for the Join Line tool, as shown in Figure 10-10.

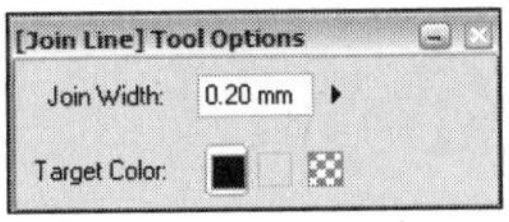

Figure 10-10:
The Join Line Tool Options palette.

[Join Line] Tool Options
Join Width: 0.20 mm ▶
Target Color: ■ ⊠

Open the Tool Options palette (if it isn't already open) by pressing F3, and then adjust the options for the Join Line tool by following these steps:

1. **To adjust the maximum size gap the Join Line tool should fix, enter a value between 0.0 mm and 5.0 mm in the Join Width text box. Or you can use the slider to adjust until you reach your desired value.**

   While the Join Line tool is great for closing gaps, it can be a bit overzealous at times. If you're trying to fill an irregular shape, it may treat a thin area of the shape as a gap and join an area you don't want it to, as shown in Figure 10-11.

Figure 10-11: Whoops. You didn't mean to *join* that gap.

Adjusting the Join Width option can help remedy the situation. This sets a maximum gap width that the Join Line tool fixes. For example, if you set the Join Width to 2.0 mm, anything larger than that is ignored. So, if there's a part of your fill section that's 3 mm, you don't have to worry about that getting closed off.

2. **Select the Target Color for your line by clicking one of the icons (black, white, or transparent).**

   This option is useful if you're working on a 2-bit (black and white) layer. You can change the color of the join line by choosing either black, white, or transparent ink. Keep in mind that color should match the color of the lines you're trying to join, so if you're joining two black lines, for example, choose the black color.

Using Airbrush and Pattern Effects with Your Line Art

I have to be honest about something. When I work on a page, I try to work as fast as possible on it. If I don't work quickly, I start to get bogged down, and it starts to get tedious. When I get bored, the art becomes flat and lackluster. And that's not good at all for anyone.

So, when I'm working on a program such as Manga Studio, I try to take advantage of whatever shortcuts it happens to provide — *especially* during the inking stage. This can be adding hatch marks to a character's jacket, adding a repetitive design to a background, or changing lines on a leather jacket from black to white.

Luckily, Manga Studio provides just such an array of tricks and shortcuts.

The Airbrush tool

If you want to add a bit of softness to your line art, without switching to grays, you can use the Airbrush tool. This is a great tool to use for spattering effects on a background, to add some dimension and texture to a piece of furniture or a vehicle, or anything else you can think of!

You can access the Airbrush tool in two ways:

 ✔ Click B on your keyboard

 ✔ Click the Airbrush button on the Tools palette.

When the Airbrush tool is selected, the cursor turns into a small image of an airbrush whenever you hover it over the page. To use the Airbrush tool, just click the page and draw away. The tool produces a stream of dots. The size of the dots depends on the airbrush you select.

To view a list of Manga Studio's preinstalled airbrushes, hold the Airbrush button down on the Tools palette for a couple of seconds. A short menu appears with your choices of airbrushes:

 ✔ **Small/Medium/Large:** These produce a uniform stream of dots with dot sizes varying, depending on the size you choose.

 ✔ **Tone:** Best used on a tone layer (which you can read up on in Chapter 11), this airbrush produces a fine stream of dots compared to the small, medium, and large airbrushes.

 ✔ **Gray Use:** Similar to the Tone airbrush, the Gray Use airbrush produces a fine mist of randomly sized dots at a lower opacity than pure black. This produces a gray color on an 8-bit layer and a dithered effect on 1- and 2-bit layers.

Using the Tool Options palette, shown in Figure 10-12, lets you fine-tune the Airbrush tool so you can get the effect you're looking for.

Figure 10-12:
The
Airbrush
Tool Options
palette.

Open the Tool Options palette (if it isn't already open) by pressing F3. Then follow these steps to adjust the Airbrush tool:

1. **To adjust the spray size, enter a value between 1.0 mm and 100.0 mm in the Spray Size text box. Or you can use the slider to adjust the value.**

   This allows you to dial in the amount you'd like the airbrush to cover. You can increase it so that it covers a wide area of the page, or narrow it down small enough that you can easily work on part of an intricate design.

2. **To adjust how thick or thin you'd like the spray to be, enter a value between 1 and 16 in the Density text box. Or you can use the slider to adjust the value.**

3. **To change the dot size, enter a value between 0.1 mm and 10.0 mm in the Dot Size text box. Or you can use the slider to adjust the value.**

4. **To randomize the size and position of the dots, select the Random Dots check box.**

5. **To adjust the opacity of the airbrush, enter a value in the Opacity text box. Or you can use the slider to adjust the value.**

The Pattern Brush tool

Sometimes I'll find myself looking for a pattern to place in a background of a panel. There's always the option to use one of the hundreds of tone patterns that Manga Studio provides. The problem is, sometimes I'd like it a bit more random and less . . . pattern-y.

Using the Pattern Brush helps because I can place and break up the pattern however I'd like. It's nice to put a personal spin on a background, while saving a bit of time compared to putting the pattern in by hand.

Another great thing about using the Pattern Brush tool instead of a tone pattern is that you can mix and match different patterns to your heart's content! Try using different patterns with the Pattern Brush tool — you can create a pattern style that's uniquely yours.

You can access the Pattern Brush tool in two ways:

✔ Press B on your keyboard until the Pattern Brush is selected. (The Airbrush and Pattern Brush share the same shortcut.)

✔ Click the Pattern Brush button on the Tools palette.

After you select the tool, you use it like you use a pencil or pen — just click and drag or draw. As you draw, each pattern reacts differently, with some following the path much like laying down a pen line, while others randomly place pattern items along the path.

Click and hold the Pattern Brush tool button on the Tools palette to access a menu with the following options:

✔ **Airbrush Based:** The pattern is sprayed on the canvas as if you were using the Airbrush tool. The Tool Options for this type of brush are based on Airbrush options, such as Spray Size and Density. Examples of Airbrush based brushes include Hazy Rings or Snow (see Figure 10-13).

✔ **Stamp Based**: Image patterns are stamped onto the canvas. The Tool Options on this brush are based on the interval between stamps. Examples of Stamp based brushes include the Butterfly Marker and Hazy Rings (see Figure 10-13).

✔ **Pen Based:** The pattern is drawn in a continuous line, much like if you were using a Pen tool.

Some brushes react to the way the mouse or pen moves and rotates by adjusting the position the pattern lays down on the canvas. Each pattern is based from one of three bases, and as such acts differently as you draw with it.

Holding down the Pattern Brush button on the Tools palette brings up the list of Manga Studio's preinstalled patterns, as shown in Figure 10-13. There are a good number of patterns to choose from, and my description of them won't do any justice.

The options for each pattern brush is going to depend on the type of pattern you're using (Airbrush, Pattern, or Pen based). So, when you look at the Pattern Brush Properties palette, certain options will not be available to you, depending on the pattern brush you're currently working on.

Instead of going through the available options for each pattern type, I compiled a generalized list that covers all of them at once. To adjust any of these options, enter a value in its corresponding numeric field, or activate its slide bar by clicking the black triangle to the right of the numeric field and adjust the bar until you've reached the desired value.

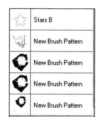

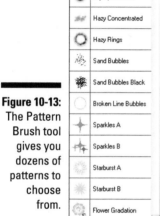

Figure 10-13:
The Pattern
Brush tool
gives you
dozens of
patterns to
choose
from.

Open the Tool Options palette (if it isn't already open) by pressing F3. You can then adjust the options for your selected pattern brush. The most common adjustments you can make include the following:

- **Size:** Enter a value between 0.1 mm and 100 mm.

- **Opacity:** Enter a value between 0% and 100% to adjust how light or dark the pattern will be on the canvas.

- **Interval:** For patterns that are stamp based, enter a value between 0.0 mm and 100.0 mm to adjust the spacing between pattern stamps.

- **Spray Area:** For those patterns that are airbrush based, enter a value between 1.0 mm and 100.0 mm to affect how far the pattern will spread as you draw.

- **Density:** For Airbrush-based patterns, enter a value between 1 and 16 to set the thickness of the pattern as you draw.

Chapter 11

Tone It Up!

Artists utilize many ways to add texture, detail, and "color" to a black and white drawing. Some like to use heavier lines in darker areas and thinner lines closer to light. Others may use a more uniform line but then render their texture with extensive and sometimes extremely detailed pen work. Then there are the ones that like to use tones. What are *tones,* you ask? Dots. Lots and *lots* of tiny dots. Many artists who work in black and white, especially manga artists, swear by tones.

Until now, the only way to use screentones with your work was to purchase sheets of the stuff, trim to fit, and then adhere them to the page. The process could be slow, messy, and expensive. (Screentone sheets aren't cheap.) Plus, you pretty much had one shot at getting it right; if you made a mistake, you'd have to carefully remove the tone and hope that you didn't ruin your drawing in the process.

The nice thing about Manga Studio is that it takes care of many of these problems at once. The tone sheets that come with the program are digital, which means you now have an infinite supply, saving you a lot of money in the long run. Cutting, pasting, and adding tone effects is easier and a *lot* less messy. Plus (and this is something I'll argue is most important), if you screw up, just delete the area (or whole layer) and start all over again!

This chapter is all about those tiny dots and how they can help add that little extra something to your manga.

Understanding How Tones Work

Have you ever seen a picture mosaic at one of those art/photography stores in the mall? If you look really closely at one of those pictures, you see hundreds or thousands of tiny images. Impressive in and of itself, but when you stand back, you see that all the tiny pictures become part of one large picture. It's all in how the mind perceives and mentally stitches together all those tiny pieces to create the one large image.

Tones work the same way. Take a look at Figure 11-1. The image on the left is a close up of a tone. Doesn't look like much, right? Now, when you look at the image on the right, you can see that those dots produce shades of gray and gradients! Your mind fills in the gaps and perceives the series of dots as shades of gray.

You'll notice many different shades of gray within the sample. If you look closely, you'll see that not all the tones are the same. Darker grays are created with bigger dots, while lighter grays have smaller dots. It's a seemingly simple technique that ultimately helps the artist to create a wide variety of "colors" on a black and white page.

There are all kinds of styles and types of tones that you may find useful to your work, depending on the situation. (See Figure 11-2.) You can choose from an array of solid screens, gradients, and patterns. Some companies even provide whole images (usually ones that have been converted to halftone) that you can use for backgrounds or scenery.

Figure 11-1: Tones don't look like much until you see the whole picture.

Figure 11-2:
Manga
artists use a
wide variety
of tones.

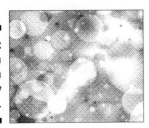

You might be asking, "Why bother with tones if all you need to do is print gray colors?" Again, it boils down to cost. It's much cheaper to print in one or two colors (in this case, black and white) than to print with 255 (or more) gray colors. If your mind can perceive thousands of tiny black dots as shades of gray, why not save a few bucks in production? It saves the reader some money as well!

Knowing Why to Use Tones

Technically, you don't have to use tones if you don't want to. Many independent comics and manga artists rely solely on their inking skills to convey exactly what they want on the page.

That said, tones are a great way to add just a little bit (or a lot) extra to your work. Much like the pencil and the pen, tones are a tool to help you shape the vision you want. Sure, it's a great way to add some color to clothes and hair, but there are other ways you can use tones to your advantage:

- **Character emotion:** In many instances of manga, you can use the background of a panel to set up more than just location. Often you'll see patterns or other types of tones used to help convey a wide range of emotions within a character or group. Figure 11-3 has an example of background tones used to emphasize emotion.

- **Ambient mood:** Much like character emotion, the use of tones can help set up the mood of a scene. You can do this by various means, including lighting effects and heavy use of shadow for dark and heavy scenes. (See Figure 11-4.)

- **Environmental boost:** Tones can be an effective means to add some dimension to a scene and help the reader become more immersed in the story. (See Figure 11-5.) This can be something as simple as adding a sky with clouds to a beach scene, a subtle white tone on a set of buildings, or light tone on a group or people to help delineate distance relative to a character.

Figure 11-3:
You can use tone patterns to convey a wide range of character emotions.

Figure 11-4:
Adding tones to a panel can change the meaning and mood of a panel.

Figure 11-5:
Tones can also help define the environment.

Artwork courtesy Teyon Alexander
(character © Merge Comics)

✔ **Directing the reader:** This is a subtle effect that the reader might not be consciously aware of. Tones can be a great way to help define where the reader should focus his attention, as shown in Figure 11-6. For example, you can cover ancillary characters in a simple tone so that all the reader's focus is on the one or two characters that matter to the scene.

These are just a few examples of what you can do with tones; I'm sure you can come up with plenty of other ideas. The point is, while tones probably aren't necessary for your story, it certainly doesn't hurt to use them, either.

Figure 11-6: They can even help direct the reader's attention in a scene.

Examining How Tones Work in Manga Studio

As I mention in the introduction of this chapter, a major problem with using tones in your work is cost. That's why the advent of digital programs like Manga Studio is so beneficial to the industry: The amount of money you save by having an almost infinite supply of tones at your disposal is outstanding.

Unlike some programs that use digital tones, the ones in Manga Studio are vector based. Much like the vector layers available to Manga Studio EX users for their ink work, the vector tones allow you to scale as large or as small as you like, without any loss of quality. This is an amazingly important feature, as the tone quality remains consistent regardless of export or print size. This practically eliminates the chances of a *moiré effect* (unwanted patterns that appear in screen tones — see the "No more moiré" sidebar later in this chapter.)

Having vector tones also means that you aren't married to a particular setting; if you don't think that the tone you selected works for you, you can change it as many times as you'd like (which I explain in the "Adjusting Your Tones" section later in this chapter).

When working with tones, I recommend working at the size you're planning to print. While you can export to any size, you'll have a much better idea towards how the final product will look when working from its print size. I've burned myself many times toning on a page at twice its print size and then seeing the tones I worked on did not look the way I thought they would when shrunk to normal size.

If you're primarily looking to use Manga Studio for producing webcomics, I still recommend working at the size you'd like your pages to be if they were going to be printed. You never know what the future holds, so you don't want to be caught without any print-quality pages! (Just remember to export your webcomic file in RGB — I explain why in Chapter 14.)

Terminology you should know

As you work with tones in Manga Studio, there are two terms you should become familiar with: *lines* and *density*. By default, tones are set at a 45-degree angle. If you look closely, you'll see that the dots form a series of diagonal lines. The term *lines* refers to the number of those diagonal lines you can fit along one inch. Fifty lines means there are 50 rows of dots that fit within one inch.

The measurement can also work in the number of dots that fit in an inch. So, using 50 lines as an example again, it means that there are 50 dots within an inch. When you see the terms *lpi* (lines per inch) or *dpi* (dots per inch) used elsewhere, that's what it's referring to.

Density measures (in percentage) the size of the dots used in the tone. The dot size defines how light or dark the tone is; smaller dots have lower percentages and result in a lighter shade, while larger dots have higher percentages and result in a darker shade. See Figure 11-7 for an example.

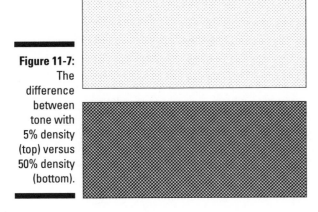

Figure 11-7:
The
difference
between
tone with
5% density
(top) versus
50% density
(bottom).

The Tones palette in Manga Studio Debut

Before you can start adding tones to your page, it would probably be a good idea to find them in the program. Fortunately, they're very easy to find: You just need to open the Tones palette, shown in Figure 11-8. To do that, either press F6 or choose Window⇨Tones.

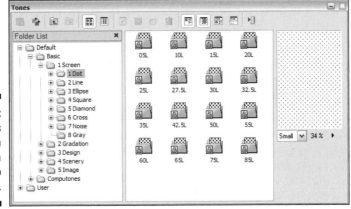

Figure 11-8:
The Tones
palette in
Manga
Studio
Debut.

It would take the rest of the book to cover all of the various types of tones available to use, so instead I point you to the Materials Catalog that comes with your program. If you have Adobe Reader (or a similar PDF reader) on your computer, you can view the catalog. From the main menu, just choose Help⇨Materials Catalog.

That said, here's a general overview of the types of tones in Manga Studio Debut you're likely to use:

- ✔ **Basic:** As its name implies, you can use this collection of basic tone styles that for objects, backgrounds, or whatever you can think of. Located in the Default\Basic folder of the Tones Palette, these tone sets include:

  - *Dot:* Tones that represent one shade of gray.
  - *Gradation:* Tones that shift from a lighter shade to a darker one.
  - *Gray:* Tones with solid shades of gray in place of dots.
  - *Line:* Tones with vertical lines instead of dots.
  - *Noise:* Tones that use a random pattern of dots and other small shapes instead of a uniform series of dots (think TV static).
  - *Figure:* Tones with crosses, squares, diamonds, and ellipses instead of dots.

- ✔ **Computones:** While Manga Studio EX has an additional function devoted to Computones (which I cover in the "Computones" section, later in the chapter), a collection of those tones has been adapted for use in the main Manga Studio program. Located in the Default\Computones folder of the Tones Palette, these tone sets include:

  - *Emphasis:* Tones that are used to convey strong emotions or actions.
  - *Feeling:* Tones that are used to express lighter emotions (bubbly, whimsical, and so on).
  - *Monologue:* Manga artists like to use a different style of word balloon when conveying the inner thoughts of a character, compared to Western-style thought balloons. This is a collection of various manga-styled thought balloons.
  - *Nature:* Tones that you can use for backgrounds of a scene. This is a collection of trees, skies and clouds, and mountains.
  - *Pattern:* Tones that you can use for the background of a scene. These are random types of patterns (animals, flowers, and so on), and you can use them to express the emotion of a character.
  - *Texture:* Tones that you can really use for anything you'd like. These are primarily noise and cross-hatching patterns.

- ✔ **CreatorsTone Vol. 2:** Located in the Default\CreatorsTone Vol. 2 folder of the Tones palette, these tones include a variety of patterns that you can use for backgrounds, clothing patterns, or anything else you can think of.

✔ **Design:** The tones here cover a wide variety of patterns and backgrounds that you may find helpful as you look and add a little something extra to your work.

Located in the Default\Design folder of the Tones Palette, these tone sets include:

- *Image:* Tone that you can use as patterns and rendered backgrounds. The patterns are broken down into folders (Clothing Patterns, Strong Emotions, and so on) to better help you find the pattern or background image you would like to use.

- *Sample:* Tones that are patterns and photographs that you can use as backgrounds to a scene.

The Tones palette in Manga Studio EX

Manga Studio EX users have almost twice the number of tones available to them compared to Manga Studio Debut. So the folder structure in EX's Tone palette is set up differently from Debut's.

EX breaks down its tones into Basic and Computones (not to be confused with the function of the same name — that's explained in the Computones section later in this chapter), incorporating all the tones and tone sets included in the Debut version. . . and *then* some (see Figure 11-9)!

The EX tone sets are set up as follows:

✔ **Basic:** This folder contains all of the basic screen tones, gradients, patterns, and backgrounds you would use in your artwork in one convenient place. The tone types are broken down into additional folders to help you easily find the tone you want for a scene or character.

Located in the Default\Basic folder of the Tones palette, these sets include (folder structure noted in parentheses):

- *Screen (Default\Basic\1 Screen):* Tones that you can use to represent shades of gray on your page. The tones are broken down into sub-folders containing Dot, Line, Ellipse, Square, Diamond, Cross, and Noise patterns, as well as solid Grays.

- *Gradation (Default\Basic\2 Gradation):* Tones that shift from a lighter color to a darker one. Like the Screen folder, the tones are broken down into sub-folders containing Dot, Line, Ellipse, Square, Diamond, Cross, and Noise patterns.

- *Design (Default\Basic\3 Design):* Tones that you can use in a background of a panel. These can be used to illustrate a character's mood, or just as a basic background pattern.

- *Scenery (Default\Basic\4 Scenery):* Backgrounds (either photographs or rendered) that you can use as the background of a scene (like a school or a wooded area).

- *Image (Default\Basic\5 Image):* Images and patterns that you can use as the background of a scene, to illustrate the mood of a character, clothing patterns, and so on.

✔ **Computones:** The tone sets here are the same as those you can use with the Computones function, although these are specifically designed to be used like Manga Studio's standard tone sets.

Located in the Default\Computones folder of the Tones Palette, these tone sets include:

- *Emphasis:* Tones that are used to convey strong emotions or actions.

- *Feeling:* Tones that are used to express lighter emotions (bubbly, whimsical, and so on).

- *Monologue:* Tones that are really a collection of manga-style thought balloons. Manga artists like to use a different style of word balloon when conveying the inner thoughts of a character, compared to Western-style thought balloons.

- *Nature:* Tones that you can use for backgrounds of a scene. This is a collection of trees, skies and clouds, and mountains.

- *Pattern:* Tones that you can use for the background of a scene. These are random types of patterns (animals, flowers, and so on), and you can use them to express the emotion of a character.

- *Texture:* Tones that you can really use for anything you'd like. These are primarily noise and cross-hatching patterns.

Time to Lay Down Some Dots!

One of the best ways to learn how something works is to use them, so how about applying some tones to a drawing?

I've included sample pages you can play around with, in case you don't have a drawing of your own to work on. You can find them in the Author/Chapter 11 folder of the CD-ROM. While you can use any of them to practice on, I use page001.cpg as an example in the following steps.

Open the page you wish to add tones to and then follow these steps:

1. **On the toolbar, select the Lasso or Polyline Marquee tool with your mouse or stylus, and start tracing area you want to add the tone to.**

   For example, I use the `page001.cpg` file and I traced the character's hair. See Figure 11-9.

Figure 11-9:
Select the area to be toned up.

2. **If it isn't open already, press F6 on your keyboard to open the Layers palette.**

3. **From the Layers palette, select the folder you want.**

   You may need to click the + sign next to the folder and drill down a few subfolders. In this example, I select the Basic\Screen\Dot\50L folder.

 4. **Highlight the tone you wish to add to your selection and click the Paste Tone button, located at the top of the palette.**

   I used the 15L 30% tone for this example, shown in Figure 11-10.

That's it! You've pasted a tone into the selection.

Figure 11-10:
The 15L 30% tone adds some color to the hair.

If you don't feel like using the Lasso Tool (or feel like going a bit more "old school"), you can always paste the tone layer as a whole, and erase all the parts you don't want with the Eraser tool.

Because this tone is its own layer, you can reuse it on as many elements in a picture as you'd like and not have to paste in a new layer. Just select another section with your lasso, make sure you have the tone layer selected on the Layers palette, and the black (foreground) color is selected. Then, use the Fill tool (G on your keyboard) to fill in the area.

Alternatively, you can use any of the drawing tools (Pencil, Pen, Marker, Pattern Brush) to draw on the tone layer with either the black or transparent colors. This is a great way to fine-tune what you've placed on the page (filling in spots you may have missed with the lasso, or trim off excess tone from an area). In the case of the Pattern Brush tool, you can add some interesting effects to the tone (especially if you try experimenting by laying down patterns using both the black and transparent colors).

As you select an area with your lasso to paste a tone in, there's always the possibility that you may miss a small section and not know it, even when you paste the tone. A good way to make sure you cover everything is to select the Tone Area check box, located on the Properties tab of the Layer Properties palette. When that's selected, the tone is covered in a blue color (or whatever color you'd like to use). This allows you to see any slivers of empty space you may have missed in the initial selection.

Adjusting your tones

It's one thing to see the tone as a sample; it's another when it's on the page. Sometimes a tone you think will look right turns out to be too dark or light. Or maybe the line count isn't to your liking. Now, you can always clear out what you just pasted on the page and paste a new tone, but there's actually a simpler way to adjust the tone to your liking.

The first thing you need to do is open the Layer Properties tab, if it isn't open already. To do that, either press F7 or choose Window⇨Properties.

With tone layers, there are actually two tabs on the Layer Properties palette, as shown in Figure 11-11. The Properties tab contains the basic layer properties that I cover in Chapter 5. You can change the name and opacity of the layer, but because it's a vector layer, you can't change the resolution (because vectors aren't affected by resolution).

What you want to focus on is the Tones tab. Here is where you can adjust the tone to practically whatever you want. (Within reason — if you placed down a computone and you want a dot tone instead, you have to replace with a new tone).

Unless otherwise noted, you can enter a value in the option's corresponding text box or use the slider (activated when you click the triangle to the right of the text box) to adjust an option to the desired value.

At the top of the Tones tab, you see three icons. You can use these to manipulate the position of the tone on the page within its pasted area (that means any areas on the page that don't have tone on them will remain unaffected).

The three buttons work as follows:

- ✔ **Grab:** Much like the Grab button on the main toolbar, this button allows you to physically move the page around. This is a good way to help reposition the page as you're adjusting the tone.

- ✔ **Move:** This tool allows you to move the tone around while maintaining all the shapes created on this layer.

- ✔ **Rotate:** The Rotate tool allows you to change the angle the tone is set in while maintaining the shapes created in the layer.

Figure 11-11:
The Tones
tab of the
Layer
Properties
palette.

Below the icons, you find the View Settings section. These two options help you adjust how you want the tones to be shown on the page.

- ✔ **Angle:** This works the same as the rotate tool; it adjusts the angle the tone is set at.

- ✔ **Method:** This sets up how you'd like Manga Studio to set up how the tones will be presented on the page and in the final exported or printed product.

  By default, the view is set to Auto. This means that high dpi tone layer (lots of dots within a square inch) will display as solid gray when zoomed out. Alternatively, you can set the Method to Gray (always displayed as a solid gray color) or halftone (will always be shown as a tone pattern — unless you *really* zoom out on the page, in which case it'll be displayed as a solid gray).

Next up is the Basic Settings section. As you might expect, these options control the basic settings for the tone.

- ✔ **Lines:** Here's is where you can change the number of lines of the tone.

  You can manually enter a value in the text box, or click the black triangle to the right of the text box, and select one of the preset line options.

✔ **Angle:** Once again, this is an option to adjust the angle of the tone.

The value entered here can work in conjunction with the View Settings Angle. (That is, setting 45 degrees here plus 45 degrees in the View Settings section, would result in a 90 degree setting.) Or if you select the Relative to Page check box, only the value in this text box is used on the tone.

Keep in mind that if you're going to change the angle for one tone layer, you should probably do that for all the other tones on the page as well. Keeping the angle uniform will help prevent any moiré patterns from happening (should two layers of different angles overlap).

✔ **Color:** By default, the tone is set to black. If you want to try a different effect, you can change the value in the Color drop-down list to white and see how that affects your scene.

✔ **Type:** While normally, tones that you may use are round dots by default, you can always switch things up and use a different shape. Using the Type drop-down list, you can change the circular tones to squares, diamonds, lines, crosses, ellipses, or random noise.

✔ **Size and Distort:** You can use these options only if you're using a noise layer.

If you wish to change the size of the noise particles, enter a value between 10 and 1,000 in the Size text box. Likewise, if you want to stretch and warp the noise particles, enter a value between 0 and 1,000 in the Distort text box.

Finally, we come to the Tone Mode section. Depending on the tone mode you wish to use, you'll see a different set of options. You can change each of the tone modes by selecting one of the options from the drop-down list at the top of the section.

✔ **Normal:** If you're using this mode, the only option available is the tone's density. All you need to do here is enter a value between 1% and 100%, or you can click the triangle to the right of the text box and use the slider to adjust the value as needed.

✔ **Gradation:** This mode gives you a few more options to help set the proper size, shape, and gradation levels. These options include:

• *Shape:* You have two options here, which you can choose by selecting one of them from the drop-down list. A line shape sets a simple gradation along a line from one shade to the other, while a circle shape provides the same function, except along a curve (as shown in Figure 11-12).

• *Flatten:* If you've selected a circular gradation, this option allows you to set how flat or thin the circle will be. Enter a value in the numeric field between 0.1 and 1,000.

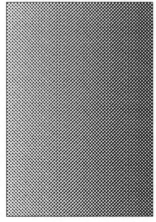
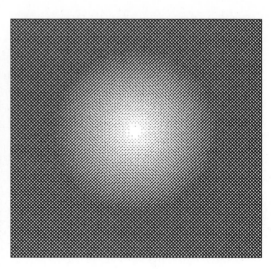

Figure 11-12:
A Line
gradation
(left) versus
a Circle
gradation
(right).

- *Density Graph:* Here's where you can adjust the gradation itself. Adjusting either of these endpoints will set how light or dark the starting and ending points will be. Adjusting the left endpoint will set the starting shade, while adjusting the right endpoint will set the ending shade.

- *Repeat Size:* This function sets up how far large the gradation pattern will be on the page. This value can be entered in the Repeat Size text box, or adjusted with the slider.

  The repeat type (shown in the drop-down list next to the repeat size) uses this value in different ways. If you choose the Repeat type, for example, the pattern will repeat once you reach the repeat size. If you decide to use the Back-to-back type, the pattern will end at the repeat size, repeat the gradation in reverse, and so on. Selecting none will end the gradation right at the repeat size.

✔ **Background (BG):** This mode is used for patterns (or images that are used as patterns) that are converted to halftone and used on the page. There are four options in this section:

- *Open File:* Click the Open File icon to bring up a directory tree dialog box. Navigate to the file you'd like to use as a BG pattern and click the Open button. The image is previewed in the window on the Open dialog box, and again on the Tones Palette (next to the Open File icon).

- *Scale:* Your drawing is now loaded, but it might not be at the size you want it for the pattern. Entering a value between 10% and 2,000% in the Scale text box (or using the slider next to the text box) helps get the pattern looking the way you'd like it to.

• *Brightness and Contrast:* The Brightness and Contrast controls can help tweak the image so it will look as you want it when it's converted into a background pattern.

To adjust these settings, enter a value between -100 and 100 (default is 0) in the Brightness and/or Contrast text boxes (or use their corresponding sliders next to the text boxes) until the image is sharp and clear enough to make you happy.

Any adjustments made to the tone affect the whole layer, so if you're looking to change only one section, the best option is to delete that section and paste in the new tone.

Deleting tones

There will come a time where you look at the tone work you've done and say — well, something that I'm sure I can't repeat in this book. When that happens, sometimes it's just best to let it go and start over. The fastest way to do that is to delete the offending tone layer.

To do that, you can either select the tone layer from the Layers palette and press the Delete button located at the top of the palette, or you can select the tone layer from the Layers palette and drag it to the Delete button.

Adding Depth to Your Tones

To paraphrase an old adage, sometimes it's best to keep things simple. In the case of tones, sometimes it just works, stylistically, to add a simple layer to an object and leave it at that. The *Trigun* manga, for example, doesn't go too crazy with tones; usually, a simple screen or gradient tone is all that you need for a character or background.

But really, what fun is that? You want to add a bit more dimension and pizzazz to your work, right? Give your page just that little extra to help it pop out from the book.

The cool thing about working with tones is that even when you want to add some dimension to a scene, you can do that with simple methods. It's pretty amazing what you can pull off simply by overlapping tones or etching and rubbing them away.

Overlapping tones to add shadows

One way to add depth to a scene is to add shadows. With tones, it's a pretty simple task: take a second tone, offset it slightly, and place it right on top of the base tone. If you look at Figure 11-13, you can see how simply adding a second layer and offsetting it slightly creates a darker color.

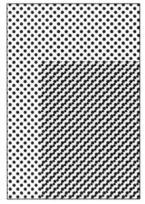

Figure 11-13:
The difference between a basic tone and two overlapping tones is dramatic.

In Manga Studio, each tone is on its own layer, so the concept of adding a layer to the page and shaping it is pretty simple — and extremely easy to correct because all you need to do is adjust the layer properties or remove the layer altogether.

To add a new tone, you just follow the same rules as when you're adding your base tone:

1. **Using your lasso, select the area you wish to add tone to.**

2. **Open the Tone palette by pressing F6 on your keyboard (or from the main menu by selecting Window ⇨ Tones).**

3. **Open the folder containing the type of tone you wish to add.**

4. **Double-click on the tone you wish to use.**

   This brings up the Tone Properties palette.

5. **Check the Show Image in the Page checkbox, located at the bottom of the palette.**

 6. **Click the Move Tone icon, located at the top of the palette.**

   Because you want to avoid a moiré effect (see the sidebar "No more moiré" for an explanation of why that's bad), the only thing in this window you want to focus on is moving the tone around to your desired offset. You can't adjust any of the other properties at this stage anyway.

7. **Using your mouse or stylus, move your tone along the page until you reached the desired offset.**

   How you offset the two tones determines the shading effect, so move the tone around until it's in a place you feel happy with.

8. **When you're done, click Paste on Page.**

When you overlap tones, keep the following helpful tips in mind:

✔ If you're planning on using this same type of layer and offset, you don't need to add a new layer each time. Just make sure you highlight the layer on the Layers palette. Now, you can select and fill in as many areas as you'd like on the layer, and you don't need to adjust the settings!

✔ If you aren't happy with the density of the shadow layer, you can change it on-the-fly. On the Tones tab of the Layer Properties palette, enter a new value in the Density text box and click OK. You can adjust this value as much as you'd like.

✔ For a different shading effect, try overlapping with a gradient tone. Just make sure that you use the same line settings as the base tone!

Overlapping tones can result in some unwanted effects, if you aren't careful. Heed these warnings, and your overlapping tones will look much better:

✔ When you add a second tone layer, you *have* to make sure that you have the same settings as the base layer and that they're at the same angle. If any of these settings are off, a nasty moiré effect will happen, and that's not a good thing. Check out the sidebar "No more moiré" for more info.

✔ Overlapping your tones is a great way to add shadow, but don't go crazy with it! Adding too many tones to a page just muddies things up, and it might not look so good in print. I suggest working with one overlapping tone at most.

Adding highlights

While overlapping tones can help bring dimensionality to a drawing by adding shadow, it doesn't do much to bring out the light. To do that, you need to remove strategic parts of the tone from the drawing.

There are several methods of adding highlights to a drawing. For this chapter, I start with the simplest method, which is to simply take your Eraser or Lasso tool, select the tone you wish to remove, and erase or delete.

No more moiré

Throughout this chapter, I constantly bring up the threat of moiré in your tone work. Specifically, I hammer home that you should avoid it at all costs and that I'm glad Manga Studio uses vector tones to help at least *try* to keep it from appearing on your completed page. That's all fine and dandy, but what exactly *is* moiré?

Moiré is an accidental (and unwanted) pattern that shows up in an image. In the case of Manga Studio, it can show up if you're using two tone patterns with different numbers of lines, or it can show up if the image has been improperly resized during export or printing.

Speaking from experience, it's extremely easy to mess up your final work if you resize the image poorly. If you take a look at the following figure, the checked patterns in the floor tiles are an unwanted moiré effect resulting from resizing an image in Photoshop.

The main reason that vectors are used in Manga Studio for their tone layers: 99.999 percent of the time, the tone should scale perfectly with whatever size you decide to use for your final image. So you shouldn't have an issue with moiré in Manga Studio due to resizing.

Moiré can also happen if you overlap the wrong kinds of tones. This can happen in a variety of ways, such as overlapping tones that are different dpi (a tone with 50 lines on top of a tone with 60 lines), or tones that are set at different angles (a tone at 45 degrees on top of a tone at 60 degrees). See the following figure for an example of a moiré effect caused by overlapping two tones.

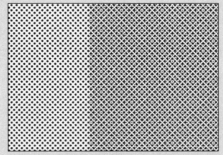

It probably doesn't seem like much to have moiré appear in your work. However, it can prove to be enough of a distraction that it takes the reader out of the reading experience — and *that* would be bad (not to mention it won't win you many jobs in the manga/comic business if publishers see that kind of mistake in your work).

Artwork courtesy Lincy Chan (character © Anthony Andora, Lincy Chan and Tokyopop Inc.)

I use the same example to add tones as I do in the "Time to Lay Down Some Dots!" section of this chapter. So, if you happened to skip that part on your way here, you need to go back and follow the instructions in that section to get to the stage I'm about to show you.

Take a drawing that you've added a tone to and remove some tone to give it some highlights by following these steps:

1. **From the Tools palette, select either the Lasso or Polygonal Marquee tool.**

   Hold the mouse button down for a couple of seconds to bring up the Polyline Marquee tool.

2. **Trace along the areas of the tone you wish to use for highlights.**

    I use the page001.cpg file for this example, so I selected areas of the girl's hair, as shown in Figure 11-14. The page001.cpg file is available in the Author/Chapter 11 folder on the CD.

3. **After you've selected the area you want to highlight, simply press the Delete key.**

   The tone disappears, and you're done!

Figure 11-14:
Adding
highlights is
a breeze!

 If you make a mistake when removing tone and remove too much, it's very simple to replace. Select the Pen tool from the Tools palette, and draw in the area you wish to replace.

If you're looking to create a softer highlight, try using the Pencil tool and selecting the transparent color (located at the bottom of the Tools palette). Use that like your Eraser tool, and you'll see it produces softer edges than the normal eraser.

If you want to get into some more advanced techniques of adding highlights, start practicing the art of etching your tones. Several books out there are dedicated to this style of highlighting and provide you with much more extensive tips and tricks than I can cover in one chapter. I list one or two of them in my top ten list of essential references in Chapter 16.

Computones

If you bought Manga Studio EX in a box, you've more than likely installed the first disc of Manga Studio EX (otherwise, it'd be pretty difficult to use the program), as well as the second disc (samples). However, that third disc may have you puzzled. What exactly are . . . Computones?

Computones are sets of screen and pattern tones that were created by the company Graphic-Sha. Initially created for use in programs such as Photoshop and Paint Shop Pro, these sets can also be used by Manga Studio EX users. It's a great place to look if you don't want to use any of the main tone sets, as there are some types of tones you won't find in Manga Studio's base tones.

If you haven't tried using the Computones function, you may find it to be a different experience than working with the base tones, and that isn't a bad thing. Personally, I find that there's almost a more natural feel when working with Computones — it's like you're working with real sheets of tones, even more so than with the Manga Studio tones.

In addition to the Computones that come with the program, you can purchase additional sets. At the time of this writing, the only way to purchase them is to buy any of the *How To Draw Manga: Computones* books (published by Graphic-Sha). Each of those books comes with a CD-ROM that contains 100 or so additional Computones.

Installing Computones

The installation process for Computones works pretty much the same as when you first installed Manga Studio:

1. **Place the third Manga Studio EX installation disc into your CD-ROM drive.**

   This step will vary, depending on how you purchased Manga Studio EX (by CD or download) or if you are installing one of the third-party Computones sets.

   • For the download version of EX on Windows, open the `mainsetup` file and click the link that says Install Computones when prompted.

- For the download version of EX on the Mac, double click the Image that says "Manga Studio EX 3 Computones Disk 3", and then double click on the "Computones" Folder when the image window appears.

- For third-party Computone sets, follow the directions that came with their CD.

2. **When the installation dialog box appears, click the resolution set you wish to install.**

   A new window appears containing a folder with the Computones for the selected resolution, and an installation program labeled Install (Installer on the Mac).

3. **Double-click the installation program. When the confirmation dialog box appears, click OK (make sure that the Computones program isn't running in Manga Studio EX).**

   The first time you install a Computone set into the computer, the Browse for Folder dialog box appears (shown in Figure 11-15), asking you to specify the destination directory or folder. You can install the Computones anyplace on the system (you aren't limited to the Manga Studio folder), so specify any location you'd like and click OK. You have to do this only once; all other Computone sets are automatically placed in this folder.

   The program then prepares the tone set for installation in your selected folder.

4. **When the Select a Tone Set dialog box appears, enter a name for the tone set (or use the default name) and click OK.**

5. **Click OK on the Tones Installer confirmation dialog box.**

6. **When all the tones finish installing, click OK to exit.**

   (Optional) When the main Computones installation menu appears, repeat Steps 4–6 for any of the other resolution sets you want to install.

If you're thinking of adding Computones to the main program's tone folder in hopes of using them in the main program, you're out of luck. Only the Computones function can read the sets. If you desperately need a Computone for the main program, be sure to check out the Computones folder in the Tones palette.

Figure 11-15:
The Browse
for Folder
dialog box.

Deciphering the differences between Computones and Manga Studio tones

I mention earlier that using Computones feels a bit more tactile or real than when working with the base Manga Studio sets. Perhaps that's because unlike using the base tones, you have a smaller margin of error with Computones:

✔ Computones don't automatically generate a new layer when you select them. So either you have to create a new layer for each tone manually, or you need to keep them all on one layer.

✔ You can't adjust the tone settings of Computones after you place them on the page. If you make a mistake, you need to erase the tone and add the corrected version.

✔ You *have* to make sure that the Computone set you work with is the *same resolution* as the layer you're working on. Using the wrong resolution results in terrible-looking tones.

✔ Unlike the base tones (which are vector based), Computones are raster based. So they aren't as friendly to you if you enlarge or shrink the page.

Applying Computones

The differences in the preceding section aside, working with Computones is not that much different than working with the base Manga Studio tones. Many of the tips I give in the book when using tones work just as well with Computones.

For the following steps, I use the `page001.cpg` file. You can find this file in the Author\Chapter 11 folder on the CD.

If you haven't installed any Computones (I use the 600 dpi Computones as an example), now's a good time to do that.

Open the page you wish to add Computones to, and then follow these steps:

1. **Create a new raster layer with a resolution of 600 dpi.**

   For the sake of time and space, I don't go into detail on how to do this. I recommend checking out Chapter 6 if you haven't already.

2. **Select a Lasso or Polyline Marquee tool from the Tools palette.**

3. **Use the Lasso to trace a selection.**

   For example, I traced along the male character's shirt. (See Figure 11-16.)

4. **From the main menu, choose Filter⇨Computones⇨Tones.**

   The Computones palette appears, as shown in Figure 11-17.

Figure 11-16: Once selected, the shirt is now set to have tone placed on it.

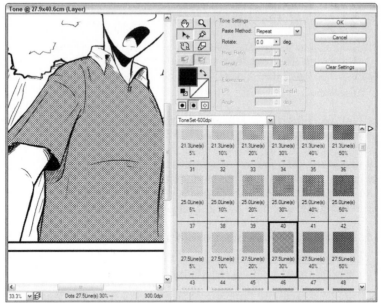

5. **Select the resolution set you want to work with from the Tone Set drop-down list.**

   The drop-down list doesn't actually have a name — just look for the drop-down list directly above the Tone window.

6. **Select the tone you want to work with from the Tone window.**

7. **You can move, zoom, and adjust the tone in the preview pane as follows:**

   - *To move around the preview pane, select the Hand tool.*

   - *To zoom the preview pane in and out, use the Zoom tool.*

     Clicking the preview pane zooms in. You need to hold down the Alt/Option key to zoom out.

   - *To adjust the tone within the preview pane, use the Move tool.*

     After you select it, you only need to click and drag the tone to wherever you want it.

   - *To rotate the tone within the preview pane, use the Rotate tool.*

     After you select it, you can click and drag the tone until it's at the angle you want it.

   - *To set an axis point to rotate the tone, select the Pin tool and click anywhere on the preview pane.*

   - *To scale the tone up or down, select the Scale button.*

Keep in mind that only certain tones can be scaled. These are usually the effects tones, such as starbursts or lightning bolts.

8. Select the color scheme you want to use for the tone.

The Color section really doesn't give you much of an option for color; you get the foreground color, background color, or transparent. What you can choose to do is set which color is rendered how.

For example, you can choose to invert the colors so that instead of black on white, you produce white on black. Or you can use the Render buttons and choose to do one of the following:

- *Render Foreground and Background Colors*
- *Render in the Foreground Color*
- *Render in the Background Color*

9. Adjust how you want the tones to lay on the page with the Tone Settings section.

Depending on the type of tone (or tone set) you select, you have the following options available to you:

- *Paste Method:* This drop-down list contains various ways the tones will lay if you want the pattern to repeat.

- *Rotate:* Like the Rotate tool, you can use this slider bar (activated by clicking the arrow to the right of the text box) to adjust the angle of your tone. Or you can manually enter a value in its text box.

- *Mag Ratio:* Like the Scale tool, you can manually adjust the scale of the tone by using the slider bar or entering a value in its text box. This option is only available for grayscale tones.

- *Density:* You can adjust how thick or thin the tone is by using the slider to set a value, or you can enter a value in its text box.

10. If you're pasting a grayscale tone, use the Expression section to set how the tone will look on the page.

You have the following options to choose from in this section:

- *Expression:* This drop-down list alters the physical shape of the tone. You can choose to use dots, lines, crosses, or a random pattern.

- *LPI:* Unlike the other resolution sets, you can adjust the number of lines in the tone. Simply enter a value between 5 and 85 lines in its corresponding text box.

- *Angle:* If you tried using the Rotate text box to adjust the angle of the tones, you probably noticed it doesn't work. That's because the only way to adjust a grayscale tone is to use the Angle text box. Just enter any value from 0 to 359 degrees, and you're all set.

11. **When you're done, click OK.**

Practically all of the tricks I mention in this chapter (and later in Chapter 14) work with both the base tones and with Computones.

Chapter 12

Words Speak Louder than Actions: Adding Text to a Page

I was once told that if you lay your pages out properly, the reader can follow exactly what's going on without the need for text. That's true, and it's a practice that I think more artists should use. But it wouldn't *hurt* to know what the characters are saying to each other. Pretty much the only way you're going to convey the sound of people talking is through text and (optionally) word balloons. The reader throws in just the right amount of suspension of disbelief to "hear" the characters on the page with words and some means of directing them to the speaker's mouth.

For the most part, Manga Studio can help you do that. Depending on whether you bought the Debut or EX version, there may be a few more steps involved, but the end result will be the same.

This chapter covers all you need to know to create text and word balloons in both Manga Studio Debut and EX versions. I first discuss the various kinds of narrative balloons you may want to use, depending on the situation. Then, I go over how to add and edit text, using the Text tool. After that, I explain how to create a simple word balloon in Debut and (more easily) in EX. Finally, I'll talk about something that the EX users out there may enjoy: the ability to create custom word balloon templates.

Adding Text

Provided you aren't working the old Marvel way (a barebones layout script with no dialogue), you likely have some words in front of you that you'd like to place on the page.

Simple enough. Break out the Text tool and add dialogue and other text to your page by following these steps:

1. **Click the Text tool on the Tools palette.**

2. **On the canvas, click the area you wish to add text to.**

   Manga Studio automatically creates a new layer to hold the text and opens the Layer Properties palette. Only this time, there is a new Text tab, as shown in Figure 12-1. As you can probably guess, the options here are what you'll be using to add the text to the canvas.

3. **Select the font you wish to use from the Font drop-down list.**

   Only the fonts that are installed on your machine appear in the drop-down list. Be sure to check out the sidebar "Knowing where to get comic and manga fonts" for instructions on finding, downloading, and installing new fonts onto your computer.

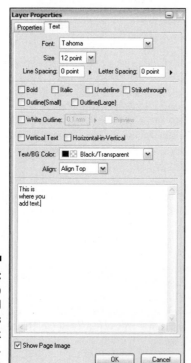

Figure 12-1:
The Text tab gives you all the options to tweak your text.

4. **Select your font size from the Size drop-down list.**

   The font sizes are measured in points. This means the font size you select remains the same relative size, regardless of the print resolution.

   To get an understanding on how large the font is on the page, there are about 72 points in an inch. So, if you were to use the default 12 point font, the text would be about ⅙-inch tall.

5. **Set the spacing between the lines of text by entering a value between 0 and 99 points in the Line Spacing text box.**

6. **Set the spacing between the letters in your text by entering a value between -99 and 99 points in the Letter Spacing text box.**

   You can see examples of differences in line and letter spacing in Figure 12-2.

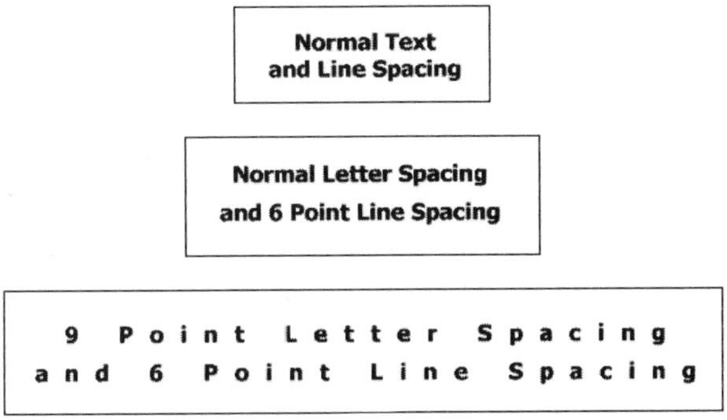

**Normal Text
and Line Spacing**

Figure 12-2:
Examples of
text at
different line
and letter
spacings.

**Normal Letter Spacing
and 6 Point Line Spacing**

**9 P o i n t   L e t t e r   S p a c i n g
a n d   6   P o i n t   L i n e   S p a c i n g**

---

7. **To format the text as bold, italics, underline, or strikethrough, select their respective check boxes.**

   You can select more than one check box to apply multiple effects to the text. For example, select the Bold and Underline check boxes to create bold, underlined text.

   If you want to apply formatting to just a word or two, or if you want to adjust formatting on any text you've already typed, you first need to select the text in the text box at the bottom of the Text tab by clicking and dragging.

8. **To convert the text into a thin outline (as shown in Figure 12-3), select the Outline (Small) check box.**

9. **To convert the text into a thick outline (as shown in Figure 12-3), select the Outline (Large) check box.**

10. **To add a white outline around the text, select the White Outline check box, and enter a value between 0.1mm and 1.0mm in its respective text box.**

Additionally, you can preview the outline on the page by selecting the Preview check box.

11. **To convert the text so that it's written vertically (as shown in Figure 12-3), select the Vertical Text check box.**

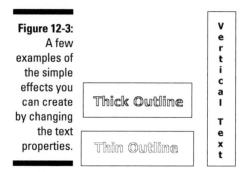

Figure 12-3:
A few examples of the simple effects you can create by changing the text properties.

12. **If you want text written horizontally when the Vertical Text check box is selected, highlight word with your mouse or stylus and select the Horizontal-in-Vertical check box.**

This function is used primarily when writing Japanese text (which is written vertically), and an exclamation (like "!!") or English word needs to be written horizontally in the dialogue.

13. **Select the color of your text with the Text/BG Color drop-down list.**

You have four options to choose from:

- *Black/Transparent:* This default value produces black text on a clear background.

- *White/Transparent:* This produces white text on a clear background.

- *Transparent/Black:* This produces clear text on a black background.

- *Transparent/White:* This produces clear text on a white background.

14. **Select the text alignment (left, center, or right justify — listed in the program as Top, Center, and Bottom, respectively) from the Align drop-down list.**

15. **Type the text in the large text box at the bottom of the palette.**

Manga Studio doesn't have an automatic word wrap, so you need to enter line breaks manually. Be sure to check out the "Formatting Pitfalls" section, later in this chapter, for tips on how to avoid any potential reader confusion.

16. **Click OK when you're done.**

17. **If you need to readjust the position of the new text on the page, click the text (it should have a red box surrounding it) and drag it along the canvas to wherever you'd like it.**

If you're feeling adventuresome, try lettering your text by hand (if you have a drawing tablet, that is)! If you use the rulers that I talk about in Chapter 8, there's really nothing stopping you from lettering the old-fashioned way. Look for some books discussing how to letter and try applying those exercises and tips in Manga Studio!

For a quick way to organize your text, simply select the Store in Text Folder check box, located on the Text tool's Options palette. Now, any text you enter is automatically placed in a text folder on the Layers palette. You can't miss the check box — it's the only option on the palette!

Editing Text

Editing text layers is easy. On the Layers palette, double-click the text layer you want to edit, and the Text Properties appear. Follow the steps I outline in the "Adding Text" section, and you can edit and reformat the text however you'd like. Alternatively, you can double-click the text on the canvas to bring up the Text Properties.

In Manga Studio EX, the Text tool always uses the default setting, regardless of what you formatted previously. Rather than redoing all your formatting, you can save time by copying the first text layer you created, placing it in the next position on the page, and then editing the text. All the formatting you apply to the first text layer is copied to the new text layer.

If you feel limited by the formatting you can apply to your text, you can convert the text layer into an image layer and then scale and transform the text as you wish. (Note that after you convert a text layer to an image layer, you can no longer edit the text.) If you want to convert a text layer into an image layer, choose Layer⇨Change Layer Type from the main menu. Select whichever layer type you would like to transform the text into, and you're all set!

Knowing where to get comic and manga fonts

There is absolutely nothing preventing you from using the default fonts your computer came with in your comic book or manga. But if you're looking to give your book's lettering a more authentic feel, grabbing a comic book or manga font off of the Internet is exactly what you need. Fortunately, there are a few places you can get them — some of them for free!

✔ Famed comic book letterer Richard Starkings created a Web site showcasing a variety of professional dialogue, title, and sound effect fonts over at www.comicbookfonts.com. Many favorite North American artists, such Dave Gibbons, Jim Lee, and Scott McCloud have fonts based on their style housed over there.

The potential drawback is that all of the fonts on the site cost money, and they aren't exactly cheap. So, if your budget is a bit tight, this place might not be what you're looking for. Even so, you should still check out the site. The folks who created Comic Book Fonts also provide a series of (free!) tutorials to help improve you lettering skills at http://balloontales.com.

✔ Like ComicBookFonts.com, Blambot (www.blambot.com) provides sets of dialogue, title, and sound effect fonts to purchase and download. They are also of superb quality, and you can use them on both PCs and Macs.

There are two distinct differences between the two sites, however: Blambot's fonts are significantly cheaper, and Blambot offers a large selection of *free* fonts!

So, if you're on a tight budget, see what Blambot has to offer. The price point is certainly right.

✔ If you check out both of the above sites and still don't find what you're looking for, try searching the Internet for sites devoted to all kinds of free fonts. One site in particular, DaFont (www.dafont.com) contains a nice collection of comic fonts, but it also carries practically every other type of font currently out there. If you're looking for a look for your book's title, for example, this might be a good area to rummage through.

✔ If all else fails, create your own font! There are several programs out there that you can purchase to create a font that you can truly call your own. If you're unsure about laying down some cash on a program you're unfamiliar with, you can see if they offer a demonstration version. Then, you're not down any money if you find it's not what you want.

Remember: I can't emphasize this enough — *always* read the user agreement before you start lettering with your new fonts. Many fonts, especially the free ones, come with a ReadMe file that contains the rules you have to follow if you want to use the font in your work. Be sure to carefully read the rules regarding using the fonts on a comic or book that will be sold for profit (as opposed to publishing the comic on the Internet) — you may need to pay a licensing fee to use them for commercial use. It's common courtesy to follow the rules the font's creator sets, considering you're saving a lot of time using a font that someone else created. (Not to mention it could save you a lot of headaches, should the creator go after you legally for not adhering to the terms of use. Not than I'm a lawyer or anything.)

Avoiding Formatting Pitfalls

Creating dialogue on a page is easy. Creating dialogue on a page that doesn't confuse the reader is a bit trickier.

There are several pitfalls when formatting the text for the page. Avoiding the following mistakes will make things easier for both you and the person reading your story:

- **Placing balloons poorly:** Make sure to place word balloons properly in a panel to give the proper flow to the dialogue. Remember that the reader is reading the balloons from left to right (unless you're formatting Japanese-style, in which case, it's right to left) and from top to bottom. So, you want to make sure that the dialogue balloons are placed in the right order in a panel, or the dialogue might inadvertently cease to make sense. See Figure 12-4 for an example.

- **Overcrowding a panel with too many balloons or balloons that are too large:** Try not to overcrowd a panel with balloons, as shown in Figure 12-5. Dialogue can become confusing to the reader if the art and balloons become too cramped inside a panel, especially when if you're trying to have more than one person speaking. You should either try to limit the amount of dialogue in a panel, or if that's unavoidable, be sure to format the panels to accommodate. To save yourself headaches, check to see if you created enough room for the dialogue in the rough layout stage.

- **Making balloons too small for the text:** Give your text some breathing room. Much like overcrowding a panel with too much text, you can confuse the reader if you try to cram too much text in a small balloon, as shown in Figure 12-6. Make sure that the word balloon is large enough to fit the dialogue, but not so small that the text is butting up to the borders. How much space you want to place between the text and the balloon borders is subjective, but try to find a buffer in between too cramped and too *much* space (to the point it hides artwork). Basically find a happy medium that's comfortable enough for you to read on the page. Odds are, it will also feel comfortable for your readers.

- **Cramming too much text into one balloon:** Try not to cram too many sentences into one balloon. It isn't much fun trying to read a large block of text in a comic. You can lose the pacing you're trying to convey if the character's speech is smooshed into one large balloon.

  If you can, try to limit dialogue within a balloon to no more than two sentences. (Optimally, you should have only one sentence per balloon.) You can always daisy-chain balloons together so that the reader understands that the character is giving a long speech.

Figure 12-4:
Which
example
flows
better?

Figure 12-5:
Too much
dialogue
can crowd
things in a
small panel.

✔ **Placing line breaks in incorrect or awkward places:** Avoid odd line breaks. This probably seems like an odd suggestion; it's only breaking the text up to fit the dialogue, right?

To a point, you'd be right. The problem is that when you throw those line breaks in odd places, they can result in a sentence reading awkwardly. That can throw your reader out of the story, and that's never a good thing.

Try to avoid the scenarios shown in Figure 12-7.

Taking the time to make sure your little cluster of text is easy to read can be just as important as providing enough padding within the word balloon. The key to all these suggestions and warnings is *reader comfort*. Readers should be focusing their energy on what's going on in the scene, not on trying to figure out how the text is supposed to be read. Otherwise, they're not going to care about the world you've spent months creating.

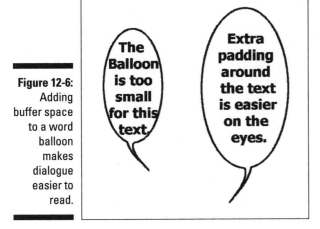

Figure 12-6:
Adding buffer space to a word balloon makes dialogue easier to read.

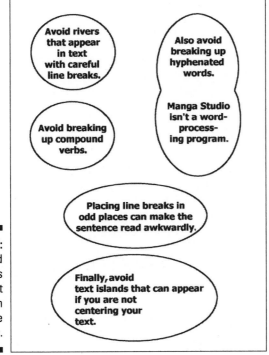

Figure 12-7:
Try to avoid line breaks in your text that result in these examples.

Creating Word Balloons in Manga Studio Debut

You've created all the dialogue for the page. Now it's time to add some word balloons so that the reader knows who's saying what to whom.

First, the bad news: Creating word balloons isn't the easiest thing to do in Manga Studio Debut. Fact is, it's a multistep process to create word balloons for your text. (Manga Studio EX really shines here — the process of making word balloons is much easier with this version. If you're using Manga Studio EX, skip ahead to the "Creating Word Balloons in Manga Studio EX" section.)

The good news is that this process can give you some artistic freedom to come up with you own style. (If you've created word balloons in Photoshop, the process isn't that much different in Manga Studio Debut. The only difference is for those who use the selection tools in Photoshop, as you won't be using that in Manga Studio.)

To create a word balloon in Manga Studio Debut, follow these steps:

1. **Create a new layer for your balloons by selecting Layer ⇨ New Layer from the main menu. Enter a name (like "Word Balloons") for the Layer Name, and click OK (the default options will work just fine for this).**

2. **Select the Shape tool from the Tools palette.**

3. **If it isn't active, press F3 on your keyboard to bring up the Tool Options palette.**

   In Chapter 5, I discuss the options on this palette in greater detail, but because you're looking to create a simple word balloon here, I discuss just the options you need to set the Shape tool up to create the balloon.

4. **If it isn't already active, click the Show Menu button on the Tool Options palette and select Advanced Settings Mode.**

   The Tool Options palette expands to include the advanced options, as shown in Figure 12-8.

5. **Select the Elliptical Shape option.**

6. **Adjust the line size to whatever size you want by entering a value in the Line Size text box.**

   The value for this option is subjective. Most artists tend to go with a thinner line for the word balloons. (Then again, you're not "most artists," now are you?)

7. **Select the Start from Center check box.**

   This option helps make the word balloon a bit easier, as it allows you to create the shape starting from the middle of the text.

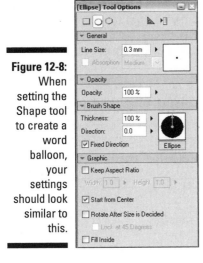

Figure 12-8:
When
setting the
Shape tool
to create a
word
balloon,
your
settings
should look
similar to
this.

8. **Make sure that the Fill Inside check box is deselected.**

   Because the fill is in the foreground color (in this case, black), it's hard to see the text when it's obscured by a black oval.

9. **From the main menu, choose Layer⇨New Layer.**

10. **When the New Layer Dialog box pops up, enter a name for your new word balloon layer.**

    You don't need to adjust the other settings in the New Layer dialog box — the settings default to a raster layer at the highest resolution relative to the page, which is fine for a word balloon layer.

11. **Click OK.**

12. **On the Layers palette, select the word balloon layer and drag it down the list of layers until it's below all of the text layers for the page.**

13. **Make sure that the word balloon layer is highlighted on the Layers palette, and then click the text you want to draw around with your mouse and stylus.**

14. **Drag the shape out from the text until it's at the size and shape you want, and release.**

    This creates the body of the balloon around your text.

15. **Select the Curve tool on the Tools palette.**

    You use the Curve tool to create the tail for the balloon.

16. **If you wish to add a slight taper to the curved lines you create for the balloon tail, select the Taper Out option on the Tool Options palette and enter a value in its corresponding text box.**

17. **Starting from the word balloon, click it and drag the tool down until it's at the length you want. Then drag the tool until it's at the bend you want.**

18. **Repeat this for the other side of the balloon tail.**

    Your word balloon should look similar to the one in Figure 12-9.

19. **From the Tools palette, select the Eraser tool.**

    You can select a smaller eraser quickly by holding down on the button for a couple of seconds and selecting from the menu that appears.

20. **Erase the excess lines from the word balloon and tail.**

    Figure 12-10 shows a balloon before and after erasing the extra lines.

Figure 12-9: Creating a tail for your balloon is a cinch!

When we were roomates, you always came up here when you were stressed out.

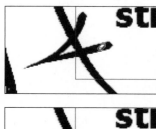

Figure 12-10: Erase the excess lines from your word balloon.

On this step, you need to make sure you don't accidentally create a gap in the word balloon, or the next few steps won't work properly. If you find you do create a gap, simply Undo (Ctrl+Z or ⌘+Z) and try again.

21. Select the Fill tool on the Tools palette.

22. Select the background color (in this case, white) on the Tools palette.

23. Click the Show Transparency button, located on the Page toolbar.

This makes it easier to see if the word balloon is filled properly. When you're done, clicking the Show Transparency button again turns the function off.

24. While making sure you're still on the word balloon layer (it won't work on a text layer), click anywhere within the word balloon.

You now have a fully drawn and filled-in word balloon, as shown in Figure 12-11. Like I mention earlier, it isn't a simple process, but the end results are definitely worth it.

You can slightly alter the preceding steps to create different types of word balloons:

✔ **To create a caption box,** simply use the Rectangle shape instead of the Elliptical shape.

✔ **If you want to create a thought balloon,** try using the Shape tool to create a series of circles around the text, and then erase the inside until only the outline you want remains. (Check out Figure 12-12 to see what I mean.)

Figure 12-11:
You now have one completed word balloon!

When we were roommates, you always came up here when you were stressed out.

Figure 12-12:
Create a
thought
balloon
using the
Circle Shape
tool.

The technique I explain in the preceding steps is only one way to create word balloons. Ultimately, the only limitation to the way you create word balloons is your imagination. Try using other Line or Shape tools to see what you can come up with. If you want to create a style that you can truly call your own, try drawing your balloons freehand!

Creating Word Balloons in Manga Studio EX

You Manga Studio EX users out there have things a lot easier than Debut users, as far as creating word balloons go. In fact, all you need to do is take advantage of the Word Balloon function, and you can use any of EX's preinstalled balloons. If none of the default templates are to your liking, you can simply create your own, which you can re-use as many times as you want! (Or you can create them by hand — see the "Creating Word Balloons in Manga Studio Debut" section, earlier in this chapter.)

After you create text on the page and click OK, you'll notice a third tab can now be seen on the Layer Properties palette. That tab, as shown in Figure 12-13, contains all your word balloon options. Just clicking that tab creates the default word balloon, so you're already halfway done. (I told you that you have it easier than the Debut users!)

Figure 12-13:
The Word
Balloon tab
in the Layer
Properties
palette.

The options on the Word Balloon tab are as follows:

- ✔ **Select Word Balloon:** This drop-down list contains all of the default and user-created balloon templates available. Simply select the balloon type you want to use, and you're all set.

- ✔ **Fit Text:** Select this check box, and the balloon automatically adjusts to the minimum size needed to incorporate the text.

- ✔ **Keep Aspect Ratio:** Select this check box, and the balloon keeps the same shape, regardless of how large or small you size it.

- ✔ **Add Tail:** Click this button to add a tail to the word balloon to help the reader know who is speaking. Click the Add Tail button, and then with your mouse or stylus, drag the tail to the speaker. You can add a curve to the tail by selecting and dragging the tail's midpoint.

- ✔ **Delete Tail:** If the tail isn't working for you, simply remove it! Select the tail with your mouse or stylus (the ruler line turns red) and click the Delete Tail button.

  If you delete the tail, you can add a new one, in case you change your mind again. Just click the Add Tail button again.

- ✔ **Tail Width:** The value entered in this text box adjusts the mouth of the tail (that is, the part that connects to the balloon). Enter a smaller value to shrink its size, a bigger value to enlarge it.

- ✔ **Line Width:** Adjusting the value in this text box adjusts the line width of the balloon.

- ✔ **Line Color:** This sets the line color for the balloon. By default, the line is black, but you can change it by clicking the color box (which brings up the Color Settings dialog box), and selecting your new color (click OK to close the dialog box).

✔ **Fill Word Balloon:** You can fill the word balloon with any color you'd like by selecting this check box and then clicking the Fill Color box to select the color. (The default option is white.)

If you leave the Fill Word Balloon check box deselected, just the outline of the balloon is added to the page.

So, word balloon creation in Manga Studio EX boils down to typing and formatting the text on the Text tab of the Layer Properties palette, and then opening and adjusting the balloon settings on the Word Balloon tab in the Layer Properties palette.

Creating your own word balloon template

Manga Studio EX users have eighteen default word balloons to choose from. It's impressive, until you discover that many of them are variations on a theme: Three are considered standard balloons, three are yelling balloons, and so on. There's a chance that you could go through all the word balloon templates provided and find that none of them match what you're looking for. So, create your own!

Much like creating your own patterns and screentones, Manga Studio gives you the option to create your own word balloons. These balloons can be either vector or raster based, each with their own advantages and disadvantages:

✔ **Vector-based word balloons**, created by using a ruler layer, can be resized without any change in the outline's width. You can also add a fill color and a tail to a vector-based balloon.

The downside is that you can use only the line or shape tools to create the rulers, so you don't get much freedom to create any wacky styles.

✔ **Raster-based word balloons,** created on either a Raster or Tone Layer, can be created by any drawing tool you like. There are no limitations to the types of balloons you can create.

However, you don't get the advantages the vector-based balloons have. The width of the balloon's outline is affected by its size. In addition, you also can't set any kind of fill color (so you'll need to add a fill to the image before you create the template), nor can you add a tail to the balloon.

Choosing one or the other boils down to personal preference, as well as your need for the particular situation.

Creating a word balloon template from a ruler layer

Using this method, creating word balloons is as simple as creating a ruler — if you need a brush-up on creating rulers, head over to Chapter 8.

Follow these steps to create a vector-based word balloon on a ruler layer:

1. **From the main menu, choose Layer⇨New Layer.**

2. **Enter a name for the new layer and select Ruler Layer from the Layer Type drop-down list.**

3. **Click OK.**

   When you click OK, you're automatically on the new ruler layer.

4. **From the Tools palette, select the Shape tool. Hold it down for a couple of seconds and select the Elliptical shape.**

5. **Using the Shape tool, create an oval of any size.**

6. **Select the Object Selector from the Tools palette.**

7. **Ctrl+click (⌘+click on the Mac) the oval you just created.**

8. **From the main menu, choose Edit⇨Save Pattern as Word Balloon.**

   The Save Pattern as Word Balloon dialog box appears, as shown in Figure 12-14.

9. **Enter a name for your new word balloon in the Name text box.**

10. **Adjust the default line width by entering a value between 0.1 mm and 5.0 mm in the Line Width text box.**

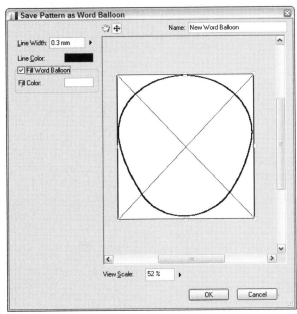

Figure 12-14:
The Save Pattern as Word Balloon dialog box.

11. (Optional) Select a color for the outline by clicking the Line Color box.

For the most part, the default color (black) will work for your outline color, but you at least have the option to change its color if you want to add some variety.

12. To make sure that the word balloon is filled in by default, select the Fill Word Balloon check box. The default color (white) will suffice.

13. Adjust the text box to fit within the word balloon.

The text box is the thin blue rectangle with the X inside it running along the border of the preview pane. (Look at Figure 12-14 to see what I mean.) If you look closely, you should see square endpoints on the corners of the rectangle. Use you mouse or stylus to click and drag the endpoints inside the word balloon until the text box fits comfortably within the word balloon. (That is, there's enough of a buffer between the text box and balloon borders that there is no risk of crowding text.)

14. Click OK when you're done.

You now have a word balloon template all ready for you to use with your dialogue. Simply select it like you would any other template, and adjust it as needed (see Figure 12-15).

The preceding steps show only one way you can create a word balloon. You can try creating a unique shape using any of the other line or shape tools.

If the shape you create isn't fully enclosed (that is, created with the Shape or Polyline tool), you can't fill it in with a default color. You also can't add a tail to the balloon later on.

Figure 12-15:
You can create word balloons that will withstand any kind of transformation.

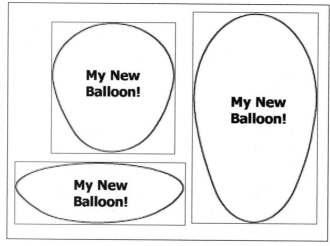

My New Balloon!

My New Balloon!

My New Balloon!

Creating a word balloon template from a raster or tone layer

Time to start flexing those artistic muscles! If you're looking to create a word balloon template that you can really say is yours, this is how to do it.

Follow these steps to create a raster-based word balloon from raster or tone layer:

1. **From the main menu, choose Layer⇨New Layer.**

2. **Enter a name for the new layer and select Raster or Tone Layer from the Layer Type drop-down list.**

   If you're working with a raster layer, be sure to set your resolution to its highest setting, relative to the page resolution. Check out Chapter 4 for more info.

3. **Click OK.**

4. **Select any drawing tool you'd like to use from the Tools palette.**

   Unlike when you create a word balloon template on a ruler layer, you aren't limited to just using the Line or Shape tools. You can design the word balloon however you like.

5. **Using any tool you wish, draw your word balloon however you want.**

   Here's where you get to be creative. So long as it's some kind of container for your text, you can draw the balloon however you like. If you're looking to fill the balloon in with a background color, however, you need to make sure that there are no gaps in the outline.

6. **(Optional) Fill in the balloon with background color using the Fill tool.**

7. **Select the Rectangular Marquee tool from the Tools palette and drag to create a selection over the word balloon.**

8. **From the main menu, choose Edit⇨Save Pattern as Word Balloon.**

   The Save Pattern as Word Balloon dialog box appears.

9. **Enter a name for your new word balloon in the Name text box.**

10. **Adjust the text box to fit within the word balloon.**

    The text box is the thin blue rectangle with the X inside it running along the border of the preview pane. (Refer to Figure 12-14.) Use you mouse or stylus to click and drag the endpoints inside the word balloon.

11. **Click OK when you're done.**

    Your custom raster-based balloon is now ready to use.

Using your custom word balloons

When you create a custom word balloon, it's automatically added to the template list on the Word Balloon tab of the Layer Properties palette. To use a custom balloon template, simply select the template from the Select Word Balloon drop-down list (shown in Figure 12-16) and then adjust it to fit the text.

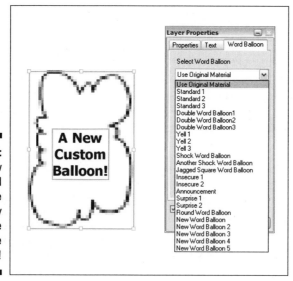

Figure 12-16:
Your new
word
balloons are
already
added to the
template
list!

Chapter 13

Printing and Exporting

· ·

· ·

*Y*ou've planned out your story, roughed it out, inked it, added tones and effects, and placed in your dialogue. The hard part's done — now all you need to do is show your comic to the masses.

Manga Studio gives you two options to share your work:

✔ Print the pages on your desktop printer.

✔ Export your pages to an external file.

   You can then post the exported file on the Web or send it to a professional printing company.

Whichever option you choose really depends on what you plan on doing with your freshly-created work.

I'm sure you're probably wondering why printing and exporting merits an entire chapter. Well, the process of printing and exporting your work is a bit more involved than simply clicking the Print or Save buttons, but I think that's a good thing. What if you want only the roughs printed? Or what if you want to export the line art, but leave out the tones? Or what if you want the print guide printed along with your image? Manga Studio gives you flexibility that not many other programs give (if at all) regarding what exactly you want to be visible in the final product.

Admittedly, that amount of flexibility can be pretty intimidating at first glance. Then again, you may have initially thought the same thing about the rest of the program, and look where you're at now.

Printing Your Work

If you're looking to sell your comic book but you don't have the money to get it printed professionally, don't worry about it! You can just as easily use your own printer to create your comic book.

If you check out any comic or anime convention, you almost always find a small press or self-publisher section. The artists there sell their goods on nothing more than a stack of 8.5-x-11-inch paper and a few staples. This is probably the simplest and cheapest way you can sell your comic in a physical form.

In Manga Studio, you can print pages either individually or as a story. For the following steps, I focus on how to print a single page (although I point out options that you use when printing a story):

1. **From the main menu, choose File⇨Print Setup.**

   The first dialog box you'll see the first time you print in Manga Studio, is the Printer Setup dialog box you usually see whenever you want to print on your computer). I discuss what I feel are the best settings for print in the "Optimal Settings for your Work" section, later in this chapter, so for now you can click the OK button to exit. (You can always change the printer settings later on by selecting File⇨Print.)

   You should now see the Print Setup dialog box, as shown in Figure 13-1.

Figure 13-1:
The Print Setup dialog box.

2. **If you're a Manga Studio EX user working off of a two-page spread, select which page (or both) you want printed in the Print Page section.**

   If you want to print out that wild two-page battle scene you concocted, you can select the Left Page or Right Page option button to print each page separately, or you can select the Dual Page option button to print both pages together on a single page.

   Keep in mind that if you choose to print the whole spread on one page, it will be smaller, and you may need to set the paper to print horizontally (Landscape mode).

3. **Choose the print size of the page by selecting one of the option buttons in the Print Size section:**

   - *Actual Size:* The size of the page in centimeters. Any part of the page outside of the paper size is cut off.

   - *Adapt to the Page Format:* The image resizes to fit inside the paper.

   - *Actual Pixels:* The size of the page in pixels, relative to the paper size. Any part of the page outside of the paper size is cut off.

   - *Spread (EX only):* Both pages of a two-page spread will be printed on one piece of paper. The spread is adjusted to fit the paper.

     If you're printing from a story file, the option is different. Instead of a Spread radio button, you have a dropdown list, where you can choose to either print two pages (Spread) or four pages (4 pages) per piece of paper. The pages will be adjusted so that any two-page spreads will be printed concurrently on the same page.

   - *Free Size (EX only):* This option allows you to set what part of the page is printed on the paper. This is useful if the page happens to be a bit larger than the paper size.

     When selected, you simply move and resize the paper (click and drag a corner of the page to resize, as shown in Figure 13-2) until it is at the size you want, and the page is positioned properly.

   - *Dual Page (EX only):* How this option works depends on if you're printing a two-page spread or a story.

     Story files are printed two pages per piece of paper. Each page in the story is treated individually, so two-page spreads (EX only) may be split up, depending on their placement in the story. (For example, a spread on pages two and three would be split up.) If you want to ensure spreads are printed on the same paper, select the Spread option instead.

     If you're printing from an individual two-page spread file, each half of the spread is printed on its own page.

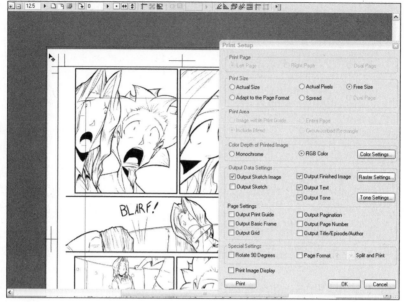

Figure 13-2:
With the
Free Size
option (EX
only), you
can size and
position the
paper
however
you'd like.

4. **Select how much of the page you want printed by selecting one of the following option buttons in the Print Area section:**

   • *Image within Print Guide:* Only the main image is printed. Anything beyond artwork from the bleed area and beyond is ignored.

   • *Include Bleed:* The image up to the edge of the bleed is printed. Anything drawn beyond the bleed is ignored.

   • *Entire Page:* Everything drawn on the page is printed.

   • *Circumscribed Rectangle:* Anything you select with the Rectangular Marquee tool is printed. Anything beyond the selection is ignored. If you haven't selected anything, this option is unavailable.

5. **Select an option in the Color Depth of Printed Image section.**

   You really have only two choices here: You can select either the Monochrome or the RGB Color option buttons. (If you aren't familiar with the term *RGB,* I suggest doing a search on the Internet for *color theory.* You'll find much more in-depth information on the subject than I can provide in this book).

   Choosing one or the other really depends on if you have color on the page. If your work is completely black and white, you can choose either option, as the result will look the same. (Although, if you want to have any extra items in color — print guide, page number, author and title, and so on — you would want to select RGB.) On the other hand, unless you want to produce a grayscale version of your work, you need to select the RGB Color radio button for any color to be printed on the paper.

6. **Select what parts of the page you want printed in the Output Data Settings section.**

   You can select by not only layer type, but also by output attribute. This is where it's good you set your drawing layers to be either Finish or Sketch. (Flip to Chapter 6 for the details on layers.)

   You have the following options to choose from. (Keep in mind that you can select multiple options in this section.)

   - *Output Sketch Image:* Any image layers where the output attribute is set to Sketch.

   - *Output Sketch:* Any sketch layers you imported onto the page. (See Chapter 5 if you aren't sure what I mean.)

   - *Output Finished Image:* Any image layers where the output attribute is set to Finish.

   - *Output Text:* Any text layers on the page.

   - *Output Tone:* Any tone layers on the page.

   EX users can also fine-tune the Raster and Tone Settings, which are explained in further detail in the "Additional Print and Export Settings" section of the chapter.

7. **Select any additional information you'd like printed in the Page Settings section:**

   - *Output Print Guide:* The area of the print guide that delineates the bleed area and page edge is printed. This option is available only if you're planning on printing the entire page.

   - *Output Basic Frame:* The area of the print guide that designates the safe area of the page (the area that is safest from being trimmed when prepping for the final book) is printed.

   - *Output Grid:* The Grid Layer overlays the artwork when printed.

   - *Output Pagination:* If you're printing a page within a story file, the user-formatted page number is printed. (Check out Chapter 4 for more information on how to paginate your story.)

   - *Output Page Number:* If you're printing a page within a story file, the page number is printed in an area of your choosing on the paper.

   - *Output Title/Episode/Author:* If you're working from a story file and fill in the requisite information, the title, episode number, and author are printed in an area of your choosing on the paper.

8. **If you use Manga Studio EX, select any other special settings you'd like for your page in the Special Settings section:**

   - *Rotate 90 Degrees:* The paper the page is printed on is rotated 90 degrees from vertical (Portrait mode) to horizontal (Landscape mode). The artwork's orientation remains the same. (That is, it stays vertical.)

- *Page Format/Split and Print:* If you're looking to print a page that's larger than the paper available, you can choose to have the image span over more than one page (up to four pages). Simply select the Page Format check box and select the number of pages you want to use from the Split and Print drop-down list.

  If you're printing a story file, only the Split and Print drop-down list is shown.

9. **Click OK to exit.**

   If you're using Manga Studio EX, you can optionally click the Print button, which starts the printing process.

10. **When you're happy with the page settings, choose File⇨Print from the main menu.**

    This brings you back to the Printer Setup dialog box you saw back in Step 1. If you made changes to the printer setup back then, you can simply click the OK button to begin printing. If you didn't and aren't sure what are the best settings, check out the "Optimal Settings for Your Work" section, later in this chapter.

Exporting Your Work to an External File

Whether it's to send to friends or family, to post on the World Wide Web, or to colorize in Photoshop, sometimes you need to save your work in a file format that isn't Manga Studio-exclusive. Fortunately, you have that option.

Using the Export function, you can export your work to one of several common image file formats, including the Photoshop PSD file. Even more, you can choose to export by either physical size (in centimeters) and resolution or by pixel size. Each has its own advantages over the other, depending on the medium you're looking to use the image. The good news is that both methods of exporting files are practically identical to work with.

To export a page or story to a file, follow these steps:

1. **From the main menu, choose either File⇨Export⇨Export by Pixel Specification or File⇨Export⇨Export by Size Specification.**

   Both types share the same kind of dialog box (shown in Figure 13-3), so to save time and words, I'm going to combine explanations. If there are any differences between the two, I'll point them out. (Granted, there's really only one difference between them, and I bet you can guess what it is.)

Figure 13-3:
The Export
Image
dialog box
(exporting
by pixel size,
Debut
version).

2. **Enter the size of the page you want to export in the Output Image Size section.**

   This section has several text boxes that you can use to set the size of the image, either in pixels or in centimeters. Three of them (Width, Height, and Pixel Ratio to Original) are locked to each other; so, you can adjust the value of any one of them, and the other two adjust automatically.

   The only one that's independent of the others is the Resolution drop-down list. When exporting by size specification, choosing the right resolution depends on what you're planning on doing with the file. Check out the "Optimal Settings for Your Work" section, later in this chapter, to find out which resolution is best for you.

   When exporting by pixel size, the resolution you choose actually doesn't matter, as a file exported at 72 dpi is the same size as one exported at 1200 dpi. So, you can ignore the Resolution drop-down list if you want.

3. **If you're a Manga Studio EX user working off of a two-page spread, select which page (or both) you want printed.**

   If you want to print out that wild two-page battle scene you concocted, you can select the Left Page or Right Page option button to export each page separately, or you can select the Dual Page option button to export both pages together on a single page.

You should keep in mind that if you choose to export the whole spread on one page, it will be smaller, and you may need to rotate the image.

4. **Select how much of the page you want exported in the Output Area section:**

   • *Image within Print Guide*: Only the main image is exported. Anything beyond artwork from the bleed area and beyond is ignored.

   • *Include Bleed:* The image up to the edge of the bleed is exported. Anything drawn beyond the bleed is ignored.

   • *Entire Page:* Everything drawn on the page is exported.

   • *Selection Only:* Anything you select with the Rectangular Marquee tool is exported. Anything beyond the selection is ignored. If you haven't selected anything, this option is unavailable.

5. **Select an option in the Output Color Depth section.**

   You really have only two choices here: RGB Color and Monochrome. Select one or the other from their respective radio buttons.

   If you're planning on exporting the page as a JPG or PNG file for the Web, I highly suggest selecting RGB Color. This will produce much better-quality inks and screentones (or gray colors) on a smaller-sized page than if you select Monochrome.

6. **Select what parts of the page you want printed in the Output Data Settings section.**

   You can select your output settings by not only layer type, but also by output attribute. This is where it's good you set your drawing layers to be either Finish or Sketch (if you read Chapter 6, that is).

   You have the following options to choose from. (Keep in mind that you can select multiple options in this section.)

   • *Output Sketch Image:* Any image layers where the output attribute is set to Sketch.

   • *Output Sketch:* Any sketch layers you imported onto the page. (See Chapter 4 if you aren't sure what I mean.)

   • *Output Finished Image:* Any image layers where the output attribute is set to Finish.

   • *Output Text:* Any text layers on the page.

   • *Output Tone:* Any tone layers on the page.

   EX users can also fine-tune the Raster and Tone Settings, which are explained in further detail in the "Additional Print and Export Settings" section of the chapter.

7. **Select any additional information you'd like printed in the Page Settings section:**

- *Output Print Guide:* The area of the Print Guide that delineates the bleed area and page edge will be included on the exported page. This option is available only if you're planning on printing the entire page. (It is grayed out otherwise.)

- *Output Basic Frame:* The area of the print guide that designates the safe area of the page (the area that is safest from being trimmed when prepping for the final book).

- *Output Grid:* The Grid Layer overlays the artwork when exported.

- *Output Pagination:* If you're exporting a page within a story file, the user-formatted page number is exported. (Check out Chapter 4 for more information on how to paginate your story.)

- *Output Page Number:* If you're exporting a story file, the page number appears in the image.

- *Output Title/Episode/Author:* If you're working from a story file and fill in the requisite information, the title, episode number, and author appear in the image.

8. **If you're planning on saving the page as a Photoshop (PSD) file, select how you want your page saved in the Photoshop File Export Settings section:**

   - *Export Merged Layer Only:* Only layers that have been merged are exported.

   - *Use Layer Set:* If you have *nested* Image Layer folders (that is, folders that are stored within other folders), you can maintain that file structure in an exported Photoshop file. You can have as many Layer folders as you want, but Manga Studio lets you export nested folders up to only five layers deep. (Any folders nested deeper are merged into the fifth layer.)

     This feature is good only for users of Photoshop CS or later; earlier versions don't support nested folders and treat them (and image layers within them) as image layers and place them within the top-most layer folder.

9. **Click OK when you're done.**

10. **When the Save As dialog box appears, enter a name for your page in the File Name text box.**

11. **Choose the type of file you want created from the Save As Type drop-down list.**

    You can export the page as a BMP, JPG, or PSD file. (EX users can also export as a PNG or TGA file.) For more information about which file type to choose, see the "Optimal Settings for Your Work" section, later in this chapter.

12. **Click OK when done.**

Additional Print and Export Settings

You may have noticed in the earlier steps in the "Printing Your Work" and "Exporting Your Work to an External File" sections that I ignore a set of buttons on the right side of the Print Setup and Export Image dialog boxes.

You can use those buttons (or button, if you're a Debut user) to make some additional tweaks to the final display of your pages. I don't know if I would say these functions will make any *vital* adjustments to your work. However, you may find that they can add just the right touch to make your work look that much better.

Color settings

The Advanced Settings dialog box (shown in Figure 13-4) gives you the option to change the color options of your text and imported sketch images, as well as any story information and guides you want included on the page.

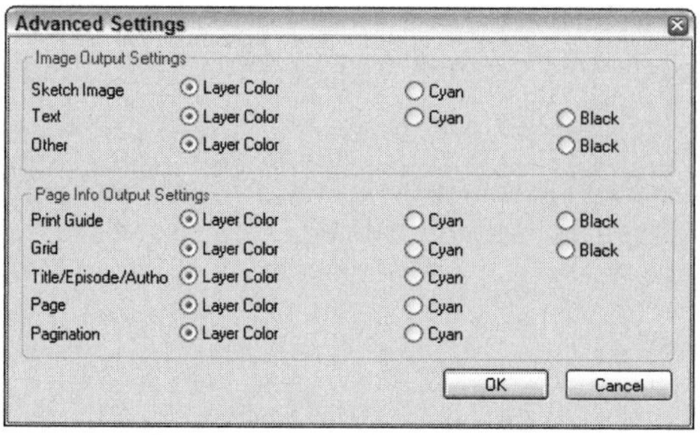

Figure 13-4:
The
Advanced
Settings
dialog box.

You have three options to choose from for each object type (though some provide only two options):

- ✔ **Layer Color:** The object type retains the original color information. If you want the exported file to look like you currently have it set on the page, this is the option to use. (This is also the Default option, so technically you don't need to make any adjustments.)

- ✔ **Cyan:** The object type is displayed in cyan. This option can be useful if you want to visually separate certain objects (such as the title and author info or the page number) from the artwork.

- ✔ **Black:** The object type is displayed in black. This option can be useful if you want to force certain objects (such as the text on the page or the print guide) to be black on the exported file.

Raster settings

A Manga Studio EX function, the Detailed Raster Settings dialog box (shown in Figure 13-5) lets you adjust how layers set to 8-bit with no color subtraction (gray layers) are printed or exported.

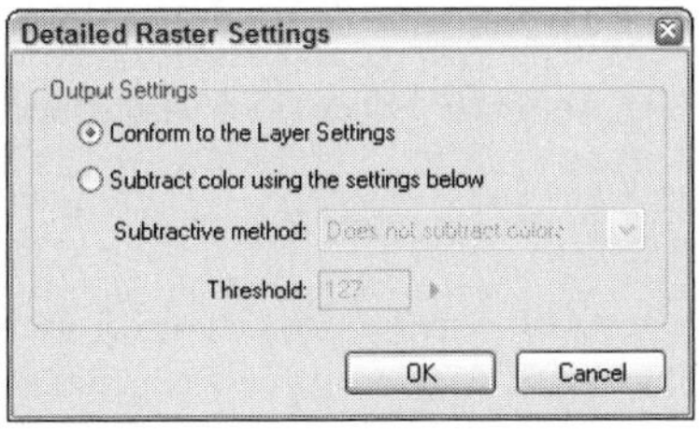

Figure 13-5:
The Detailed
Raster
Settings
dialog box.

Figure 13-5:
The Detailed
Raster
Settings
dialog box.

Detailed Raster Settings

Output Settings

◉ Conform to the Layer Settings

○ Subtract color using the settings below

Subtractive method: Does not subtract colors

Threshold: 127

OK   Cancel

There are two options to choose from in this section:

✓ **Conform to the Layer Settings:** The gray layer settings remain as they are.

✓ **Subtract Color Using the Settings Below:** This option allows you to change how gray layers are displayed in the final exported image.

• *Subtractive Method:* You can convert the display settings for the gray layers by selecting from the drop-down list. (It doesn't subtract colors, Threshold, Dither, or Convert to Tone.)

• *Threshold:* If you select the Threshold Subtractive Method, you can set the threshold level by entering a value between 0 and 255 in its numeric field.

Tone settings

A Manga Studio EX function, the Detailed Tone Settings dialog box (shown in Figure 13-6) adjusts how the tone layers display either when printed or when exported to a file.

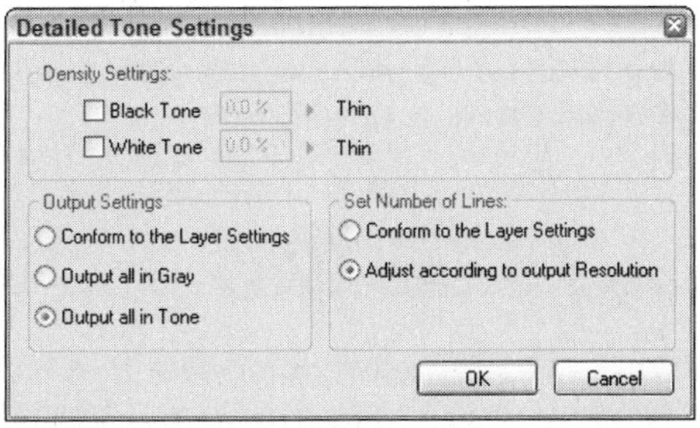

Figure 13-6:
The Detailed
Tone
Settings
dialog box.

Detailed Tone Settings

Density Settings:

☐ Black Tone 0.0 %   Thin

☐ White Tone 0.0 %   Thin

Output Settings
○ Conform to the Layer Settings
○ Output all in Gray
◉ Output all in Tone

Set Number of Lines:
○ Conform to the Layer Settings
◉ Adjust according to output Resolution

OK   Cancel

✔ **The Density Settings section adjusts the thickness of the tone dots.**

To adjust the density of either the White or Black tones you have on the page, follow these steps:

1. *Select the check box of the tone you wish to adjust (the Black Tone or the White Tone check box).*

2. *Enter a value between -20% (to increase density) and 20% (to decrease density) in its respective text box.*

✔ **The Output Settings section adjusts how the tones are displayed when printed.**

In this section, you can choose to:

- *Conform to the Layer Settings:* All tone layers remain as they are, depending on how you set them in the Layer Properties palette. (See Chapter 11.)

- *Output All in Gray:* All tone layers are displayed as gray layers, regardless of what you set in the Tone Properties.

- *Output All in Tone:* All tone layers are displayed as screen tones, regardless of what you set in the Layer Properties palette. (See Chapter 11.)

✔ **The Set Number of Lines section adjusts how the tones are printed or exported.**

You have two options to choose from in this section:

- *Conform to the Layer Settings:* The Tone Layer properties remain the same regardless of how large or small you make the page. This means that a tone layer will retain the same size and shape if it's 700 pixels wide or 3000 pixels wide.

- *Adjust According to Output Resolution:* The Tone Layers adjust relative to the size of the page being printed or exported.

Optimal Settings for Your Work

Sadly, it isn't enough to simply print or export the file and be done with it. You need to make sure that the settings you've adjusted are the right ones for the medium. Otherwise, you could end up with poor-quality pages, and that's not going to please any of your readers.

Tips for exporting for the Web

It can be tricky to get your work to look the way you want it to in a Web-compatible format. When I started using Manga Studio and tried to export for the Web, I ended up with pages that flat-out looked terrible; either the lines were too jagged or the tones weren't coming out how I wanted them. It was certainly frustrating at first to get things to look how I wanted them to.

So, to save yourself the initial headaches I went through, here are some suggestions for what I think are the best settings for creating a file for the Web:

✔ **Export your file by pixel size by choosing File⇨Export⇨Export by Pixel Specification.**

Unlike the physical world, where images are measured in centimeters or inches, on your computer monitor, images (and most everything else) are measured in *pixels* (dots on the screen). So, to avoid confusion about what size and resolution you want for the computer screen, work with the units of measurement that matter digitally.

✔ **Keep the file size as small as possible.**

While the percentage of people using broadband Internet connections is growing, there are still a good number of users in the United States that don't have broadband Internet connections. So, you're not going to win any fans from the dialup camp if you create a file that's more than 500K in size.

Manga Studio does a pretty good job optimizing the exported file. Still, you should be mindful of the file size and be prepared to reduce the physical size of the page (while still maintaining quality and legibility, of course) to reduce the number a bit.

✔ **Save your exported file as a JPG file.**

Web browsers these days can read only a handful of image types. You can export your work to two of those types: BMP and JPG (and PNG if you own Manga Studio EX).

✔ **Save your exported file in RGB color.**

When you're working on a file that's full size and is eventually going to be put in a book (either by yourself or a printing company), you want to use monochrome, as it produces the sharpest lines and tones possible. However, when you're exporting a file to be shown on the Web (which needs to be shrunk down from its original size), exporting in monochrome actually hurts the quality of the line, which you can see in Figure 13-7 on the left.

What exporting the file as an RGB file does is add some anti-aliasing to the lines and tones (adding shades of gray to soften them slightly), which helps the artwork shrink down to Web size while basically maintaining the same quality as the full-size image (which you can see in Figure 13-7 on the right).

Figure 13-7:
The
difference
between
RGB color
(left) and
Monochrome
(right) can be
pretty drastic
when
exporting for
the Web.

✔ **Avoid making a page larger than the monitor's width.**

This is a tricky one, as most people have their monitors set up differently.

The average user's display resolution is 1024 pixels by 768 pixels (1024 x 768), although some people still prefer to use 800 x 600. The point is, you really don't have a clue who's reading your comic at what resolution, so, you should prepare your page for the lowest resolution.

What you consider the lowest resolution is up to you. For example, some have sworn off 800 x 600 entirely and have set 1024 x 768 as the lowest resolution to read their webcomic. Whatever you decide to be the lowest resolution, the thing that you have to make absolutely sure is that the page you create fits within that resolution's width (and also the dimensions of the web page design, should you decide to include navigation and/or advertisements along the sides of the page). Unless the page is designed to read that way, you don't want the reader to scroll horizontally. It's just going to irritate them if they have to scroll along two axes to read your page.

Personally, I suggest having an image no larger than 650-700 pixels, as it's a good compromise of page dimensions on the screen, as well as the size of the file itself (which means it will load faster on the Web site for the reader).

Tips for printing (locally or professionally)

I think when you either print your own comics or have them done profession-ally, you want any judgments on your work to be based on your own artistic merits, not on a technical glitch or bad print job. I've flipped through many books from small press and self-publishers over the years, and more than a few times I've been taken out of the story because they produced some extremely shoddy prints of their art work.

Taking your reader out of the experience is, *I* think, the kiss of death for any repeat patronage. While it's extremely important to have a gripping story, you need to keep in mind that comics and manga are a visual medium. So, you need to make sure that the pages you print or have printed for you are as professional-looking as possible.

The good news is that Manga Studio tries to make creating the best-quality prints and images you can get as foolproof as possible. That said, things can still get messed up if you don't have the correct settings. So, the following two lists provide tips that I think are helpful, along with suggestions to ensure that your work is accurately represented, whether you print the pages on your own desktop printer or use a professional printing service.

Getting the best prints with your desktop printer

If you're printing your pages on a desktop printer (such as an inkjet or laser printer), keep these tips in mind:

✔ **When you first create your new page or story file, make sure the resolution is at a minimum of 300 dpi.**

Optimally, the higher the resolution, the smoother and crisper the line work is on the page. But not everyone has a fast enough system to work at 1200 dpi. So, you should try to work at a minimum of 300 dpi, as it's the lowest resolution to work at before the quality of your line work begins to take a hit.

✔ **Keep in mind the size of the book you want to create.**

It isn't going to do you much good if you're creating a book that's going to be larger than the 8.5-x-11-inch standard printing paper you have available. You may need to go to your local print shop if you're looking to create a large-format comic.

✔ **When printing, set the highest ink quality for your printer (and use black ink only if you're printing a black-and-white manga).**

✔ **If your comic is black and white, save or print your file in monochrome.**

✔ **When printing, match your printer's resolution to the page resolution.**

This helps to keep things consistent between your page and the printer.

Getting the best results from a professional printing service

If you're exporting files to send them to a professional printing service (local or out-of-town) to be printed, keep these tips in mind:

✔ **Don't be afraid to shop around and ask questions.**

If you have only one print shop in town, your choices are going to be more limited than those who have a couple shops to select from. Still, it never hurts to find out more information on the print shop (or shops) you're considering using to print your comic.

Try to talk to them over the phone or pay them a visit in person. This way, you can get a good grasp on their process, what they can or can't do, and what you'll need to provide to make the process easier for both you and them (aside from the pages themselves). Plus, you can find out better which shop will best fit what you need or want.

Above all else, don't be afraid to ask questions. If this is the first time you've ever done this and you aren't sure exactly what to do, they may be able to provide suggestions you never thought of before. It may save you a lot of time, headache, and money in the long run.

✔ **Find out the print shop's requirements for file specifications and adjust your export settings to match.**

To make sure that you and your printer are on the same page (no pun intended), it's good to find out exactly what requirements the printer has for your work to look its best. This may include the minimum requirements for file resolution (at least 300 dpi, for example) or how large they'd like the bleed area to be. (See Chapter 1 if you don't know what the bleed area of the page is.)

✔ **When sending files out to be professionally printed, make sure you save the *entire* page (including print guide) in the file.**

The print shop needs to know what areas of your pages are important and what they can trim from the final product. So, printing the print guide along with your artwork helps them avoid accidentally cutting off a vital part of the page.

If you've drawn outside of the safe area of your page, you want to make sure that the Basic Frame is deselected from the Print or Export Setup dialog boxes, unless you want that printed in the middle of your page.

Part IV
Advanced Tips and Tricks

The 5th Wave   By Rich Tennant

"I'm going to assume that most of you – but not all of you – understand that this session on 'masking' has to do with Manga Studio."

In this part . . .

If you've already looked through the first three parts of this book, you have a pretty good grasp of what you can do with Manga Studio. Or do you?

This part is all about the more advanced tips, tricks, and functions in Manga Studio, with a heavy emphasis on the EX version of the program.

Chapter 14 covers advanced features of both Manga Studio Debut and EX, while Chapter 15 focuses on the many exclusive EX tools that help make things just that much easier for you.

This part shows you what you can *really* do with Manga Studio!

Chapter 14

General Tips, Tricks, and Shortcuts

*I*f you're reading this chapter, odds are you've either worked through all the basics covered earlier this book and you're looking to see what else you can do with Manga Studio. If that's the case, you're gong to be pleased, as I really only scratched the surface of what you can do with the program in Chapters 1–13.

For users of both Manga Studio Debut and EX, this is a good chapter to start learning some of the more advanced functions and tricks of the program, as it covers everything that both programs can do. Granted, EX users have even more functions to learn than Debut, and I cover those in the next chapter. But, everyone has to start *somewhere*.

System Preferences Tips

Here's some good news for those that like to tweak program settings: You aren't married to the default system preferences of Manga Studio. You can adjust parts of the program to best suit your needs. These can range from changing the computer's memory allocation to the system to changing the color of your rulers. All of this is located in the Preferences dialog box, accessible from the main menu by choosing File⇨Preferences.

It would take way too many pages to cover every single option in the Preferences dialog box, so instead I go over some of what I think are the important performance and comfort tweaks you can set to help make your experience with Manga Studio just that much more enjoyable.

Increasing the display quality

By default, Manga Studio has the page display set at a standard quality. However, if you have a strong enough system (and really, you'd need a pretty weak system for this not to work well), you can increase the display quality a bit so that lines don't look quite as jagged as you rotate a page.

On the Page tab of the Preferences dialog box, shown in Figure 14-1, the first option you see is the Display Quality drop-down list. When you click the list, you see three options (Standard, High, and Maximum). Try each of them out and see how your system likes the adjustments.

You don't see any major difference in quality when the page is in its normal (zero-degree) position. The only time you see any difference is when you use the Rotate tool to turn the page as you work. As you can see in Figure 14-2, the differences are slight, but you might find it more comfortable to work at High or Maximum quality than at Standard.

Figure 14-1:
Check out the Page menu in the system Preferences to change the display quality.

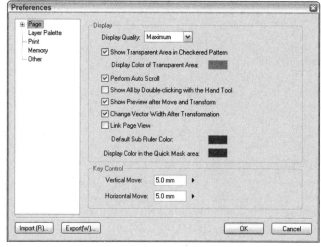

Figure 14-2:
Use the
Rotate tool
to best see
differences
in display
quality.

Rotated page at
standard quality

Rotated page at
maximum quality

Changing the Drawing tool's cursor

If you aren't happy with the default cursors for your drawing tools, don't use
them! Manga Studio provides several different cursors that you can use in
place of what the Pen, Pencil, Marker, Eraser, Airbrush, and Pattern Brush
tools offer initially.

Follow these steps to change the cursors:

1. **Choose File⇨Preferences; in the Preferences dialog box, click the +
   to expand the Page tree on the left and select Cursor (as shown in
   Figure 14-3).**

2. **From the Tool drop-down list, select the drawing tool you wish to
   change.**

3. **From the Select Cursor drop-down list, select the cursor you wish to
   use in place of the default one.**

   You can see the cursor options available to you in Figure 14-4.

4. **Repeat as necessary for the other tools in the list.**

5. **Click OK when you're done.**

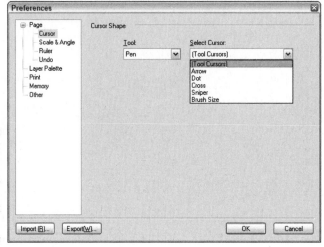

Figure 14-3:
Use the
Cursor tab
to change
the default
cursors.

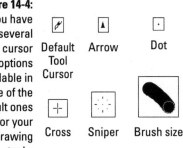

Figure 14-4:
You have
several
cursor
options
available in
place of the
default ones
for your
drawing
tools.

Default Tool Cursor   Arrow   Dot

Cross   Sniper   Brush size

Maximizing your undos

I do say earlier in the book to be careful to not become too dependent on the Undo function, as it can result in you tweaking your page more than is probably necessary. That said, it never hurts to maximize the number of undos available, just in case.

To change the number of undos, follow these steps:

1. **Choose File⇨Preferences; in the Preferences dialog box, click the + to expand the Page menu tree and select the Undo menu.**

2. **Enter a value between 1 and 20 in the Undo Levels text box.**

   If you're looking to maximize the number of undos, enter **20**.

3. **Click OK when you're done.**

Changing your default layer settings

If you find yourself constantly changing the settings of any new layers you create, it's safe to say you aren't too happy with the default settings. Changing those settings is easy to do in Manga Studio.

To change the default layer settings, follow these steps:

1. **Choose File⇨Preferences; in the Preferences dialog box, select Layer palette on the left. (See Figure 14-5.)**

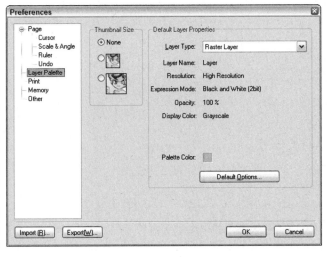

Figure 14-5: You can change the default layer settings from the Layer palette menu.

2. **If you want to simply change the layer type, select a new layer type from its respective drop-down list.**

3. **To change all of the default layer settings, click the Default Options button.**

   The Layer Properties dialog box appears, as shown in Figure 14-6.

4. **(Optional) Enter a name for the layer in the Layer Name text box.**

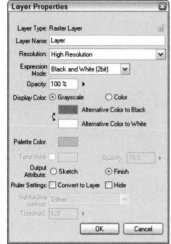

Figure 14-6:
The default
Layer
Properties
dialog box.

5. **From the Resolution drop-down list, select the resolution you wish the default layer to use.**

   You have four options in this list:

   • *Low Resolution (150 dpi)*

   • *Medium Resolution (300 dpi)*

   • *High Resolution (600 dpi)*

   • *Maximum Resolution (the page file's resolution up to 1200 dpi)*

6. **From the Expression Mode drop-down list, select the expression mode of the layer (1bit, 2bit, or 8bit).**

   Check out Chapter 6 for an explanation of the various expression modes.

7. **Adjust the opacity of the layer by entering a value between 0% and 100% in the Opacity text box.**

8. **From the Display Color radio buttons, choose whether you want to display the layer in grayscale or color by selecting one option.**

9. **If you choose to display in color, select your foreground and background colors by clicking the Alternative Color to Black/White color boxes and picking the new color from the Color Settings dialog box.**

10. **Click the Palette Color box and select the color the layer will appear in the Layers palette from the Color Settings dialog box.**

11. **From the Output Attribute radio buttons, select whether the layer will be a Sketch or Finish layer.**

12. **Set whether the layer-specific rulers are created on the image layer or on its own by selecting the Convert to Layer check box.**

13. **Set whether you want the rulers visible by selecting the Hide check box.**

14. **If you chose an 8-bit expression mode, select the subtractive method (Does Not Subtract, Threshold, Dither, or Convert to Tone) from the Subtractive Method dialog box.**

    Check out Chapter 6 for more info on subtractive methods.

15. **If you chose the Threshold subtractive method, set its threshold by entering a value between 0 and 255 in the Threshold text box.**

16. **Click OK when you're done.**

Drawing Tool Tips

Whenever I talk about the drawing tool settings in this book, I mention that you should check out the advanced tips chapter, as I go over the additional settings you can use to tweak things further. Well, here we are!

Adjusting the brush settings

The default brushes work just fine as is. But there's the possibility that they don't feel "right" to you. Maybe you'd like to increase the pressure sensitivity of the Thin Pencil tool or remove the tapering from the brush Pen tool?

Well, there's nothing stopping you from customizing these tools to better suit your style of working. After all, you're going to be using them to create your next great masterpiece, so why not make them comfortable to use? The good news is that it's quite easy to adjust the settings of your drawing tools.

Follow these steps to adjust your brush settings:

1. **Select the drawing tool you want to change (Pen, Pencil, Marker, Eraser, Airbrush, or Pattern Brush).**

2. **Open the Tool Options palette. (Press F3 on your keyboard.)**

3. **Click the Show Menu button and select Advanced Settings Mode.**

    The advanced options vary, depending on the drawing tool you're adjusting. The [Pencil] Tool Options palette is shown in Figure 14-7.

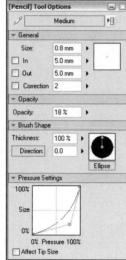

Figure 14-7:
The Pencil
Drawing
tool options
in Advanced
Mode.

Depending on the tool you're adjusting, you see some, if not all, of the following options:

- *Thickness:* Entering a value between 0% and 100% in the text box adjusts the roundness of the brush.

- *Direction:* If you've adjusted its roundness, you can change the angle the brush sits at by entering a value between 0 and 360 degrees in this text box.

- *Pressure Settings:* If you think this option looks a lot like a graph, you're right. The curve you see sets the size of the line drawn relative to the pressure sensitivity of your drawing tablet. This allows you to adjust how much pressure you need to place on your tablet. The lower you set the curve, the more pressure you need to exert, and vice versa. (Compare settings between the Magic Marker and the G Pen, for example; try each of them out on the canvas to see and feel the difference.)

- *Affect Tip Size:* You can set whether the line drawn with the tool is affected by the pressure settings graph. When selected, the size of the brush adjusts according to the amount of pressure you place on the tablet. When deselected, the line width remains constant. If you're using the Pencil Tool, only the opacity is affected by the pen pressure.

Tweaking the Pattern Brush tool's advanced options

The Pattern Brush has a completely different set of advanced options, as shown in Figure 14-8, than the other drawing tools. As I mention in Chapter 10, it would almost take forever to go over the available options for each type of Pattern Brush, so I list all of the options you see on the palette. Keep in mind that not all of the options are available, depending on the type of Pattern Brush you're adjusting — options you can't use will be grayed out.

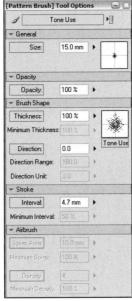

Figure 14-8: The Pattern Brush advanced options. There's a lot to choose from.

To adjust the Pattern Brush tools advanced options, follow these steps:

1. **Select the Pattern Brush tool on the Tools palette.**

2. **Open the Tool Options palette by pressing F3.**

3. **Click the Show Menu button and select Advanced Settings Mode.**

   The [Pattern Brush] Tool Options palette offers the following advanced settings:

   - *Thickness:* Entering a value between 0% and 100% in the text box adjusts the roundness of the pattern.

- *Direction:* If you've changed the pattern's Thickness, you can change the angle the pattern sits at by entering a value between 0 and 360 degrees.

- *Direction Range:* If you want the pattern to rotate depending on the angle of your stylus, you can set the rotation angle by entering a value between 0 and 180 degrees. This option is available if you set the Brush Control for Direction to anything but None. (I explain this in the "Brush control" section of this chapter.)

- *Direction Unit:* If the pattern rotates as you draw, you can set the rotation interval by entering a value between 0.1 and 90 degrees. This option is available if you set the Brush Control for Direction to anything but None. (I explain this in the "Brush control" section of this chapter.)

- *Spray Area:* If the Pattern Brush is airbrush-based, you can set the size of the spray area by entering a value between 1.0 mm and 100 mm.

- *Minimum Spray:* If the airbrush-based pattern is pressure sensitive, entering a value between 1% and 100% sets the minimum amount of spray when you lightly draw on the canvas. This option is available if you set the Brush Control for Spray Area to anything but None. (I explain this in the "Brush control" section of this chapter.)

- *Density:* This sets the density of the airbrush-based pattern. You can enter a value between 1 and 16 in its text box.

- *Minimum Density:* If the airbrush-based pattern is pressure sensitive, you can enter a value between 1% and 100% to set the minimum amount of density as you lightly draw on the canvas. This option is available if you set the Brush Control for Density to anything but None. (I explain this in the "Brush control" section of this chapter.)

Brush control

The Size, Opacity, Thickness, Direction, Interval, Spray Area, and Density of the pattern brush can be adjusted even further if you want to. If you look closely at the titles of these options, they're actually buttons you can click with your mouse or stylus. Clicking any of them brings up the Brush Control dialog box. You can switch between any of the options by clicking on their respective tab.

The controls you can set vary, depending on the option you're adjusting. So I compiled a list covering the various controls you can adjust the option with:

✔ **None:** The option is left unchanged.

✔ **Stroke Speed:** The option is affected by how fast or slow you draw a line.

✔ **Pressure:** The option is affected by the amount of pressure placed on the tablet by the stylus. This works only with tablets that support pen pressure. The pressure can be further tweaked by adjusting the Fixed settings graph, located to the right of the Select Control list.

✔ **Tilt:** The option is affected by the way the stylus is tilted on the drawing tablet. The tilt can be further tweaked by adjusting the Fixed settings graph, located to the right of the Select Control list. This control works only with tablets that support pen tilt.

✔ **Orientation:** The option is affected by the orientation of the pen on the tablet. This works only with tablets that support pen orientation.

✔ **Rotation:** The option is affected by the rotation of the stylus on the drawing tablet. This works only with tablets that support pen rotation.

✔ **Stroke Direction:** The option is affected by the direction you draw.

✔ **Random:** The option is altered randomly. If you're working with a mouse or a tablet that doesn't support the above options, you can always select this to try and simulate a tablet that can support them.

Creating a custom brush

If you want to keep the default brushes as they are, but you'd still like to have a few custom ones to work with, you can easily create new brushes.

Follow these steps to create a custom brush:

1. **From the Tools palette, click the drawing tool you'd like to create a new brush from.**

   For example, you may want to select the Pen or Magic Marker tool.

2. **Open the Tool Options palette (F3 on your keyboard).**

3. **Click the Show Menu button and select New Tool Option Settings.**

4. **When the New Tool Option Settings dialog box appears, enter a name for your new brush in the Name text box.**

5. **Optionally, if you want to use a custom icon for your new brush, click the Browse button and navigate to the icon file.**

   Keep in mind that the icon has to be either a bitmap (BMP) or jpeg (JPG) file and should be kept to a reasonable size.

6. **Click OK when you're done.**

Now that you've created your new brush, you can do whatever you want! Feel free to adjust the opacity, thickness, pressure settings, any of the options I cover in the "Adjusting the brush settings" section earlier in the chapter. Now you can tweak the settings however you'd like while maintaining the default settings of your other brushes.

Tone Tips

In Chapter 11, I go over the basics of using tones in Manga Studio; namely, how to add, remove, and create simple effects like shadows and highlights. This section delves a little bit deeper, with three tips — one that can help you produce more authentic effects, one that gives you the chance to create a tone that you can truly call your own, and one that provides a quick means of keeping track of all those thousands of tones that the program provides.

Etching with drawing tools

When used with the Transparent Ink color, you can use the main drawing tools of the program to etch away the unwanted sections of tones and create effects you can't do with the Eraser.

- ✓ **Pencil tool:** If you're looking to create an effect similar to rubbing away tones with a block or pencil eraser, try using the Pencil tool. Unlike the Eraser tool, which gives you a complete hard-edged erasure, the Pencil tool can give you something that's softer and a more subtle. This can be useful if you want to add highlights to a shiny yet soft material, like leather, as shown in Figure 14-9.

  Something to keep in mind when you're rubbing tone away with the pencil tool: you can really see the subtleties in the pencil rubbing only when you're zoomed in closely. When you zoom out, the rubbing looks like it's solid white. Don't worry — that's not how it'll look in the final exported/printed product. My suggestion if you want to use this tip is to work while zoomed in pretty close to the page (at least around 66.7% or so).

- ✓ **Pen tool:** The Pen tool, depending on the type you use, can give you more control over how much you etch away. Depending on your pen settings, you can quickly and easily adjust the size of the erasure by how hard or soft you press down on your drawing tablet. The pen tool can also be useful when you want to create a pointillism effect on the tone by erasing a single dot at time. See Figure 14-10.

- ✓ **Airbrush tool:** To create a spattering or fading effect on a tone, use the airbrush tool. Simply go over the tone area as if you were airbrushing on an ink layer to create a more subtle transition between the tone and canvas, as shown in Figure 14-11.

Figure 14-9:
The pencil
tool can
create
a softer
removal of
tone from
the page.

Figure 14-10:
The Pen tool
can give you
more control
over the
way you
erase the
tone.

Figure 14-11:
The airbrush
tool can
help create
a soft
transition
between the
tone and
page.

Creating your own tone

There's always the possibility that none of the tone patterns that Manga Studio has are what you want. You may be looking for something a bit more unique — something that you can call your own.

So, make your *own* pattern! It's easy to do in Manga Studio; any drawing or picture will work. Simply choose the pattern you wish to create and add it to the program as your own custom tone. Then, you can use and reuse it as often as you like!

To create your own pattern tone from a drawing, follow these steps:

1. **Draw the pattern you'd like to create on the page.**

2. **From the Tools palette, select the Rectangular Marquee tool.**

3. **Click and drag a selection around the drawing. Be sure to include any buffer space between drawings for the pattern.**

4. **From the main menu, choose Edit⇨Save Pattern as Tone.**

   The New Pattern Tone dialog box appears.

5. **Enter a Name for your new pattern in the Name text box.**

   If this is the first time you're creating a new pattern, you need to have a folder to put the new tone pattern in before you can save it. The User folder in the Tones palette already contains one folder (called My Tone) that you can use to place your new tone patterns in. Simply click the User folder in the folder tree and then click on the My Tone folder.

   If you're looking to separate your tones into different sets, creating more folders may prove to be useful.

6. **Click the New Folder button to create a new folder for your tone pattern.**

   The New Tone Folder dialog box appears.

7. **Enter a name for the folder in the Name text box and select an icon from the Icon list. Click OK when you're done.**

8. **Select the new folder from the list in the New Pattern Tone dialog box and Click OK.**

Using the Materials Catalog for quick reference!

Manga Studio comes preinstalled with thousands of tones and patterns to use. (That number is even larger if you own Manga Studio EX.) So, it can be a bit daunting to find the right type of tone for your work. Fortunately, the hunting process is easier than you may think.

The Materials Catalog that comes with the program in electronic form contains every single tone and pattern type available to Manga Studio Debut and EX users. It also covers all the default and EX-exclusive Computones, as well as all of the 2DLT and 3DLT materials that EX users can work with. (I go over 2DLT and 3DLT in Bonus Chapter 2 on the CD.)

To access the Materials Catalog, simply choose Help⇨Materials Catalog from the main menu. The catalog is in PDF format, so make sure you have a PDF reader installed (such as Adobe Acrobat Reader or Foxit Reader).

Layer Tips: Coloring Your Work

In Chapter 1, I say that one of the things that Manga Studio doesn't do easily is color work. Note that I don't say it's *impossible* to do; it's just not *easy*. Actually, coloring your work in Manga Studio can be a fun little exercise to practice. It certainly proves to be a useful trick to know if you really want to add color to your page but don't have access to a program better suited to digital coloring, such as Photoshop. Just expect to have *many, many* layers if you're planning on using lots of different colors, because each color has to be on its own layer.

If you're looking for an alternative to working in black and white, it's a nice alternative to work with color layers. How in-depth you'd like to go with colors on your page (and, subsequently, how many layers you're willing to work with) is up to you.

While it'll look best at the final (inked) stage of your work, you can add your color layers at any time of your creative process. If you're still roughing things out, you may find it to be a good time to test out what colors will work.

To add some color to your page, follow these steps:

1. **From the main menu, choose Layer⇨New Layer.**

   The New Layer dialog box appears.

2. **Enter an easily identifiable name in the Layer Name text box.**

   The default layer type (raster) and resolution (high) will work just fine, so leave those as they are.

3. **Select the type of Expression Mode you want for the layer from its respective drop-down list.**

The expression mode you choose is a matter of personal preference, as all of the layers will work in color. Personally, I like to use a Gray (8bit) layer with the "Does Not Subtract Colors" Subtractive Method, as it produces solid colors without any dithering.

4. **Click OK.**

5. **Open the Layer Properties palette (F7 on your keyboard).**

6. **Click the Color radio button.**

7. **Click the Alternative Color to Black color box. (On an 8-bit layer, it says Alternative Color to Gray.)**

   The Color Settings dialog box appears.

8. **Select the color you want to work with and click OK.**

9. **From the Tools palette, select a drawing tool (Pen, Marker, Fill, and so on).**

10. **Start drawing in the color on the canvas.**

11. **Repeat Steps 1–11 for each additional color you want to include.**

If you are on a black-and-white (2-bit) layer and want to cut down on the number of potential color layers, use the background color as well as the foreground color. Click the Alternative Color to White color box and pick your secondary color. Then, just switch between the foreground and background colors as you work.

For a quick way to add shadows and highlights, create a simple black-and-white image layer. Then, adjust the opacity from the Layer Properties palette until the blacks and whites are at the level of transparency you want to work at.

If you want to stick with screentones in your work, there's nothing stopping you from coloring them. Simply select the Color radio button on the Layer Properties palette of the tone you want to colorize and click the Tone Color box to select the color you want. It's a cool way to add a pop-art or old-school-color newsprint look to your work!

Using Filters

There are times when I'm glad I use a computer program to create art — especially when I get to use shortcuts to quickly complete what would normally be a mundane and monotonous task. With Manga Studio, you can take advantage of three filters (focus lines, speed lines, and vanishing point rulers) to quickly generate special effects or drawing aids to help speed the process along just that much more.

Adding focus lines

Focus lines are a staple of manga that help to create the trademark look of the genre. It's a simple effect that you can use in a variety of ways, including expressing motion towards the reader, focusing attention towards an item or person, or (when created with reverse colors) creating effects, such as starbursts. Check out Figure 14-12 for some examples of focus lines in action.

Figure 14-12: You can use the Focus Lines filter in a variety of ways.

To use the Focus Lines filter, follow these steps:

1. **From the Main menu, choose Layer⇨New Layer.**

   You're placing the focus lines on this layer. (It helps the other line art remain untouched.)

2. **In the New Layer dialog box, enter a name in the Name text box that will help you easily identify it and select the highest-resolution raster layer relative to your page's resolution.**

   Check out Chapter 4 for a more in-depth explanation on how to create a new image layer.

3. **From the Tools palette, select the Rectangular Marquee tool.**

4. **Using your mouse or stylus, click and drag a selection over the panel you'd like to add speed lines to.**

5. **Open the Focus Lines dialog box by choosing the appropriate commands from the main menu:**

   • *Debut version:* Filter⇨Focus Lines

   • *EX version:* Filter⇨Render⇨Focus Lines

   The Focus Lines dialog box appears.

6. **From the Preview drop-down list, select the quality (High, Mid, or Low) you'd like to preview the focus lines on the page.**

   For Steps 7-12, you have the additional option to randomize the values set. This allows you to add a bit more variety to the lines (the spacing between lines could become more erratic, for example) — leaving the values as they are produces a simple, uniform look to the lines. For each of these values, select the Random check box for the corresponding value and enter a value between 0.0 (no randomization) and 4.0 (heavy randomization) in its respective text box.

7. **In the Length text box, enter a value between 1 mm and 600 mm to adjust the length of the focus lines.**

8. **In the Width text box, enter a value between 0 mm and 10 mm to adjust the width of the focus lines.**

9. **In the Angle text box, enter a value between 0.5 and 50.0 degrees to adjust the angle at which the focus lines are drawn.**

10. **In the Curve text box, enter a value between -100% and 100% (the default value is set to 0) to adjust the curve of the focus lines.**

11. **In the Shift text box, enter a value between 0 mm and 300 mm to adjust the starting points of the focus lines.**

12. **In the Distance text box, enter a value between 0 mm and 150 mm to set the gap between lines.**

13. **To set the distance of the focus lines from the focal point, select the Distance check box and enter a value between 0 mm and 150 mm in its respective text box.**

14. **To taper either the inside points or outside points (or both) of the focus lines, select the Inside and/or Outside check boxes.**

15. **From the Drawing/Background Color drop-down list, select the color of the focus lines.**

    You have the following options in the list:

    • *Black*

- *White*
- *Transparent*
- *Transparent on a Black Background*
- *Transparent on a White Background*

16. **Select the Clear Layer check box if you want to delete everything on the current layer, replacing it with the speed lines.**

    This is useful if you happen to rough out how you'd like the speed lines to look, for example.

17. **Select the Perform Oversampling check box to minimize the aliasing (jagged edges) on the speed lines.**

    This option adds a slight dithering effect to the speed lines. This doesn't perform a true anti-aliasing effect that you see in Photoshop.

18. **Click OK to add the focus lines to your new layer.**

If you aren't happy with how the lines are initially generated in the preview, click the Generate button (located below the Preview Quality drop-down list) to create a new set of speed lines.

You can quickly adjust the position of the focus lines using the Positioning tools (see Figure 14-13), located at the top of the Focus Lines dialog box.

Figure 14-13:
The
Positioning
tools.

- ✔ **The Grab tool**, much like the one on the Tools palette, allows you to quickly adjust the position of the canvas on the screen.
- ✔ **The Move tool** sets the focal point on the page. As you move the focal point, the Focus lines pointing to it adjust accordingly.
- ✔ **The Draw Position Move tool** allows you to draw where you want the focus lines to end. (Check out Figure 14-14 for an example.)
- ✔ **The Draw Position Transform tool** allows you to alter the read area you adjusted with the Draw position Move tool by rotating and resizing it as need be. The general shape of the area is unaffected by this tool.

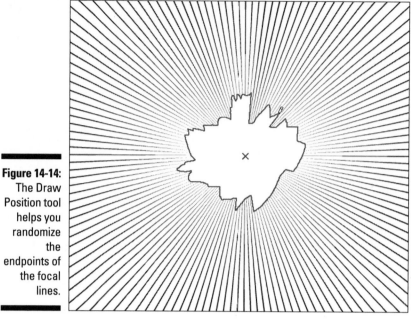

Figure 14-14:
The Draw
Position tool
helps you
randomize
the
endpoints of
the focal
lines.

Creating speed lines

Probably one of the most identifiable effects in Manga is the use of speed lines to express motion on a static page. Take a look at Figure 14-15 and tell me which of the two images feels more kinetic and dynamic.

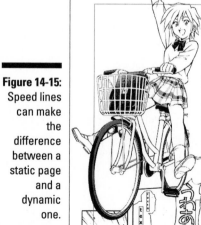

Figure 14-15:
Speed lines
can make
the
difference
between a
static page
and a
dynamic
one.

Artwork courtesy of e frontier.

The Speed Lines filter in Manga Studio helps you to create as many or as few lines as you need for a panel or page. You can create them as simple and uniform or wild and random, all with a few changes to the filter's options.

Follow these steps to use the Speed Lines filter:

1. **From the Main menu, choose Layer⇨New Layer.**

   This is the layer your speed lines will be placed on.

2. **In the New Layer dialog box, type a name in the Name text box and select the highest-resolution raster layer relative to your page's resolution.**

   (Check out Chapter 4 for a more in-depth explanation on how to create a new image layer.)

3. **From the Tools palette, select the Rectangular Marquee tool.**

4. **Using your mouse or stylus, click and drag a selection over the panel you'd like to add speed lines to.**

5. **Open the Layer Properties dialog box by choosing the appropriate commands from the main menu.**

   - *Debut version:* Filter⇨Speed Lines
   - *EX version:* Filter⇨Render⇨Speed Lines

   The Layer Properties dialog box appears with the Speed Lines tab selected, as shown in Figure 14-16.

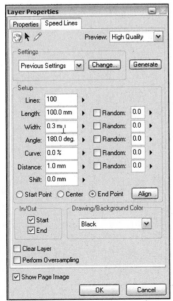

Figure 14-16: The Speed Lines tab of the Layer Properties dialog box.

6. **From the Preview drop-down list, select the quality (High Quality, Mid Quality, or Low Quality) you'd like to preview the speed lines on the page.**

7. **In the Lines text box, set the number of speed lines generated by entering a value between 1 and 300.**

   To keep things from looking *too* uniform, Manga Studio provides the option to randomize the values of the next group of options (Steps 7-11 on this list). If you want to change things up a bit, select the Random check box for the corresponding value and enter a value between 0.0 and 4.0 in its text box.

8. **In the Length text box, enter a value between 1 mm and 600 mm to adjust the length of the speed lines.**

9. **In the Width text box, enter a value between 0 mm and 10 mm to adjust the width of the speed lines.**

10. **In the Angle text box, enter a value between 0 and 359.9 degrees to adjust the angle at which the speed lines are drawn.**

11. **In the Curve text box, enter a value between -100% and 100% (the default value is set to 0) to adjust the curve of the speed lines.**

12. **In the Distance text box, enter a value between 0 mm and 50 mm to set the gap between lines.**

13. **In the Shift text box, enter a value between 0 mm and 150 mm to randomly adjust the starting points of the speed lines.**

14. **Select either the Start Point, Center, or End Point radio button to adjust the alignment of the speed lines and click the Align button to reset the lines.**

15. **Select the Start and/or End check box(es) to taper either the start points or end points (or both) of the speed lines.**

16. **From the Drawing/Background Color drop-down list, select the color of the speed lines.**

   These are the options you have for a drawing color:

   - Black
   - White
   - Transparent
   - Transparent on a Black Background
   - Transparent on a White Background

17. **Select the Clear Layer check box if you want to delete everything on the current layer, replacing it with the speed lines.**

   This is useful if you happen to rough out how you'd like the speed lines to look, for example.

18. **Select the Perform Oversampling check box to minimize the aliasing (jagged edges) on the speed lines.**

This option adds a slight dithering effect to the speed lines. This doesn't perform a true anti-aliasing effect that you would see in Photoshop.

19. Click OK to add the speed lines to your new layer.

If you aren't happy with how the lines are initially generated in the preview, click the Generate button (located below the Preview Quality drop-down list) to create a new set of speed lines.

You can quickly set and adjust the position of the speed lines using the Move tools (see Figure 14-17), located at the top of the Speed Lines dialog box.

✔ **The Grab tool**, much like the one on the Tools palette, allows you to quickly adjust the position of the canvas on the screen.

✔ **The Move tool** sets the focal point on the page. In this case, the focal point is the center-most speed line. So, moving the focal point sets where you want the middle of the line set to lay.

✔ **The Draw Position tool** allows you to draw where you want the speed lines to rest (depending on the alignment option — Start Point, Center, or End Point — you selected). (Check out Figure 14-18 for an example.)

Figure 14-17:
The Move
tools.

Figure 14-18:
The Draw
Position tool
helps you
quickly set
where the
speed lines
end.

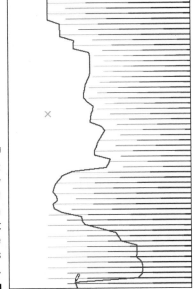

Inserting vanishing points

For those unfamiliar with the concept of perspective lines, the short definition is it's a means to create three-dimensional objects easily and accurately. I could go into great detail about the various types of perspective lines you can create, but you can find many wonderful books on drawing that explain the technique *far* better than I can in this book. Be sure to check out Chapter 16 for one of my personal favorite books on drawing comics.

If you've done work with perspective lines before, you know that setting up the perspective grid can be tedious, especially when you're making sure that each line matches up with the vanishing points correctly. Even worse, if a vanishing point is well off the page, it becomes that much more difficult to match up the line.

What the Vanishing Points filter does is take the tedious part out of the equation. All you need to do is place the vanishing points on the image layer, and the filter draws in all the perspective lines for you. Placement isn't even limited to the page — you can place vanishing points anywhere on or off the canvas, giving you more freedom to quickly generate the lines you need to make sure your work looks as accurate as possible in three-dimensional space.

To use the Vanishing Points filter, follow these steps:

1. **From the main menu, choose Layer⇨New Layer.**

   To keep the Vanishing points separate from your artwork, it's a good idea to keep the perspective lines on a separate layer. It beats having to erase the lines later on.

2. **On the New Layer dialog box, enter an easily identifiable name in the Name text box and select the Sketch Output Attribute.**

   The other default options for the layer will work just fine.

3. **Click OK.**

   Unlike when you use the Focus or Speed Line filters, the Vanishing Point filter creates perspective lines that take up the entire page, regardless of whether you make a selection — so don't bother trying to constrain the lines. You can always erase them later.

   When laying down vanishing points, it's good to have a basic idea where the horizon will be (For those curious, the *horizon* is the imaginary line that separates the ground from the sky in your drawing and resides at eye level — see Figure 14-19).When working with one or two-point perspective, the horizon is the line on which you set your vanishing points. So before you start working with the Vanishing Points filter, be sure to know where the horizon is in the panel.

Figure 14-19:
It helps to
know where
the horizon
is in the
panel before
you start
placing any
vanishing
points.

4. **Open the Layer Properties dialog box by choosing the appropriate commands from the main menu:**

   • *Debut version:* Filter⇨Vanishing Points

   • *EX version:* Filter⇨Render⇨Vanishing Points

   The Vanishing Points tab of the Layer Properties dialog box appears, as shown in Figure 14-20.

Figure 14-20:
The
Vanishing
Points tab.

5. **Click the Arrange Vanishing Points button. (It's a black arrow, as shown in the margin.)**

6. **Click the canvas where you'd like to place the vanishing point.**

   The default perspective lines automatically generate around the vanishing point. You can add as many vanishing points as you want.

You can adjust the position of the vanishing point by clicking the focal point (designated by the blue X in the middle) and dragging it to the new position.

To remove a vanishing point, select the one you want to delete and click the Trash button, located at the top of the dialog box.

7. **In the Degrees/Line text box, enter a value between 0.05 and 30 to change the number of perspective lines generated.**

   The value you enter is the angle at which a line is generated, so a smaller number results in more lines, and vice versa.

8. **Select the Apply to All the Vanishing Points check box before you adjust the value if you'd like the Degrees/Line value reflected in all the vanishing points created.**

   If you want the value to affect only the current vanishing point, deselect the check box.

9. **In the Width text box, enter a value between 0.1 mm and 1.0 mm to adjust the line thickness of all the perspective lines.**

10. **If you aren't happy with how things are looking and just want to start fresh, you can click the Delete All button, and all the vanishing points (and their respective lines) are removed from the page.**

11. **Select the Clear Layer check box if you want to remove any other art from the image layer.**

    This option is useful if you happened to draw on the layer before you started the filter, for example.

12. **Click OK when you're done.**

To make things easier to read while working, you can adjust the color of the perspective lines. Simply open the Layer Properties dialog box by pressing F3 on your keyboard and change the Display Color from Grayscale to Color. Click the Color box to change the value to a different color.

If you're working in two- or three-point perspective, try creating each vanishing point on a separate layer. That way, you can make each set of perspective lines a different layer. When you're working with many different perspective lines, this can help reduce confusion when staring at a jumble of lines.

Chapter 15

Manga Studio EX Only!

Here's where spending the extra money for Manga Studio EX pays off. Fundamentally, there aren't any major differences between Manga Studio Debut and Manga Studio EX. Both versions do an excellent job with exactly what they're intended to do — help you digitally produce the finest work you can. In fact, if you compared a page created in Debut and a page created in EX, you wouldn't be able to tell the difference (unless the EX user decided to use a lot of funky effects on the page).

I think that the real difference between the two versions boils down to *convenience*. Both versions can perform the same tasks — but Manga Studio EX can perform some of them *easier* and *faster*. The advantages that EX has over its little brother Debut ranges from setting the color density of all the drawing tools at once to drawing correctly in perspective simply by drawing on the screen. EX also has a few functions and abilities that Debut simply can't do, such as applying special effects. This chapter is all about the advantages you have with Manga Studio EX.

Understanding and Taking Advantage of the Manga Studio EX Palettes

The basic palette that users of Manga Studio Debut and EX have has been covered throughout the course of this book. However, I'm sure you EX users have noticed an additional group of palettes that I haven't touched on . . . yet.

To avoid confusion for the Debut users, I set aside these exclusive palettes to this chapter, where I would be able to discuss them in further depth. Considering the cool features you now have at your disposal, you'll be glad I saved these palettes for last.

The Gray palette

If you want to lighten the color of your line work when penciling, you'd normally open the Tool Options palette and adjust its opacity. However, if you notice, that setting is good for only the particular pencil you're working with; if you want all your pencils to have the same opacity level, you need to go through each pencil type and set its corresponding opacity. Of course, if you change your mind and want a darker color, you have to go though each type again and . . . I think you get the point.

What the Gray palette (shown in Figure 15-1) does is save you time. Instead of going through each pencil type, you simply adjust the gray level in the palette, and all your pencil tools now draw in that same shade of gray. Even more, *all* of your drawing tools use the same gray level. If you need to change colors on-the-fly, simply adjust the level in the Gray palette again and keep working with any of the drawing tools you want.

While I've established in this book that you aren't really working with colors other than black and white, I use "colors" to refer to the drawing opacity level. It rolls off the tongue better than "gray levels"

To use the Gray palette, follow these steps:

1. **Either click the Gray palette button, located on the main toolbar or press F9 on your keyboard.**

2. **Choose whether you want to adjust the color of the foreground or background colors by clicking their respective color boxes.**

3. **Use the slider to adjust the color to the value you want. Or you can enter a value between 0 % and 100 % in its corresponding text box.**

4. **If you'd like to save the color to use later, click the Register Color button and it's saved in the color repository.**

5. **When you want to reuse a color you've saved, click its color box in the repository and you're ready to go.**

If you don't want to save your own colors, you can use one of the preinstalled gray sets instead. Click the Temporal Gray Set button (located below the color slider) and you can then select the set you'd like to use from the drop-down list.

TIP

If you're trying out the trick to color your work (which I describe in Chapter 14), you may find this tidbit useful. If you're working on an 8-bit gray layer, you can use the color sets on the Gray palette to draw in different shades of your chosen color. What's more, you can draw over a darker shade with a lighter shade if you want (something you can't do on any other kind of layer). Check out Figure 15-2 to see what I mean.

Figure 15-1:
Change the opacity of drawing tools with the Gray palette.

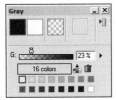

Figure 15-2:
You can draw a lighter color over a darker color if you're using a pen or shape tool on an 8-bit gray layer.

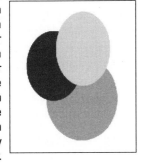

The Materials palette

The Materials palette works as your "one stop shop" for the various image layers, rulers, and 2D or 3D objects you can apply to a page. These materials serve as templates that you can simply add to the page instead of manually creating and adjusting each time you need to add a new one.

Using the default materials

Located in the Default folder of the Materials palette are a variety of preset layers and tools that you can use right away on your page, simply by selecting what you want and either pasting it with the Paste Materials button or by dragging it directly onto the page, as shown in Figure 15-3.

The materials provided in the Default folder include the following:

- ✔ **2DLT Sample and 3DLT Sample:** These folders contain two dimensional images and three dimensional objects that you can import onto a page. I discuss how they work in further detail in Bonus Chapter 2 on the CD, but basically you can drag and drop these objects onto the page, where you can then adjust to your liking using the respective 2DLT (setting threshold and posterization levels of the image) and 3DLT (setting position, angle, lighting, threshold, and posterization levels of the object) filters.

- ✔ **Layer:** The materials in the Layer folder are preset layer types, which are almost like layer templates in that you can simply paste them onto the page as is rather than create and adjust your own drawing layers.

- ✔ **Rulers:** In Chapter 8, I talk about how you can create a ruler from practically any kind of shape. The rulers in the Rulers folder prove just that — you can choose from a variety of rulers ranging from simple shapes to (fairly) complex objects. For you traditional artists who like to work with French curves and other drawing guides, you can select virtual versions of those tools as well!

- ✔ **Ver2 Layer:** These are additional layer types that you can add to a page, including specialized ruler layers such as the focus line, parallel line, and perspective line rulers, (each of which I discuss later in this chapter in the "Filters as Rulers: Using the Parallel, Focus, and Perspective Line Rulers" section.)

- ✔ **Word Balloons:** All of the word balloon types I discuss in Chapter 12 are located right here.

You can use the Paste button . . .

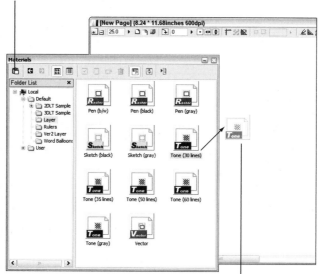

Figure 15-3:
Adding
materials to
the page is
easy to do!

. . . or drag the material onto the page.

Creating your own material

The default materials do cover a lot of ground, but it's still possible that the particular preset you're looking for isn't included. The good news is that you aren't limited to the default materials — you can create layers, artwork, word balloons, and rulers exactly as you need them and then save them in the Materials palette to use over and over again!

Follow these steps to add your own material to the Materials palette:

1. **Make sure that the User folder is selected on the Materials palette, as shown in Figure 15-4.**

   Manga Studio won't let you save your custom material in the Default folder, so you need to be sure you have the User folder selected before you can go any further.

2. **Click the New Folder button to create a folder for your material and name it according to the type of material you plan on storing. When created, double-click the folder.**

   Technically, you don't need to do this. You can just as easily use the Materials folder already created in the User folder, if you want. You can even place everything right in the main User directory itself. However, it might be a bit difficult to find a particular template or image if you have lots of them stored in one location.

   It's good practice to try to keep your materials organized in separate folders. You'll thank yourself later.

3. **Prepare the layer you want to save as material.**

   How you prepare the layer obviously varies, depending on the type of material you're looking to save. The idea here is that if you want to save a particular item to the Materials palette, you need to make sure that said material is ready to be saved.

   Because a layer is what ultimately is saved to the Materials palette, everything that's on the layer is saved as well. If you're looking to save only one ruler, for example, you need to make sure there are no other rulers on the layer.

4. **Highlight the layer you want to save on the Layers palette.**

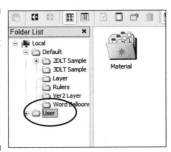

Figure 15-4: You can't create your own materials until you select the User folder.

5. **From the main menu, choose File⇨Save as Material.**

   And there you go! Your image, drawing layer, ruler, or other material has been saved to the Materials palette, ready for you to use whenever you want!

The only layer types you can't add to the Materials palette are basic frames, grids, guides, and sketch layers (images imported as sketch layers, — not to be confused with the raster layers with the sketch attribute selected).

You can include other files in this folder by clicking the Show Menu button and selecting Import. You can save any kind of file to the Materials folder — even ones that you can't use in Manga Studio! For non-Manga Studio files, the native program used to open the item starts up when you double-click it.

To delete a material from the palette, select the item from the window and click the Delete icon.

Custom Tools palette

The Custom Tools palette (shown in Figure 15-5) works like an art supply box. With this palette, you can pick and choose which pens, pencils, markers, and other tools or functions you like to use most frequently from one location. No more needing to hold a tool button down for a few seconds and choose from a list; each tool is laid out on the Custom Tools palette for you to select quickly. Even better, you can create and use custom sets, which can store just the tools you want to use for a particular phase of development!

Figure 15-5:
Use only the tools you want with the Custom Tools palette.

The palette comes installed with four custom sets. You can choose between them by clicking the set name, and selecting the new set you want to work with from the drop-down list.

To customize this palette, follow these steps:

1. **Click the Show Menu button and select Custom Settings. (You can't miss it — it's the only option on the menu!)**

   The Custom Settings dialog box appears.

2. **Select one of the sets you want to customize from the Set Name drop-down list.**

   Alternatively, you can choose to either delete a set or create a brand-new one. To delete the highlighted set, click the Delete Set button and click Yes when the confirmation dialog box pops up. To add a new set, click the New Set button and enter a name when the New Custom Tool Settings dialog box pops up.

3. **To add a new menu command to a set, highlight the command you want on the Menu tab and click the Add button.**

   Adding a menu command to a set gives you one-click access to a command you'd normally have to choose from the main menu.

4. **To add a new tool to a set, highlight the tool you want on the Tool tab and click the Add button. (See Figure 15-6.)**

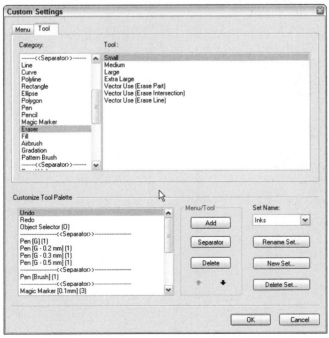

Figure 15-6:
Use the Custom Settings dialog box to choose what tools and functions you want for each custom set.

Adding tools to this palette give you faster access to the variant tools you use. For example, if you normally wanted to switch between the G pen and the Brush, you would have to bring up the list of pens from either the Tools or Tool Options. Now, you can add each pen type to the Custom Palette, and to switch between them, simply click their respective button.

It probably doesn't seem like much, but it's certainly a nice convenience to have.

5. **To delete one of the existing commands or tools from a set, highlight the tool in the Customize Tool palette list and click the Delete button.**

6. **Click OK when you're done.**

Actions palette

Actions are much like macros in some other programs: They're a series of commands that you can program to perform in a particular sequence. Using actions, you can eliminate some of the more mundane tasks by simply grouping them together.

Using default actions

Manga Studio comes preinstalled with a series of actions. They're all pretty basic, and while I think you may find them useful, I believe the default actions are more useful to give you an idea of what you can do with your own customized actions.

The descriptions of each action are self explanatory, so I'll point you to Figure 15-7, which lists all of the default actions on the Actions palette.

Figure 15-7: Save some time by using any of the preinstalled actions, or create your own!

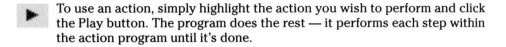

To use an action, simply highlight the action you wish to perform and click the Play button. The program does the rest — it performs each step within the action program until it's done.

Organizing action sets

Like with the Custom Tools palette, you can choose to organize your actions by placing them in different sets. You can switch to any of these sets by clicking the set name and selecting from the drop-down list that appears.

You can organize your action sets by clicking the Show Menu button and choosing from the following functions:

- ✔ **To create a new set,** select New Settings and enter a name for your new set when the dialog box appears.

- ✔ **To delete a set,** select Delete Settings and click OK when the confirmation window appears.

- ✔ **To rename a set,** select Rename Settings and enter a new name when the dialog box appears.

- ✔ **To copy a set,** select Duplicate Settings and enter the new name when the dialog box appears.

Creating your own actions

To create your own action, follow these steps:

1. **Select the set your new action will reside in.**

2. **Click the Show Menu button and select New Action.**

3. **When prompted, enter the name of your action.**

4. **When you're ready to create the action, click the Record button, located at the top of the Actions palette.**

5. **Start performing the functions you want to add to the action.**

   For example, you can:

   a. *Use the Marquee tool. (Hold down the button to select the rectangle tool.)*

   b. *Draw a rectangle on the page.*

   c. *Select a tone from the Tones palette.*

   d. *Paste the tone into the selection.*

   e. *Clear the selection from the page (Selection⇨Clear Selection from the Main Menu).*

6. **When you're done, click the Stop Button.**

If you find you made a mistake when recording your action, you can go back and delete it from the program. Just highlight the offending step and click the Trash button. Then, click the record button and rerecord the step or steps you *wanted* to perform.

The Gradation Tool

The Gradation tool, located on the Tools palette, gives you the ability to manually create a gradient of any size or angle, directly on the page. Actually, it's much like the Gradation (or Gradient) tool that you've probably seen in other programs, like Photoshop. What those other art programs don't let you do, however, is adjust the gradation after you've created it on its own tone layer.

Used on any other layer in the program, the Gradation tool produces its own tone layer, which you can then adjust using the Tone Layer Properties palette. I like to think of the Gradation tool as a quick setup of a tone gradation, which I can then tweak later on to get it exactly how I want it to look.

When you use the Gradation tool on a raster layer, you have the option to create a new tone layer or to draw the gradient directly on the raster layer. Depending on the expression mode, the raster layer can produce an effect ranging from a dithered (2-bit) to a solid (8-bit gray) gradient.

To use the Gradation tool, follow these steps:

1. **Select the Gradation tool on the Tools palette.**

   If you want to add a gradient to the entire page, go to Step 2. If you want to add the gradient to a selection, select the Marquee tool from the Tools palette and create a selection on the page.

2. **Drag the Gradation tool on the page (or inside the selection).**

If you want more control over the gradient you create with the Gradation tool, follow these steps:

1. **Create a selection if you want to keep the gradient contained and then click the Gradation tool icon on the Tools palette.**

2. **Open the Tool Options palette by pressing F3.**

   The [Gradation] Tool Options palette appears.

3. **If you want to use one of the preset options, click the gradient name and select from the drop-down list that appears.**

4. **Choose whether you want to create a line or elliptical gradient by clicking its respective buttons.**

If you choose to make an elliptical gradient, you have the additional option to constrain the gradient within the ellipse you create. To do this, select the Inside Circle Only check box.

5. **If you're currently on a raster layer and you don't want to place the gradient on it, deselect the Draw on Selected Layer check box.**

   When deselected, any gradients drawn on a raster layer are created on their own tone layer.

6. **Select the colors for your start and end points (or center and ring if elliptical) from the Density Graph.**

   This works much like the Pressure Settings Graph you use to adjust your drawing tools. (See Chapter 14.) To adjust, click and drag the starting color and ending color until they're at the shades of gray you want to work with. Optionally, you can click the middle of the graph line to create a curve and give some additional variety to the gradient created.

7. **From the Repeat Type drop-down list, choose how you would like the gradient pattern to repeat:**

   • *Repeat:* The pattern repeats when the end of the gradient is reached.

   • *Back-to-Back:* The pattern repeats in reverse when the end of the gradient is reached.

   • *None:* The gradient pattern doesn't repeat.

8. **If you want to adjust the lines or angle of the gradient, click the Show Menu button and select Advanced Settings Mode.**

   When the two options appear (see Figure 15-8), you can enter new values for the angle and number of lines in their respective text boxes.

9. **Using the Gradation tool, click the area of the page or selection you want to start from and drag to the end point.**

   If you're creating an elliptical gradient, you start from the center point of the ellipse, drag it out to its end point, and rotate it until it's at the angle you want.

If you create a gradient on a tone layer, remember that you can tweak the gradient on the Layer Properties palette. So if you make a mistake or just aren't happy with how the gradient comes out, you don't have to delete it and start over!

If you create the gradient on a raster layer, you can't adjust it like you can on a tone layer. So if you aren't happy with how the gradient comes out, you need to delete or undo the gradient and try again.

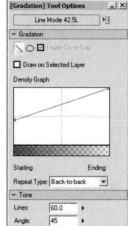

Figure 15-8:
The
Gradation
Tool Options
palette in
advanced
mode.

Spicing Up Your Work with Filters

Are you feeling avant-garde? Do you want to really go wild with special effects? Manga Studio EX has that covered, with a series of rendering, transformation, and other effect filters that you can add to a scene or panel to really give it an extra level of pop.

Because there are so many filters to work with and because there's only so much space in this chapter, this section is intended to give you just a taste of the various effects filters at your disposal.

Rendering filters

Both Manga Studio Debut and EX come with the speed line, focus line, and vanishing point filters. Manga Studio EX boasts one additional rendering filter: clouds.

The clouds filter produces a random cloud effect on an 8-bit gray layer (see Figure 15-9), which can be good for a background or pattern effect in a scene. To use the Cloud filter, choose Filter➪Render➪Cloud Pattern from the main menu, and the program takes care of the rest.

No two renderings will be the same, so if you don't like how one rendering comes out, simply undo and try it again.

If you want to produce a darker cloud effect, run the Cloud filter over the same selection a few times. The more filters you add to the image, the darker it becomes.

Figure 15-9:
The clouds
filter
produces
clouds (to
the surprise
of no one,
I'm sure).

Transformation filters

You use the transformation filters to take your image and *really* mess with
it. You can pull, twist, and distort the image however you'd like, as shown in
Figure 15-10. If you're looking to create a really crazy effect on your page,
these filters may do just the trick.

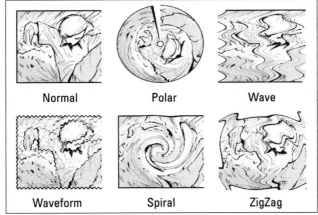

Figure 15-10:
You can
create some
zany effects
with the
transforma-
tion filters.

To use a transformation filter, select Filter➪Transform from the main menu,
and select the filter you wish to apply.

These are the transformation filters available to you:

- **Polar Coordinates:** Depending on the option you choose, the image
  is distorted into a circular shape. This is done by either by taking the
  rectangular coordinates of the image and converting them into polar

coordinates (and vice versa) or by projecting the image as though they were on a sphere. The Polar Coordinates dialog box gives you options on how to apply the filter:

- Convert From X and Y Coordinates to Polar Coordinates: Converts the linear (x,y) coordinates of the image, into polar (north and south) coordinates, as though the image was on a globe.

- From Polar Coordinates to Rectangular Coordinates: Converts the polar (north, south) coordinates of the image, into to linear (x,y) coordinates.

- Project on a Sphere: Converts the image into a spherical shape.

✔ **Wave:** Produces a watery wave effect on the image. When the Wave dialog box appears, you have the following options to adjust:

- Set the angle of the wave effect by entering a value between 0 and 180 degrees in the Direction text box.

- Set the amplitude (the strength of waves generated) can be by entering a value between 0.1 and 200.0 percent in the Amplitude text box.

- Set the number of waves generated by entering a value from 1.0 and 20.0 in the Number of Waves text box.

✔ **Waveforms:** Produces a ruffling effect by applying horizontal and vertical waves to the image. When the Waveforms dialog box appears, you have the following options to adjust:

- Set the type of waveforms created (Sine Wave, Triangular Waveform, or Rectangular Wave) by choosing their respective Waveforms radio button.

- Set the number of waves generated by entering a value from 1 and 20 in the Number of Waves text box.

- Set the wavelength of the vertical and horizontal waves by entering a value between 0.1 % and 100.0 % in their respective Wavelength text boxes.

- Set the vertical and horizontal wave amplitude (strength) by entering a value between 0.1 % and 100.0 % in their respective Amplitude text boxes.

- Set the size of the horizontal waves by entering a value between 0.0% and 100.0 % in the Horizontal Scale text box.

- Set the size of the vertical waves by entering a value between 0.0% and 100.0 % in the Vertical Scale text box.

- Set how the filter will treat the edge of the image (*Rewind*, which reverses the image, or *Repeat to fill in the edge color*, which repeats the image) by selecting one of their respective Processing Outside the Area radio buttons.

If you're not happy with the way the effect looks, you can always try regenerating it by clicking the Regenerate button. Click OK to apply the effect.

✔ **Spiral:** Distorts the image with a spiral effect. When the Spiral dialog box appears, you have the following options to adjust:

- Set the amount that the image will be distorted by entering a value between -900 and 900 in the Skew text box. A positive value distorts the image clockwise, while a negative value distorts the image counter-clockwise.

- Set the amount of the image that will be distorted by entering a value between 0.1 (large amount) and 4.0 (small amount) in the Pull text box.

✔ **Zigzag:** Adds a zigzag distortion to the image. When the Zigzag dialog box appears, you have the following options to adjust:

- Set the amount that the Zigzag effect rotates on the image by entering a value between 0.0 degrees and 180 degrees in the Rotate text box.

- Set the number of zigzag waves generated by entering a value between 0.1 and 30.0 degrees in the Number of Waves text box.

Adjustment filters

Best suited to 8-bit gray layers, the adjustment filters help adjust the light levels of an image, as well as clean up and fine-tune the line work of a drawing.

To use an adjustment filter, choose Filter⇨Image Adjustments from the main menu, and then select the filter you wish to apply.

You have the following adjustment filters to work with:

✔ **Brightness and Contrast:** Adjusts the brightness and contrast of the image. When the Brightness & Contrast dialog box appears, you can enter a value of -100 to 100 in the Brightness and Contrast text boxes. You can have the program automatically adjust the brightness and contrast by clicking the Auto Adjust button, and can preview the effect on the image at any time by selecting the Preview checkbox.

✔ **Tone Curve:** Adjusts the brightness and contrast of image by setting its *contrast density curve* (which is a fancy way of saying a graphical line you can fine-tune the brightness and contrast with). When the Tone Curve dialog box appears, you can use your mouse or stylus to adjust the contrast density curve by clicking and dragging anywhere on the graph line (which creates a control box you use to adjust the graph — you can add as many of these as you'd like). You can reset the graph at any time by pressing the Reset button, and can preview the effect on the image by selecting the Preview checkbox.

✔ **Adjust Levels:** Fine-tunes the brightness and contrast of the image by adjusting its *histogram levels* (the amount of shadow, midtones, and highlights in an image). When the Adjust Levels dialog box appears, you set the shadows, midtones, and highlights of the image by clicking and dragging the left, center, and right triangles (respectively), located at the bottom of the histogram graph. Moving any of the triangles to the right will darken the image, while moving them to the left will lighten it.

Additionally, you can set the general brightness of the image layer by clicking and dragging the triangles located at the bottom of the brightness map (which is below the histogram graph). Moving the triangles to the right will lighten the layer, while moving them to the left will darken it.

You can have the computer automatically set the levels by clicking the Auto Adjust button, and you can preview the effect on the image at any time by selecting the preview checkbox. Click OK to apply the filter.

✔ **Bitmap:** Converts an image into a bitmap image, similar to changing the layer type. (See Chapter 6.) When the Bitmap dialog box appears, you can change the image by choosing Threshold, Dither, or Diffusion from the Type (normally labeled Expression Mode elsewhere) drop-down list. If you set a Threshold Type, you can enter a Threshold value of 0 to 255 in its text box. You can preview the effect on the image at any time by selecting the preview check box.

✔ **Dust Cleaner:** Helps remove any dirt that may have scanned in with an image. When the Dust Cleaner dialog box appears, you have the following options to adjust (note that you can preview the filter at any time by selecting the Preview check box.):

- Set the maximum size of the dust to remove by entering a value between 0.0 mm and 2.0 mm in the Size text box.

- Set the color of the dust particles to remove (black, white, or transparent) by selecting their respective Dust Color box.

- Set the color the dust will be converted to (black, white or transparent) by selecting their respective Category Color box.

✔ **Line Smoother:** Helps smooth out any shaky or wobbly lines on an image. When the Line Smoother dialog box appears, you can adjust the following options:

- Set the amount of smoothing you want applied to the image by selecting the Smoothing check box (it's selected by default), and entering a value between 1 and 5 in the Intensity text box.

- To fill in gaps between lines, select the Join Line check box (it's selected by default).

The following options will differ, depending on the type of layer you're working on:

- *For Raster Layers:* Set the maximum gap size by entering a value between 0.10 mm and 5.00 mm in the Join Line text box. You can then set the Reference (the lines that will be joined) and Drawing Color (the color of the join line drawn) by selecting black, white, or transparent from their respective color boxes.

- *For Vector Layers:* Set the strength of the join line function by entering a value between 1 and 20 in the Intensity text box.

  If you're working on a Vector Layer, you can choose to have the entire line smoothed out as a whole, or only the ends by selecting the Correct Entire Line check box.

✔ **Line Width Correction:** Adjusts the thickness of the lines in the image. When the Line Width Correction dialog box appears, you can select from one of the following options by clicking on its respective radio button:

- To widen the lines, select Widen to the Specified Width, and enter a value between 0.00 mm and 2.00 mm in its text box.

- To thin out the lines, select Narrow to the Specified Width, and enter a value between 0.00 mm and 2.00 mm in its text box.

- *For Vector Layers,* you can enlarge the lines by a certain magnification, select Expand to the Specified Magnification, and enter a value between 1.00 and 5.00 in its text box.

- *For Vector Layers,* you can shrink the lines by a certain magnification, select Reduce to the Specified Magnification, and enter a value between 1.00 and 5.00 in its text box.

- *For Vector Layers,* you can set all the lines to a specific width, select Set Constant Line Width and enter a value between 0.1 mm and 10.0 mm in its text box.

If you are working on a Vector Layer you can adjust the lines as a whole (as opposed to only a portion of them) by selecting the Correct Entire Line check box.

Effect filters

The effect filters perform a much more subtle effect on an image than the transformation filters do, although you can used effect filters to distort the image just the same. Examples of these effects can be seen in Figure 15-11.

To use an effect filter, choose Filter⇨Effects from the main menu, and select the effect you wish to apply. You have six filters to choose from:

✔ **Mosaic:** Adds a pixelated effect to the image. When the Mosaic dialog box appears, you can set the size of the mosaic blocks by entering a value from 0.1 mm to 99.0 mm in the Mosaic Block text box.

- ✔ **Blur/Blur More:** Softens a raster layer image. The amount of blurring depends on which of the two functions you choose. There are no dialog boxes for either of these functions.

- ✔ **Gaussian Blur:** Adds a customized softening to a raster layer image. When the Gaussian Blur dialog box appears, you can set a blurring range from 0.1 mm to 10.0 mm in the Range text box. You can also adjust the preview quality (before the filter is applied) by selecting High or Low Quality from the Preview Quality drop-down list.

- ✔ **Sharpen/Sharpen More:** Sharpens a raster layer image. The amount sharpened depends on which of the two functions you choose. There are no dialog boxes for either of these functions.

- ✔ **Posterize:** Reduces the number of gray colors in an image. When the Posterize dialog box appears, you can set the amount of posterization by entering a value from 2 to 20 in the Posterization Level text box.

- ✔ **Invert:** Inverts the foreground and background colors of the image. Transparent areas aren't affected by this filter. There is no dialog box for this function.

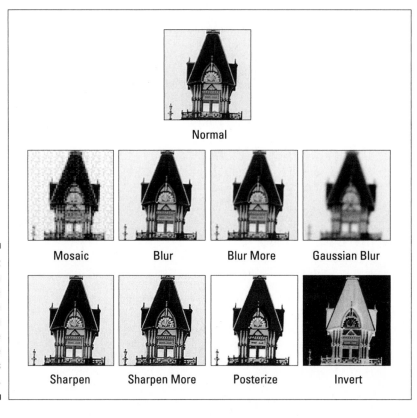

Figure 15-11: You can create subtle effects on an image using the effects filters.

Normal

Mosaic | Blur | Blur More | Gaussian Blur

Sharpen | Sharpen More | Posterize | Invert

Special effect filters

Special effect filters perform additional enhancements to your image or line art.

To use a special effect filter, select Filter⇨Special Effects from the main menu, and select the filter you wish to apply. You have two filters to choose from:

- ✔ **SHD:** You use the SHD, or Super High Density Filter, to beef up the quality of a lower-resolution image by either applying a diffusion, dither, or threshold effect to the line work. This helps to smooth out the jagged lines that appear in a low-resolution image or line art. See Figure 15-12 for an example — the image in the top-left corner is a low-resolution image that's jagged; the bottom-right corner shows how the image appears after applying the SHD filter.

    When the SHD dialog box appears, you can set the resolution of the image (150dpi to the maximum resolution of the image) by selecting from the Resolution drop-down list. You can also set the Expression mode of the image by selecting Threshold, Dither, or Diffusion from the Type drop-down list (if you select Threshold, you can enter a threshold value between 0 and 255 in its respective text box).

- ✔ **2DLT:** This filter performs 2DLT effects to turn a scanned image into line art and tones. Check out Bonus Chapter 2 on the CD for a more in-depth discussion on how 2DLT works.

Figure 15-12:
The SHD filter helps smooth out the jagged lines of a low-resolution image.

Filters as Rulers: Using the Parallel, Focus, and Perspective Line Rulers

I think the speed line, focus line and vanishing point filters introduced in Chapter 14 are a great way to create special effects or prepare drawing guides when you just want it done quickly. But what if you want something a bit more hands-on?

Manga Studio EX actually provides an alternative version to all three of those filters; the parallel, focus, and perspective line rulers. Each of these perform the same basic function as their respective filters. The big difference is that instead of the computer rendering the lines . . . you do! Even better, you don't have to do anything more than simply draw on the page. The rulers take care of the rest.

For each of these rulers, you can choose to place them on either their own ruler layer or on the image layer you're currently working on. Be sure to check out Chapter 8 for more information on setting up rulers on your page.

The parallel lines ruler

The idea behind the parallel lines ruler is pretty straight forward: You use it to draw parallel lines. (I know, it's a big shock.) What's really cool about this function is that you don't need to do anything special after you set the drawing angle for the ruler — you just draw freehand! The ruler takes the lines you draw and automatically straightens them and snaps them to the ruler's angle. It's definitely one of the fastest and simplest means to draw up some speed lines on a page (for example) without having to break out a ruler (or in Manga Studio's case, the Ruler tool).

Follow these steps to use the parallel lines ruler:

1. **From the main menu, choose Ruler⇨Create Parallel Lines Ruler.**

   The focus lines ruler appears as a series of three lines in the middle of your page.

2. **From the Tools palette, select the Object Selector.**

3. **Click the Parallel Lines ruler and drag out and up or down along the page to rotate the ruler angle.**

4. **If you created the parallel lines ruler on a ruler layer, select the image layer you'd like to work on from the Layers palette.**

5. **Select a drawing tool from the Tools palette.**

6. **Start drawing! (See Figure 15-13.)**

You can change the ruler angle as you work. Simply switch back to the Object Selector to rotate the ruler to the new direction.

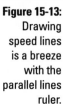

Figure 15-13:
Drawing
speed lines
is a breeze
with the
parallel lines
ruler.

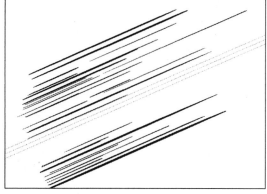

The focus lines ruler

The focus lines filter (see Chapter 8) is a great way to quickly add focus lines to a scene. However, if you're looking to add a bit of personal flair (or you're the type that prefers to not have *everything* done automatically), you can always use the focus lines ruler.

The focus lines ruler automatically straightens and aligns any lines you draw freehand to a single focal point. All you need to do is set the focal point on the panel (or page) you want to add the focus lines to, and sketch away!

Follow these steps to use the focus lines ruler:

1. **From the main menu, choose Ruler⇨Create Focus Lines Ruler.**

   The focus lines ruler appears in the middle of your page.

2. **From the Tools palette, select the Object Selector.**

3. **Click the focus ruler and drag it to wherever you want it on the page.**

4. **If you created the focus lines ruler on a ruler layer, select the image layer you'd like to work on from the Layers palette.**

5. **Select a drawing tool from the Tools palette.**

6. **Start drawing! (See Figure 15-14.)**

As you draw, you should see the lines converge to the focal point of the ruler. Now you can draw lines as large or small, long or short as you'd like for the scene you're working on!

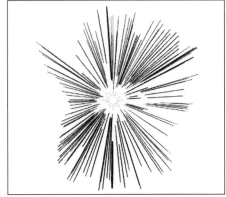

Figure 15-14:
You can
draw focus
lines
however
you'd like
with the
focus lines
ruler.

The perspective ruler

The perspective ruler was probably the single most important item that influenced me to purchase Manga Studio EX, and I'll bet once you use it, you'll wonder how you ever drew digitally without one.

The concept is simple: All you need to do is set the focal point (or points if you're working on two or three-point perspective) on the scene you're working on. Then, you just draw! The ruler will automatically straighten the lines drawn, and snap them to whichever focal point you are drawing towards. (Check out Chapter 16 for suggestions on books on perspective if you're unfamiliar with the topic.)

If the idea of drawing in perspective has ever been a cause of stress for you, this tool will certainly help to make the concept a bit easier to handle. To use the perspective ruler, follow these steps:

1. **From the main menu, choose Ruler⇨Create Focus Lines Ruler.**

   The Focus Lines Ruler appears in the middle of your page.

2. **From the Tools palette, select the Object Selector.**

   Initially, the ruler defaults to three-point perspective. If you want to reduce it to a one- or two-point perspective, you need to select a ruler line or point with the Object Selector, right-click, and select One-Point Perspective or Two-Point Perspective from the pop-up menu.

3. **To move a vanishing point, click it with the Object Selector and drag it to wherever you want it on the page.**

   If you're unsure which is the vanishing point, look for the ruler point that two lines are converging towards.

4. **If you created the perspective lines ruler on a ruler layer, select the image layer you'd like to work on from the Layers palette.**

5. **Select a drawing tool from the Tools palette.**

6. **Start drawing! (See Figure 15-15.)**

As you draw, the lines drawn automatically snap towards one of the vanishing points! Suddenly, drawing in perspective just became a whole lot easier!

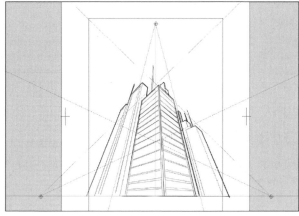

Figure 15-15:
You can whip up a perspective drawing in no time with the perspective ruler.

As you switch from one ruler to another, you need to make sure the drawing tool snaps to the ruler. Check the Snap To buttons located at the top of the Page toolbar (see Figure 15-16) and see if the ruler type has its snap function on. If not, simply click the button to activate.

Snap to Perspective Rulers

Snap On/Off | Snap to Parallel Rulers

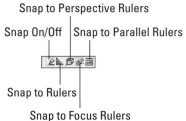

Figure 15-16:
Activate the Snap To function.

Snap to Rulers

Snap to Focus Rulers

Putting Miscellaneous Functions to Use

These are the hodgepodge functions that, while not exactly fitting into a specific category, continue the convenience theme that Manga Studio EX provides you. They might not seem like much, but when you're working towards a deadline, you may find these small things can help build up some extra time that you can devote to other things.

Consecutive scanning

The consecutive scanning function in Manga Studio EX allows you to do pretty much what you'd expect it to do, considering its title: It allows you to scan in several pages of work at once. What's really nice about this function is that instead of scanning the pages into separate page files, they're all combined into pages of a story file.

Considering all the other functions that you get in this program, the idea of consecutive scanning might seem like a small thing to crow about. However, those of you who have a large stack of pages you need scanned in are going to find this *very* useful to use. It's certainly a great way to quickly build up a story file.

Follow these steps to use the Consecutive Scanning function:

1. **From the main menu, choose File⇨Import⇨Consecutive Scanning.**

2. **When the New Story dialog box appears, enter all the necessary information for your story.**

   I go over the New Story options in greater detail in Chapter 4.

3. **When the Consecutive Scanning dialog box appears (see Figure 15-17), enter the number of pages you plan on scanning in the Page text box.**

Figure 15-17:
The Consecutive Scanning dialog box.

4. **Assign the page alignment of the scanned pages (Left Page, Right Page, or All Pages) from the Page drop-down list.**

5. **To set the image options for all the scanned pages, select the Sets the First Page by Opening It check box.**

   It's a confusing name for a check box, to be sure. The idea here is that when selected, the Import Image dialog box appears for the first scanned page. This is your opportunity to adjust the initial settings for the page. (Check out Chapter 5 for an extensive explanation on how to import images from a scanner).

   When those settings are made, all subsequent scans in this group have the same settings. This way, if all the pages are essentially the same, you don't need to go through and adjust the options for each individual scan.

6. **Select whether you want a normal or 2DLT scan from the Import Method after Scan section.**

   If you're unfamiliar with 2DLT importing, check out Bonus Chapter 2 on the CD, where I go over how it works in detail.

7. **Click OK when done.**

8. **When the scanning program for your scanner starts up, follow its directions to scan your work into the program.**

When you've scanned your work into the program, your story file is chock full of manga goodness!

Filling and outlining selections

Something familiar to Photoshop users is the ability to take a selection and fill it in or draw an outline around it. What's unique to Manga Studio, at least for filling selections, is the ability to choose exactly *what* is filled in.

After you create a selection, fill it by following these steps:

1. **From the main menu, choose Edit⇨Fill Selection.**

   The Fill Selection dialog box appears, as shown in Figure 15-18.

2. **Choose the fill color (black, white, or transparent) by clicking its respective color box.**

3. **Choose how you want to fill the selection.**

   You can choose by selecting one of the following radio buttons:

   - *Fill All:* The entire selection is filled in.

   - *Fill Closed Area:* Only areas that are completely closed (that is, an ellipse or rectangle) are filled in within the selection.

   - *Protect Transparent Area:* Only areas of the selection that aren't transparent are filled in.

   - *Draw in Transparent Area:* Only the transparent area of a selection is filled in.

   - *Draw in Transparent and Closed Area:* Only areas that are either completely enclosed or are transparent are filled in.

4. **Click OK when you're happy with the settings.**

If you simply want to fill in the selection with the current color you're working with, choose Edit⇨Fill Selection with Drawing Color.

Figure 15-18:
Choose how
you want a
selection
filled.

To outline a selection you created, follow these steps:

1. **From the main menu, choose Edit⇨Outline Selection.**

   The Outline Selection dialog box appears, as shown in Figure 15-19.

2. **Select the drawing color for the outline (black, white, or transparent) by clicking on its respective color box.**

3. **Choose how you want the outline drawn.**

   You have three options you can choose among by selecting its respective radio button:

   - *Draw Outside:* The outline is drawn on the outside of the selection border.

   - *Draw on the Border:* The outline is drawn in the middle of the selection border.

   - *Draw Inside:* The outline is drawn on the inside border.

4. **Choose the outline's width by entering a value between 0.1 mm and 10.0 mm in the Line Width text box.**

5. **When you're happy with the settings, click OK.**

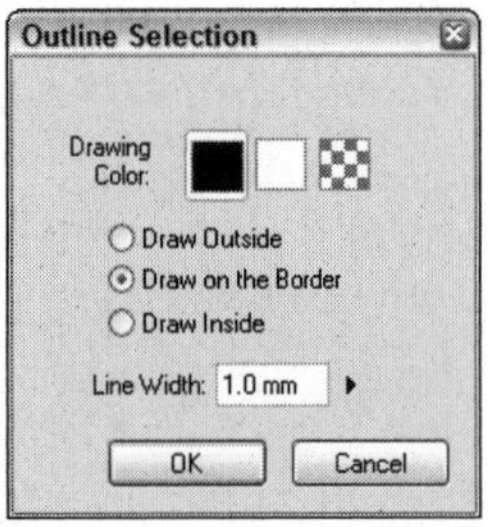

Figure 15-19:
The Outline
Selection
dialog box
helps you
set up
exactly how
you want
the
selection
outlined.

Creating pattern brush material

Creating your own pattern brush is much like creating your own tone pattern (which I cover in Chapter 14). The main difference here is that unlike the tone pattern, you can work with your custom brush pattern like you would with any other drawing tool. So, you now get the freedom to come up with a much more random pattern than you would with a pattern tone.

Creating a new pattern brush is quite easy:

1. **Either import an image you'd like to use or draw your own image.**

2. **Select the Rectangular Marquee tool from the Tools palette.**

3. **Using your mouse or stylus, click and drag a selection around the image. (See Figure 15-20.)**

4. **From the main menu, choose Edit⇨Save Pattern as Brush Material.**

5. **When the Save Pattern as Brush Material dialog box appears, enter a name for your new pattern in the Name text box.**

6. **If you'd like this pattern to become listed as an option for the Pattern Brush, select Create a New Tool Options from Brush Material check box.**

   Not selecting the check box places your new pattern in the Brush pattern repository, which you can access from the Pattern Brush Tool Options palette.

7. **Click OK when you're done.**

Now when you use the Pattern Brush, you can draw up your new pattern however you'd like. Because the Pattern brush is pressure sensitive, the pattern image becomes as large or as small as you want, depending on how hard you press on the tablet. (Check out Figure 15-21 to see what I mean.)

Figure 15-20: To create your pattern brush, select the image or drawing with the Rectangular Marquee tool.

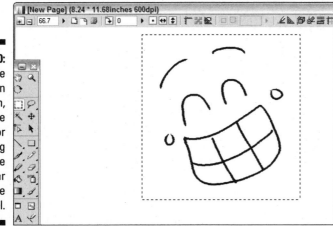

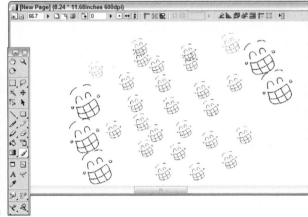

Figure 15-21:
Your image
has now
become a
pattern you
can use
over and
over again!

The expression mode of the layer you used to create the image for the pattern brush is the expression mode for your pattern. So, a drawing made on a 2-bit layer becomes a 2-bit pattern.

Part V
The Part of Tens

The 5th Wave   By Rich Tennant

"Are you using that 'clone' tool again?!"

In this part . . .

This part contains two chapters. Chapter 16 covers ten (or so) books and Web sites that I think you'll find useful to look through as you reach the next stage in your artistic evolution. During those times when you're ready to put your fist through your computer, check out some of these suggestions. It's cheaper than replacing a monitor.

Chapter 17 is all about comfort and convenience. In there, I offer ten suggestions to help improve your overall Manga Studio experience, from making sure you're comfortable enough for those marathon sessions to reminding you to always — *always* — save your work. Repeatedly.

Chapter 16

Ten (Or So) Books and Web Sites to Check Out

*I*f you're an old pro who's been at this whole "making comics" thing for a while, this chapter might be a bit boring or redundant. However, for those of you who are brand new to the concept of drawing manga — or have been doing this for a little while but aren't sure how to reach that next creative level — you might be interested in the books and sites I describe in this chapter (if you haven't already seen them, of course).

Because I personally don't see anything *fundamentally* different between American and Japanese comics (and because I'm influenced by both in my work), you'll see references that can apply to just one or the other, when in fact I think they apply to both. I think it's important to understand that while stylistically they may be different, there's still an underlying structure that's shared by all comics.

The references and suggestions in this chapter cover a wide range of topics, from drawing basics to distributing your work. I hope you'll take the opportunity to check out a few (or all) of them and see if they'll help you find the missing piece of your artistic puzzle you may have been looking for and not been aware of it.

Drawing Manga

Resource: *Manga For Dummies,* by Kensuke Okabayashi (Wiley)

Of *course* I'm going to reference a fellow For Dummies author!

Seriously though, Kensuke Okabayashi's book is perfect for the beginning manga artist. He works to include many of the basics of drawing and character design in this book, with many simple tips and instructions to get you started down the path towards creating your own work.

I think the thing to keep in mind when you're first starting out is to not lose faith. It's easy to get discouraged when you start drawing because the drawings you produce don't look at all like what you may see in the book. That's fine. You have to crawl before you can walk. Kensuke does a fine job in helping you along those first steps. It isn't easy (despite what you may hear the experts say), but if you read and pay close attention to what Kensuke has to say in his book, you'll get the hang of it faster than you may think.

Oh yeah, and he shows you how to draw big robots. Who wouldn't like to learn that?

Drawing Characters

Resource: *Creating Characters with Personality: For Film, TV, Animation, Video Games, and Graphic Novels,* by Tom Bancroft (Watson-Guptill)

It's one thing to create a character. It's another to create an icon.

While I'm not saying that this book tells you how to create the next Superman or Goku, Tom Bancroft does a fantastic job in helping you understand what it takes to create a character that the audience will care about.

I think it's something that happens to every beginning artist (I know it happened to me): When he or she draws people, they all have a tendency to look the same (and no, changing the character's hair or adding a beard doesn't count as creating a "different look"). Tom's book helps you get over that hump, as he shows how you can create unique characters of all ages, shapes, and sizes. Even more important is how choosing the right kind of design can really help you bring out the character's personality (hence the name of the book). I think that's a vital aspect to consider because knowing the character's personality certainly helps you know how that character can act or react in a scene. (Hey, the writer's words can only do so much, y'know?)

Tom's book also helps point out what I mention in the intro to this chapter — that these principles of character design are applicable to whatever style you work in.

Inking Your Comics

Resource: *The Art of Comic-Book Inking,* 2nd Edition, by Gary Martin with various authors (Dark Horse)

Using Manga Studio to ink your work digitally is great. You don't need to worry about running out of ink, or ruining a pen tip because you forgot to properly clean it, or cursing the high heavens when your cat knocks the ink well all over the page you just finished. (Now you just need to pray the cat doesn't accidentally pull the plug on your computer before you get a chance to save you work.)

But you still need to have a basic understanding of how inking works and how it's more than just tracing the pencils with a thin line and hoping that the tones or colors will add dimension to the page. Regardless of the medium, inking is easy to pick up and extremely difficult to master.

That's why I suggest checking out Gary Martin's *The Art of Comic-Book Inking.* While the book is primarily focused on Western-styled inking, there are plenty of basic facts of inking that can work just as easily on your manga work. And while traditional inking tools are used, the tips and suggestions translate quite easily to inking in Manga Studio. Remember, by default the program comes with settings for a variety of real-world pens.

The book includes the basic discussion you'd expect from an instructional book, such as how to ink backgrounds, how to treat inking a character depending on the lighting of a scene, and how brush work can create different results than using a G Pen. What I think you'll find interesting is the second half of the book, where the same page is inked by a variety of different artists, who also discuss what tools they used and why they tackled the page the way did.

I think that's a great way to see not only how a page can be interpreted by different people, but how you may agree or disagree with what they did (or didn't do). You may find your own inking "voice" in the process.

Drawing Backgrounds

Resource: *Perspective! For Comic Book Artists: How to Achieve a Professional Look in Your Art,* by David Chelsea (Watson-Guptill)

It's amazing to see comics from new artists where character drawings are spot-on but the backgrounds are either extremely sloppy, off kilter, or worse yet, not done at all. It's hard to get a feel for a scene when there's no scene to look at.

It's understandable, actually. Most of the time when you're reading a comic, you're obviously going to focus your attention on the characters. They're why people read the books. So, when new artists want to start drawing comics themselves, they may focus entirely on drawing the people and just ignore or crudely draw a background so that *something* is there. I know I was guilty of this when I started drawing.

Backgrounds are an important part of comics. If a drawing has no background, the reader has no sense of place for the scene. The characters could be in the country or the city, but without scenery, the reader isn't going to know what you have in mind.

Backgrounds are also extremely difficult to master. Hearing things like "using one/two/three-point perspective will help you draw realistic scenes" is nice, but it doesn't help when you want to draw a cityscape and aren't sure exactly how to tackle that. Plus, many books dedicated to perspective work and technical drawing can be a bit confusing and dense to read.

David Chelsea's book takes a different approach to handling the explanation of perspective work. Taking a cue from Scott McCloud, Chelsea wrote the whole book in an illustrated form. It's almost like watching a video tutorial, as the book guides you visually through various methods, tips, and tricks in hopes that you'll understand how to apply it to your work.

If you're new to the concept of drawing backgrounds — or maybe you try drawing them and find it's all too confusing and daunting — have patience. Reading this book can help you down the path, but practicing the methods and taking chances by drawing things you've never drawn before (a car, a lamppost, a living room, and so on) can help you improve. Then, much like your character drawing has become second nature, so too will creating the environment around them become.

Using Tones

Resources: *How to Draw Manga: Computones,* Volumes 1–5, by Knife Senno (Graphic-Sha)

Obviously, a perk to purchasing any of these books is the bonus CD containing additional Computones that Manga Studio EX users can use. That isn't why I'm suggesting you check this series of books out, though.

When I first started playing with tones, I was surprised to find very little information on exactly *how* to work with them. It was a while later that I discovered the first of Graphic-Sha's books on using tones. While the first series of books focuses on the traditional use of screentones, it was the next series, which focuses on Computones, that helped me to understand how to work with their digital counterparts.

As of this writing, five volumes of *How to Draw Manga: Computones* are out, each covering a basic theme. The books cover the basics of using tones to add flavor to your work, but then delve in deeper to cover how to tone for certain situations. These can include action scenes, interactions with others, emotional expressions, special effects, and so on.

The art of toning is much harder than it first seems. It can be a daunting task trying to figure out exactly what to do, or even where to start. The *How to Draw Manga: Computones* series really does help to give you a better idea on how to use tones more than just to add some color to a shirt and pants.

And yes, the bonus CDs are nice, too.

The Books of Scott McCloud

Resources: *Understanding Comics: The Invisible Art, Reinventing Comics: How Imagination and Technology Are Revolutionizing an Art Form,* and *Making Comics: Storytelling Secrets of Comics, Manga and Graphic Novels,* by Scott McCloud (Harper Paperbacks)

Scott McCloud is a very interesting person.

Mention his name to other artists and you'll hear the words "genius" or "crackpot," and most certainly "controversial." One thing is absolutely certain though; he makes you think, and that's why I happen to like him.

Scott takes his vast knowledge and understanding of the medium and presents it in an entertaining graphic-novel-styled format. It's a really cool idea, in that not only are you presented with a series of very interesting theses on the subject of sequential art, but you're seeing what he's talking about applied in real time (or as close as one can when reading a book).

In *Understanding Comics,* Scott deconstructs comics to their purest essences, in order to help the reader understand exactly how and why comics are the way they are. With *Reinventing Comics* (the book that garnered him that "controversial" moniker), Scott explains what he thinks were the major revolutions that helped comics over the years, and he heavily pushes the concept of digital distribution and webcomics as a means of thinking outside the box. Finally, in *Making Comics,* Scott once again deconstructs the comics medium, this time breaking down the creative process. Here, he not only explains how character expression or panel transitions work, but also why.

I think that's what I like the most about Scott's books — they make you think beyond what you see on the page. Perhaps when you get the chance to read any of these books, you'll look at your collection a little bit differently.

Closely Read Other Manga and Comics

Around, I'd say, 1992, I picked up a video cassette that covers how to draw comic book characters, hosted by *Spawn* creator Todd McFarlane. I don't remember too much from that tape, except there's this one statement he makes to the audience. He says that you should study other comics if you want to learn how to draw because it's that exaggerated and surreal style that you want to understand if you want to make it in the business of comics.

To a degree, I think he's right; you should look at other comics. They can be a great source of inspiration, as far as learning how certain artists draw the way they do. Where I differ from him, though, is while he suggests focusing on the "how," I suggest paying attention to the "why."

While it's true that the writer dictates how many panels are on a page and has a general setup of the point-of-view for each panel, it's still the artist who decides how those panels are laid out on the page. He or she is the one who has to look at the page and decide what the best way to convey the story visually is.

This probably doesn't sound like a big deal. All you do is draw some stuff, make sure there's enough room for dialog, and you're done, right? It isn't as easy as you would think. Ask any professionals how many times they may go through a series of thumbnail sketches before they find the perfect setup that best expresses what the writer is trying to convey.

I'm sure you have a least a small collection of your favorite comics and/or manga. You've read really good ones multiple times, I bet. The story is really compelling, or the artwork is top-notch, or maybe it's one of the modern classics, where you get the best of both worlds.

Well, I suggest you read them again. (I know . . . I really have to twist your arm.) Here's the catch, though: This time, pay close attention to how the story is told through the artist's eyes. As you do that, start asking yourself questions, like:

- ✔ Why did the artist decide to draw the page (or a specific panel) that way?

- ✔ Did the artist convey the scene or mood that the writer intended? (Does the art match the writing?)

- ✔ Is the storytelling on the page easy to follow?

✔ What is it about the artwork and storytelling that makes it his or her style? Or is there a unique style to begin with, or is it just a copy of someone else?

✔ What would you have done differently if you were given the script?

While you're at it, pick up an older book you haven't read before, but maybe have heard a lot about. Check out Osamu Tezuka's *Metropolis*, or Jack Kirby's early *Fantastic Four* run, or Katsuhiro Otomo's *Akira*, or Will Eisner's *A Contract with God*, or many other classic books out there. Look at how they convey the story and ask yourself the same questions as before. You'll be surprised at how much your work can evolve as a result.

It doesn't hurt to look at your favorite artists' drawing styles for inspiration and personal education. Keep in mind that you have to be careful not to emulate them too much in your work. I'll say about 80 percent of artists out there start off with their artwork looking like their mentors', but eventually they do find their own style. So be sure to learn from your favorites, but try to find your own style in the process. It's better to have a fan say, "Hey, you're So-and-so!" than being told "Hey, you're that artist that draws like So-and-so."

On-Demand Publishing

Resource: Lulu (www.lulu.com)

Your manga is done. You see the finished project in front of you in Manga Studio, and you're ready to print it out and distribute it to the masses, either through the mail or possibly at a comic or anime convention. So the next question on your lips is probably, "How do I do that?"

The simplest and least expensive option is to create an ashcan comic. All you need to have is a printer, a large stack of paper, a paper cutter, and a stapler. As you can probably surmise, the idea here is to simply print out the pages, trim off the excess, fold them in half, and staple them together. It's a perfect low-cost means of creating a comic for distribution, although it doesn't have the professional look of some contemporary comics and manga.

If you're looking for something more professional-looking, you can always contact a local printer and have them print the comics out for you. All you need to do is provide the pages in a high-quality format and the printing company can make the book in any form you'd like, from a traditional-styled floppy comic to the perfect-bound digests you see on the manga shelves of your local bookstore. It's great . . . if you have the money. The problem with this route is that in order to get the lowest print cost, you have to buy in bulk. Even then, it can cost you a bit of cash. So, you're working from a loss right off the bat.

More recently (as in the last year or two), a new option has emerged that helps take the whole production and distribution arm of the creation process out of your hands. Companies like Lulu and have started what is called *on-demand publishing*. This is how it works:

- ✔ You create an account with the company.
- ✔ You follow the directions to set up your new comic. This includes setting up the cover price.
- ✔ You provide the pages to the company to print in whatever file format they want them in.

That's all there is to it! The on-demand companies take care of the sales, the printing, and the mailing of your manga or comic. The best part of this deal is that it costs you *nothing* to do this. No membership fee, no printing fee . . . not one red cent!

How this works is that each comic has a base price on the site. This price helps the company cover the cost of printing and distribution. Because you control the price of the book beyond the base price, you set your own royalty rate. This can be a few cents or a few dollars. But those profits are yours, and you don't have to worry about rushing down to the post office to bulk mail your comics and hope that they make it to your readers.

The Joy of Webcomics

Now we're getting into a topic I'm *very* familiar with.

I believe some of the earliest webcomics can be traced back to the early to mid 1990s. Nowadays, thanks to the massive success of comics and manga such as *MegaTokyo* (www.megatokyo.com), *Penny Arcade* (www.penny-arcade.com), *PvP* (www.pvpcomics.com), and so on, it seems like you can't go anywhere on the World Wide Web without running into a webcomic.

And why not? Producing and distributing your comic on the Internet is probably the fastest and cheapest way to bring your product to the masses. You don't need to worry about making sure you have the exact number of pages needed for a print book. If you're really avant-garde, you don't even need to worry about sticking to a traditional comic page format. The possibilities are endless, creatively.

However you tackle it, with just a few clicks of the mouse, your comic is up and available for hundreds (or if you're lucky, thousands) of readers in an instant. There's nothing quite like instant gratification. Add on a message board or blog (or at least an e-mail address), and you can cultivate a loyal fanbase that eagerly anticipates the next installment of your series (or who may purchase a trade paperback of your series should you decide to print it).

Of course, the first thing you need to think about is where you're going to host your comic. You can always purchase your own space from one of the many Web hosts out there. Then, if you're code savvy enough, you can generate a Web site to house your comic. If there's a potential downside, it's that this path costs you money, depending on the type of service you purchase. And if you're just starting out in the world of webcomics, and you aren't even sure if people will like your story, it can prove to be a costly gamble.

That said, there is a place I think to be a great starting point to cultivate your comic and fanbase, while not costing you a dime. In the early 2000s, a Web host was formed that was designed purely to be a repository for anyone who wanted to create a webcomic. In exchange for banner ads, people could place their comic on their servers and take advantage of their automated functions and code that would make updating the comic (and blog if you wanted to have one) a breeze. Originally it was called Keenspace but more recently changed its name to Comic Genesis (`www.comicgenesis.com`).

To paraphrase an old advertisement, I'm not just endorsing them, I was originally a client. The first webcomic I created, *Place Name Here*, was a Keenspace comic. I can tell you that it was a great way to get my feet wet and start building a fanbase before I moved to my own Web space (and that was only because I'm also a Web programmer and I wanted to program my own site from scratch).

If you're looking to dive into the world of webcomics but don't have a lot of money to spend, start at Comic Genesis. You get to do a lot there for very little.

Online Forums

You can read all the books and visit all the sites I suggest in this chapter, and it hopefully helps build your knowledge of creating comics. But knowledge can be nothing without application, and what better way to find out how well you're applying what you've learned than by getting real-time feedback from a group of your peers?

Sprinkled throughout the comics community are many message boards devoted to sharing art with others, with users ready to give critiques to anyone brave enough to step up. Some can be cruel, others more forgiving, but all are ready to let you know exactly what you've done wrong and what you've done right.

It's easy to feel intimidated when you check out one of these places for the first time. There's definitely a "new kid at school" vibe when you first start out, and you may be very reluctant to post any kind of messages there, much less your artwork. My suggestion is to spend a few days checking out the community and how the users interact with both newbies and regular users. That way, you can tell whether the forum is a good fit for you, personality-wise. Then, if you're serious and confident enough in your work to take critiques, politely introduce yourself and post some of your art.

I suggest being gracious and polite as you start off in a new forum. If anything, you want to show the regulars there that you aren't an obnoxious user who's just going to be a jerk while you're there. I'm not saying you should kowtow and grovel at their feet or anything; just be nice and polite, and you'll get the same in return. (Well, there are no guarantees, really. Some people are just jerks. You just have to roll with the punches with those people.)

This is also a great way to prepare yourself, should you decide to show your work to professionals or potential employers at one of the hundreds of various anime and comic conventions out there. It's possible that the people you meet could be extremely tough on you, and it can be discouraging at first. If you start showing off your work in some of the comic art forums, if anything it's a great way to thicken your skin for the convention circuit. If you can survive the feedback from your peers, you should have no problem with a few editors.

Some of the sites you can check out include:

- Digital Webbing (www.digital-webbing.com)
- Penciljack (www.penciljack.com)
- Ten Ton Studios (www.tentonstudios.com) Okay, in full disclosure, I'm a founding member there. But it's still a great place to hang out . . . honest!

So, what are you waiting for? Start posting some work!

Chapter 17

Ten Ways to Improve Your Manga Studio Experience

The title of this chapter is probably a bit misleading, as only three of the tips actually involve Manga Studio itself. The rest of the chapter cover things you might not think of while working on the computer, ideas and suggestions that will help you feel comfortable both mentally and physically. When you feel comfortable, nine times out of ten you'll feel more creative. And when you feel creative, lots of art gets drawn.

So, here are a few ideas that I think will help your Manga Studio (and digital art in general) experience go a bit more smoothly.

Find the Right Place to Work

Are you the type of person that likes to sit at a desk in a studio, where you can just crank up your stereo and draw away? Or do you prefer absolute silence? Or maybe you feel more creative far away from the desk, and would rather sit outside at the local coffee shop or under a tree?

While it sounds silly to think about such things when you're talking about using a computer program, it really isn't. One factor toward producing the best art you can is comfort. If you don't feel like you can work in one kind of environment or another, you're not going to *want* to work. And that's no good.

So, consider where and how you feel your most creative and productive. From there, it will help you with the next suggestion.

Purchase the Right (Digital) Tools for the Job

Odds are you may already have the computer that best fits the environment you like working in. If not, and you have some money to invest, look into the right computer for you. If you happen to like working outside, purchase a good laptop that you can take anywhere. If you prefer working at home, a solid desktop machine will be fine. (Or if you already have a laptop, look into a docking station and treat it like a desktop.)

The good news with this program is that it doesn't require the absolute top-of-the-model system; any computer from the last couple of years will work just fine with Manga Studio, with no significant (or very little) drop in performance. So, if you don't have the budget for the latest computer, check out some online auction sites and see what used and/or refurbished machines are available.

Regardless of the type of system you want to work from, the one item you should seriously look into buying is a drawing tablet. Oh sure, you *can* use a mouse if you really want to. If you're looking to do simple tasks, like selecting areas to fill in with tones, a mouse works just fine. If you plan on doing any intricate drawing with a mouse though, let's just say it can prove to be difficult. Actually, it feels like trying to draw with a brick — not very intuitive, and you're going to spend a lot of time trying to clean up mistakes.

Several manufacturers produce drawing tablets, but the 800-pound gorilla is most certainly Wacom (www.wacom.com), and rightfully so. Wacom produces some of the highest-quality tablets around, both in construction and functionality. And they cover a wide range of tablet styles that tailors to both skill level and budget. For the beginner digital artist with a small budget, the Graphire series is a great entry-level tablet. For more advanced users with a bit more money to spend, there's always the Intuos series of tablets, which provide additional functionalities (such as shortcut keys) and increased *pressure sensitivity* (which is the ability to accurately simulate light and heavy strokes while drawing).

If money's no object, or if you happen to have a decent budget to work from, you can consider a couple of (relatively) more recent innovations. Both let you draw directly on the screen, but choosing one or the other goes right back to tip number one of this chapter: Where are you most comfortable working?

If you prefer working at a desk, the Wacom Cintiq may be perfect for you. Much like the Intuos series, this 21-inch monitor has 1,024 levels of pressure sensitivity (compared to the 512 levels of the Graphire series), as well as a series of programmable hotkeys that you can use for shortcuts while you work. It's probably the closest you'll come to drawing directly on paper in a digital plane. Also, because it's a monitor, you can hook it up to either a PC or a Mac (or even a machine running Linux!). The expensive catch is that the monitor costs (as of this writing) around $2,500. So start saving now!

Another option, especially for those that prefer to work on the go, is a tablet PC. While there are various types of tablet PCs on the market, they all have one thing in common: They're all laptops with screens you can draw directly upon. Compared to the Cintiq, tablet PCs have much lower pressure sensitivity (256 levels) and no programmable keys. Oh, and they're only for PC (although the third-party Apple Modbook should be out by time this book sees print, so you Apple users may be in for some luck). But, most Tablet PCs cost about the same as or less than the Cintiq, and you can take your Tablet PC *anywhere*. (The Cintiq weighs more than 20 pounds, and it's a 21-inch monitor tethered to a desktop — not exactly the easiest thing to port around.)

The moral here is that if you have the chance, find the right setup to go with where you feel most comfortable working.

Create a Comfortable Workspace

What constitutes a "comfortable workspace" is extremely subjective, if only because we're all different.

I happen to like taking my tablet PC to the various coffee shops in town, sitting down, plugging in my iPod, and sketching away (or at this particular moment, writing a book). That doesn't mean my nomadic style works for everyone; you might find the idea of working anyplace but at home revolting. It all boils down to the first tip in this chapter: Find the place you feel your most creative. When you've done that and you have the best equipment to help you achieve that, the next thing to do is make sure you have a comfortable workspace. Not only will it help you mentally stay focused on your work, but physically, it could help you prevent any kind of repetitive-stress injuries.

For desk people, try to make sure that the desk you work at is the right height for your body and that your chair is both comfortable and offers good back support. Try to set your tablet at an angle that is easy on your wrist. (Or if you prefer to use a mouse, try to use a gel wrist rest.) If you're the type that likes to use the keyboard shortcuts while you're working, try to move the keyboard so that it's easy to reach with your nondrawing hand.

For the laptop crowd, you obviously don't get the luxury of a comfy chair and desk combo (I guess it really depends on the type of coffee shop or bookstore you hang out in), but some of the above suggestions can still apply. First and foremost, try to find a table that's the right height for you (or grab a cheap foam-backed lap desk if you like working away from a table). You can always brace your tablet along the edge of the laptop (or on top of the keyboard) to assist in the hand-eye coordination, as well as save a bit of space if you happen to be working in a smaller area.

Depending on how you set up your laptop and tablet, you might not have easy access to the available keyboard shortcuts. If that's the case, you can purchase a programmable minikeyboard to use. Or if you don't have the money to spend, grab an old game controller and do an online search for the program Joy2Key. That program can help you customize the controller's buttons to whatever keys or key combinations you want.

Regardless of where you work, you need to be aware of your posture. Working digitally is obviously different from working over a piece of paper, especially in how your body is positioned. So, you can't hunch over your work quite the same way you do with traditional tools.

That's why I mention having a good comfortable setup while working. If you're not comfortable, you may find yourself working in a position that could put pressure on your neck, shoulders, and/or drawing wrist. Those kinds of repetitive stress injuries only kill your productivity in the long run. At best, you may have to take longer and more frequent breaks; at worst, there may be surgery to deal with.

Just because you may have found a comfortable setup doesn't mean you can't change things up now and then. Try to switch your position and tool placement around occasionally. It can help keep your body from becoming too accustomed to working in one position.

Take a Break Now and Then

I admire the people who can stare at a computer monitor for hours on end without a break. They seem to have the superhuman ability to not wear out their corneas or get a splitting headache. I may have had that ability when I was younger, but it's certainly long gone now.

It doesn't hurt to take a step back from the computer every now and then. Getting up to stretch, walk around, play some video games, or whatever you want to do is a good way to recharge your batteries.

At the very least it's a good way to come back to a particular panel that's frustrating to work on. Sometimes walking away from the point of irritation for a while, and then coming back to it can set off a light bulb in your head, and suddenly you find yourself finishing the problem in no time. It's certainly cheaper than punching your fist through the computer monitor in frustration.

Also, much like finding a comfortable setup to work, taking a break is good for the body that may have been stuck in one position for a while. Do whatever it takes to get the blood flowing in your system: Stretch your muscles, roll your neck around, grab a sandwich, anything. It'll help you both mentally and physically, and that's good for your artwork in the long run.

Don't Overburden Your System

Manga Studio is a pretty robust program that doesn't take up too much of your system resources. However, depending on the machine you're using, that doesn't mean you should overburden the system while working.

If you happen to have large amounts of system RAM, it's probably not much of a hassle or problem to run six or seven different programs at once on your computer. If you have a basic 512MB of RAM, though, running that many programs at once is just going to run your poor computer into the ground. Okay maybe not, but it's certainly going to affect your system's performance, especially when you're working in Manga Studio.

For those unfamiliar with what RAM is, it's memory that's used by the system to run programs. You have only so much space on RAM, so chunks of a program you're running cycle between the hard drive and the RAM as the computer needs it. The more programs running means there's going to be more swapping between the hard drive and the system to keep them all running optimally. The more swapping there is, the slower the computer performs, resulting in a very frustrated user.

If you can afford it, look into purchasing additional RAM for your system. You should run with a minimum of 1GB of RAM while working in Manga Studio anyway. If you can't afford any kind of hardware purchasing at this point, try to limit the programs running on your system while working on Manga Studio.

Take Advantage of Manga Studio Tools

There's a reason that Manga Studio comes chock full of tools for you to use; it's to help you streamline your work and increase your productivity. It's also nice to use a program that you don't have to necessarily shoehorn into working for you.

I happen to like this program because I get to use real-world tools on a digital plane. Sure, Photoshop and Painter have line and curve tools, but they can't create rulers and guides on the fly and treat them like the real thing! Add to that the myriad of pens, pencils, airbrushes, and screen tones (and a large number of each type of tool) that Manga Studio places at your disposal.

For EX users, it's even better, with tools like the perspective, speed, and focus line tools. Being able to set up vanishing points on the fly and just draw away like you're drawing normally is a very satisfying feeling.

There are also the various filters you can use, such as the speed and focus line filters to automatically generate lines you'd be spending time drawing by hand. Even taking advantage of the fill tool to quickly fill in large black areas shaves minutes off of your production time.

It never hurts to take advantage of the fact that this *is* a computer program you're working with. If there are ways that Manga Studio can save you time and headaches, by all means, use them!

Save! Save! Save! And Save Again!

I mention the importance of saving often in Chapter 3, but it's significant enough to bring this topic up again. Computer programs are fickle. One second they'll work just fine — the next . . . poof. All the work you just toiled away on for who knows how long, gone in an instant. That's why it's imperative that you save, and save, and save. Be obsessive about it if you must; it's better to be obsessive than to regret it later.

On that note, it also doesn't hurt to take your projects and other work and back them up. Much like computer programs, you never know when your seemingly stable computer or hard drive may suddenly die on you.

Again, it's always better to be safe than sorry. Burn your documents to a CD or DVD, or to an external hard drive if you have one. Heck, if you have one of those old-school tape drives, use that. Just think about how happy and relieved you'll feel should something catastrophic happen to your machine. You may have to pony up for a new one, but at least you'll have a backup of your data.

Avoid Perfectionism

You could also call this section "Don't Be a Slave to the Undo Button."

If there's a pitfall to working digitally, it's that you can spend a lot of time working on things you really don't need to. While I mention in Chapter 16 the need for backgrounds to help get a sense of place in a scene, you probably don't need to spend six hours working on every individual leaf on the furthest tree in the panel just because you can zoom in insanely close on the page.

By the same token, you need to be careful you don't spend too much time working on a particular section of a page or panel where you're constantly drawing and undoing and drawing and undoing until that one strand of hair on the heroine is "perfect."

If you have an endless amount of time and are in no rush to produce something, you can go to town making the perfect page. Most of us, though, have that deadline looming overhead, and we really don't have that kind of time to devote to insignificant details. Yet I've still caught myself repeatedly making one or both of the above mistakes, just because I have that ability to make the page absolutely perfect!

If All Else Fails, Try a Different Medium

Trying something else when you're stuck may sound like familiar advice. You know what you want to draw on the page or in the program. You visualize it perfectly in your mind. The problem is, what you have in your head won't translate to a doodle, let alone a final drawing.

I don't know if there's a proper term for this kind of situation, but I like to call it Artist's Block. It's that frustrating, helpless feeling you get when you can't seem to draw anything you want. The feeling can be exacerbated if a deadline's looming, and you start to feel the pressure to get your work done by yesterday.

While the initial feeling is probably to throw something through a wall, it may just be that a change of scenery is in order. I'm not necessarily talking about location; rather, it may be a change of drawing medium that's in order.

For example, while I draw primarily on the computer these days, there are those times when I'll just turn off the monitor, grab a paper and pencil, and just try to work through my Artist's Block that way. Most of the time that seems to do the trick, and then I'll just scan the work onto the computer and continue on to the next step.

So, if you're a digital artist and getting bogged down with lack of creativity, try going analog for a little while. Conversely, if you're a traditional artist and happen to have a drawing tablet you'd normally use for color or tone work, why not try to do some sketching right on the computer? Drawing on a different medium may be just the thing to break you out of the artistic doldrums.

Have Fun!

Sometimes when you're knee deep in a project with a deadline looming overhead, and the stress begins to build up, you may have a tendency to forget why you decided to become an artist. Well, I'm here to remind you why: because it's fun!

You get to work (in a business) where you can spend hours at a time creating amazing and wonderful pieces of sequential art on a regular basis. If you're even luckier, you may be getting paid to do this! But even if you're not, who cares? Whether it's for a major company or for your own Web comic, what matters is that you're getting to do what you've been dreaming of doing for who knows how long. When you step back, it's really crazy to believe, isn't it?

It's frustrating business at times. I've lost track of the number of hours lost staring at a blank canvas, cursing the high heavens as I try to figure out why I can't seem to draw a stick figure, let alone a complete page. Sometimes my wife has to come by and give me a metaphorical swift kick in the rear, reminding me that I'm getting to draw for a living and that I shouldn't stress out so much over it.

So, consider this a literary kick in the rear whenever you feel frustrated and stressed. Take a step back, take a deep breath, and remember that you get to draw comics and manga on a regular basis. Have fun!

Appendix

About the CD

*T*his appendix describes the system requirements your computer needs to meet so that you can use the CD. It also shows you how to install the demo version of Manga Studio EX, as well as access the included sample art files.

System Requirements

Make sure that your computer meets the minimum system requirements shown in the following list. If your computer doesn't match up to most of these requirements, you may have problems using the software and files on the CD. For the latest and greatest information, please refer to the ReadMe file located at the root of the CD-ROM.

✔ A PC running Microsoft Windows 98, Windows 2000, Windows NT4 (with SP4 or later), Windows Me, or Windows XP. (Manga Studio has some issues with Windows Vista at the time of writing.)

✔ A Mac running Apple OS X version 10.2.8, 10.3.9, 10.4.1, or later.

✔ A minimum system processor speed of 500 MHz.

✔ A minimum of 256MB of RAM (512MB for the Mac). Realistically, you need 1GB (or more) of RAM to run Manga Studio smoothly.

✔ A CD-ROM drive

If you need more information on the basics, check out these books published by Wiley Publishing: *PCs For Dummies,* by Dan Gookin; *Macs For Dummies,* by Edward C. Baig; *iMacs For Dummies,* by Mark L. Chambers; *Windows 2000 Professional For Dummies, Windows XP For Dummies,* and *Windows Vista For Dummies,* all by Andy Rathbone.

Using the CD

To install the items from the CD to your hard drive, follow these steps.

1. **Insert the CD into your computer's CD-ROM drive. The license agreement appears.**

   Note to Windows users: The interface won't launch if you have autorun disabled. In that case, choose Start⇨Run. In the dialog box that appears, type *D:***\Start.exe**. (Replace *D* with the proper letter if your CD drive uses a different letter. If you don't know the letter, see how your CD drive is listed under My Computer.) Click OK.

   Note for Mac Users: The CD icon will appear on your desktop. Double-click the icon to open the CD and double-click the Start icon.

2. **Read through the license agreement, and then click the Accept button if you want to use the CD.**

   The CD interface appears. The interface allows you to install the programs and run the demos with just a click of a button (or two).

What You'll Find on the CD

The following sections are arranged by category and provide a summary of the software and other goodies you'll find on the CD. If you need help with installing the items provided on the CD, refer to the installation instructions in the preceding section.

Shareware programs are fully functional, free, trial versions of copyrighted programs. If you like particular programs, register with their authors for a nominal fee and receive licenses, enhanced versions, and technical support.

Freeware programs are free, copyrighted games, applications, and utilities. You can copy them to as many PCs as you like — for free — but they offer no technical support.

GNU software is governed by its own license, which is included inside the folder of the GNU software. There are no restrictions on distribution of GNU software. See the GNU license at the root of the CD for more details.

Trial, demo, or *evaluation* versions of software are usually limited either by time or functionality (such as not letting you save a project after you create it).

Manga Studio EX 3.0 from e-frontier

30-Day Trial Version for Windows and Macintosh.

This is a fully featured demonstration version of Manga Studio EX that you can use for 30 days. All of the functionality of the full program is available for you to try out during the 30 days, after which you are reminded to purchase the full version (and you'll no longer be able to use the demo).

If you're using the demo version of Manga Studio, you won't be able to open all the sample files on the CD. You'll have to buy the full version to use all the sample files.

Author-created material

For Windows and Macintosh.

All the examples provided in this book are located in the Author directory on the CD and work with Mac and Windows 98/2000/Me/XP. The files include sample artwork created in Manga Studio, as well as 2-D images and 3-D objects you can import into the program for your own testing. The structure of the examples directory is Author/Chapter *X*.

- **Author/Chapter 3:** This folder contains a sample page file that is used during the quick-start walkthrough. It contains the digital pencil roughs, the completed inks, a folder containing the screentones used on the page, a folder containing the word balloons and dialogue, and a layer containing the panel borders. (I had removed the white gutter space from the borders in this example.)

- **Author/Chapter 4:** This folder contains a sample story file containing five pages from my webcomic, *Chibi Cheerleaders From Outer Space*. This is to show an example of how you can place multiple pages into one story file.

- **Author/Chapter 5:** This folder contains a sample of a scanned pencil drawing that you can import into Manga Studio.

- **Author/Chapter BC1:** This folder contains a sample page file of a character roughed out on a raster layer, cleaned up on a second raster layer, and inked on a vector layer. Manga Studio Debut users can view the vector inks but can't draw on it.

- **Author/Chapter BC2:** This folder contains several digital photo samples that you can use to import as 2-D objects into Manga Studio.

Bonus Chapters

The CD also includes three bonus chapters. Bonus Chapter 1 covers the advanced topic of using vectors; Bonus Chapter 2 describes importing 2-D and 3-D objects into Manga Studio. Bonus Chapter 3 gives you background information on manga that may help you if you intend on publishing the comics you create in Manga Studio.

Troubleshooting

I tried my best to compile programs that work on most computers with the minimum system requirements. Alas, your computer may differ, and some programs may not work properly for some reason.

If you're having problems, the two likeliest culprits are that you don't have enough memory (RAM) for the programs you want to use, or you have other programs running that are affecting installation or running of a program. If you get an error message such as `Not enough memory` or `Setup cannot continue`, try one or more of the following suggestions and then try using the software again:

- ✔ **Turn off any antivirus software running on your computer.** Installation programs sometimes mimic virus activity and may make your computer incorrectly believe that it's being infected by a virus.

- ✔ **Close all running programs.** The more programs you have running, the less memory is available to other programs. Installation programs typically update files and programs; so if you keep other programs running, installation may not work properly.

- ✔ **Have your local computer store add more RAM to your computer.** This is, admittedly, a drastic and somewhat expensive step. However, adding more memory can really help the speed of your computer and allow more programs to run at the same time.

Customer Care

If you have trouble with the CD-ROM, please call the Wiley Product Technical Support phone number at (800) 762-2974. Outside the United States, call 1(317) 572-3994. You can also contact Wiley Product Technical Support at `http://support.wiley.com`. John Wiley & Sons will provide technical support only for installation and other general quality control items. For technical support on the applications themselves, consult the program's vendor or author.

To place additional orders or to request information about other Wiley products, please call (877) 762-2974.

Index

Wiley Publishing, Inc.
End-User License Agreement

READ THIS. You should carefully read these terms and conditions before opening the software packet(s) included with this book "Book". This is a license agreement "Agreement" between you and Wiley Publishing, Inc. "WPI". By opening the accompanying software packet(s), you acknowledge that you have read and accept the following terms and conditions. If you do not agree and do not want to be bound by such terms and conditions, promptly return the Book and the unopened software packet(s) to the place you obtained them for a full refund.

1. **License Grant.** WPI grants to you (either an individual or entity) a nonexclusive license to use one copy of the enclosed software program(s) (collectively, the "Software") solely for your own personal or business purposes on a single computer (whether a standard computer or a workstation component of a multi-user network). The Software is in use on a computer when it is loaded into temporary memory (RAM) or installed into permanent memory (hard disk, CD-ROM, or other storage device). WPI reserves all rights not expressly granted herein.

2. **Ownership.** WPI is the owner of all right, title, and interest, including copyright, in and to the compilation of the Software recorded on the physical packet included with this Book "Software Media". Copyright to the individual programs recorded on the Software Media is owned by the author or other authorized copyright owner of each program. Ownership of the Software and all proprietary rights relating thereto remain with WPI and its licensers.

3. **Restrictions on Use and Transfer.**

    (a) You may only (i) make one copy of the Software for backup or archival purposes, or (ii) transfer the Software to a single hard disk, provided that you keep the original for backup or archival purposes. You may not (i) rent or lease the Software, (ii) copy or reproduce the Software through a LAN or other network system or through any computer subscriber system or bulletin-board system, or (iii) modify, adapt, or create derivative works based on the Software.

    (b) You may not reverse engineer, decompile, or disassemble the Software. You may transfer the Software and user documentation on a permanent basis, provided that the transferee agrees to accept the terms and conditions of this Agreement and you retain no copies. If the Software is an update or has been updated, any transfer must include the most recent update and all prior versions.

4. **Restrictions on Use of Individual Programs.** You must follow the individual requirements and restrictions detailed for each individual program in the "About the CD" appendix of this Book or on the Software Media. These limitations are also contained in the individual license agreements recorded on the Software Media. These limitations may include a requirement that after using the program for a specified period of time, the user must pay a registration fee or discontinue use. By opening the Software packet(s), you agree to abide by the licenses and restrictions for these individual programs that are detailed in the "About the CD" appendix and/or on the Software Media. None of the material on this Software Media or listed in this Book may ever be redistributed, in original or modified form, for commercial purposes.